AN INTRODUCTION TO SANSKRIT GRAMMAR

AN INTRODUCTION
TO
SANSKRIT GRAMMAR

Manish Kumar Pathak

BHARATIYA KALA PRAKASHAN
DELHI (INDIA)

First Published : 2004
2011

Published by **C.P. Gautam**
BHARATIYA KALA PRAKASHAN
3421-A, IInd Floor, Narang Colony, Tri Nagar,
Delhi-110035. Phone : 27153083(O) 27522129 (R)

ISBN : 81-8090-037-1

Laser Type Setting by
A-ONE GRAPHICS
X-4, Gali-2, Brahmapuri, Delhi-110053
Phone : 2218 3470

Printed at
Santosh Offset Press
Delhi

CONTENTS

INTRODUCTION

Our purpose in studying this highly inflective ancient language of non-verbal communion is to feel the meanings of the terms and not to rely solely on translations or sectarian points of view. The basic terms are intensified inwardly when you can recognize the verbal root energy forms springing forth from the construes. Keep in mind the importance of the vowel changes, the prefixes, suffixes and infixes for the terms, and above all be sure to review the propositional prefixes in the terms.

The Indic Philosophy is perhaps the most intensified reason why so many students in the Occidental countries want to learn Sanskṛit. Due to its inner-non-verbal implosive meaning of the philosophical terms and ancient sacred texts, one will find this text a gentle means for feeling the concepts and not having to rely upon translations.

The first language were onomatopoetic, reproducing the sounds of nature. By human usage and long custom these became understood as the means of conveying the human thoughts, needs and wishes.

Sanskṛit has words for the higher teachings of the inner mysteries of the Soul and Spirit; the many after-death states, the origin and destiny of worlds and of man, human psychology, the level of human consciousness in and above the human stage, and a storehouse of philosophical and religious terminology. Every term is a living symbol of one of the Eternal Vibrations of Nature. It is a revealed language scholastically substantiated to around 3,000 B.C., and even older within the ancient Vedic texts.

The Sanskṛit language was developed by means of affixes, prefixes, suffixes, and so on. It was continued on by the word of mouth tradition of the Brahmins, and was not written down until the Sage Panini set forth the grammatical writings.

To try to translate such common words as *dharma*, *karma*, *bhakti, yoga*, etc., would involve the comparative comprehension of the translator's understanding. The ancient Sastras, or scriptures, eternally spoke of the uniqueness of Monotheism, oneness, and non-dual attainment. In India religion and philosophy are not divorced; they are a total interplay of inner attainment and development for action in this lifetime. Sectarianism is as prevalent in India as elsewhere, but this is perhaps the one reason one would want to learn Sanskṛit. The name Sanskṛit itself means "highly-polished" and the actual script is called Devanāgarī. It is an inner-implosive feel-language, non-verbal and highly sophisticated. Each letter of the alphabet has a numerical vibratory force which allies with the rhythmic vibrations of the human body—blood pressure, respiration rate, and so on. When the sound of a letter is made either vocally or inwardly, the vibratory force is activated, especially in meditation. Within each *Chakra* there is a lotus, and on each petal appears one distinct letter of the alphabet. For meditation purposes one will choose a phrase, *sutra, mantra*, or merely a letter of the alphabet, which will help the psychic subconscious to move in the realms of Cosmic contact. It is this slow process which leads to Self-Realization, enlightenment, and *samadhi*. This is described definitively in the Vedas. In A U M, "A" is the first letter of the alphabet, "U" signifies the second part of the Trinity—"Brahmā-Viṣṇu-Śiva," and "M" represents the total body vibration for life sustenance.

It includes exercises of both Sanskṛit to English and English to Sanskṛit with an appendix of the answer to help guide the student. Also at the end is a series of intensely interesting verbal glossaries of a comparative nature to expand the students appreciation.

CHAPTER I

Devanāgarī : The Alphabet and the Script

The script of Sanskṛt language is "Devnāgarī." Sequence of its alphabet is from "A" (अ) to"Ha" (ह). The consistence of pronunciation is excelent feature. The structure and logic of this language is unique. In English pronunciation of a letter varies time to time, for example one can pronounce "c" in three different ways, and 'a' in six different ways. But in Sanskṛit pronounce of each letter is very definite, the sound never varies. In Sanskṛit each consonant has an inherent 'a' like America, and each vowels has both a long nad short form of pronunciation **i.e**. a - ā, i - ī, etc.

At first to get the order of Devanāgarī "alphabet" by heart is essential. for the new aspirant of this language, the following table may help them to understand the structurr of the alphabet, and pronunciation of every letter.

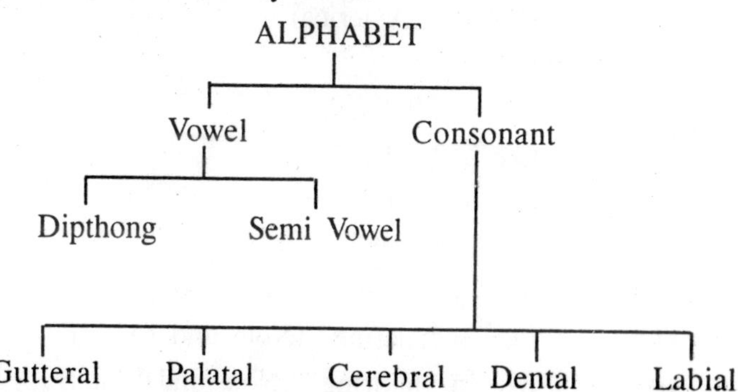

There are 5 kinds of "n's" (nasal letters) and 3 kinds of "s's" sibilants)

In Sanskrit the beauty of the sound is in the diaphragmatic aspirant sounds (h's), and the body sounds of the nasals, (n's).

These should flow effortlessly and unobstructed, devoid of volume or strain. This is the essence of the mantra used in meditation. The alphabet appears in each of the Cakras.

DO NOT CONFUSE THESE NAMES :

1. A vowel is any letter where air flows freely and unobstructed.
2. A consonant is any letter where the air is obstructed by either the tongue, lips or teeth.
3. A diphthong is a double-vowel sound:

   e = a + i

   o = a + u etc.
4. A semi-vowel is an open sounded vowel which can alternate with other vowels under specific conditions in grammatical constructions.
5. A sibilant is the consonant "s".
6. An aspirant is the diaphragmatic "h" sound.

CORRECT ALPHABETICAL ORDER, COMMENCING WITH VOWELS :

a = uh (as in America)

ā = ah :

i = like in "Indian"

ī = like in "police"

u = like in "put'

ū = like in "rude"

ṛ = like in "merit" (Note carefully the underdot :)

ṛī = like in "marine" (Note underdot :)

ḷrī = like in "bullring" (Note underdot :)

ḷrī = like in "jewelry" (Note underdot:)

Diphthongs : Double-vowel reflected sound :

e = like in "prey" (Never confuse with the Sanskṛt "a" *OR* first letter of English ABC's

ai = like in "aisle" (Note double-vowel sound:)
o = like in "gō" (Note double-vowel sound:)
au = like in "out!" or "Ow!" (Note double-vowel sound:)

Consonants : Letters where the air is blocked by either the tongue, lips or teeth. In Sanskṛt a special consonant is the cerebral, (sometimes called retroflexive or lingual,) where the tongue touches the roof of the mouth. It is a very soft body sound.

Gutteral Consonants : Harsh sound from back of throat.
Palatal Consonants : Produced from palate placement.
Cerebral Consonants : See above note:
Dental Consonants : Tongue touches the teeth.
Labial Consonants : Explosive lip motion for sound production.

Step One : There are only two letters in each of the 5 groups.

PLEASE NOTE : CONSONANT "C" IS ONLY PRONOUNCED

LIKE "CH" IN THE WORD "CHURCH" ... NO OTHER WAY!!

Review : Complete, correct order of all consonants :

Column	**1.**	**2.**	**3.**	**4.**	**5.**
Gutteral :	ka	kha	ga	gha	ṅa
Palatal :	ca	cha	ja	jha	ña
Cerebral :	ṭa	ṭha	ḍa	ḍha	ṇa
Dental :	ta	tha	da	dha	na
Labial :	pa	pha	ba	bha	ma

Step Two : Alphabetically, first vowels, second diphthongs, third consonants + nasals, and now the *semi-vowels* :

Palatal : ya, in sound has affinity to "ī" and"e"
Cerebral : ra, in sound has affinity to "ri" and "ar"
Dental : la, in sound has affinity to "ḷri" and "al"
Labial : va, in sound has affinity to "ū" and "wa".

Review of Semi-Vowels :

ya ra la va (column 6)

Step Three : Sibilants are the "s" sounds, exacting in placement.

Palatal : śa, like in word "session" or "seizure" (very heavy:)

Cerebral : ṣa, note under dotting: Like in "*sh*: be quiet:"

Dental : sa, air rushing through teeth, hissing sound (all in column 7).

Step Four : The final letter of the alphabet is the "Aspirant." It is pronounced just like the "h" in English. "ha" appears in column 6

In addition to the letters of the alphabet, there are also two special letters (sounds) for specific grammatical usage : (The visarga appears in column 7).

1. The Anusvāra: this is the inner body sound transliterated as: aṁ. It is not a part of the alphabet but co-relates to the various nasals. Part of the 'AUM:"
2. The visarga : is a declensional ending which reflects: "aḥ" It is most commonly pronounced like the English sound of agreement, aha. It can be attached to any vowel or diphthong:

aḥ, āḥ, iḥ, īḥ, uḥ, ūḥ, ṛḥ, ṛīḥ, ḷṛḥ, ḷṛīḥ, eḥ, aiḥ, oḥ, auḥ

Review : Total alphabet listed in correct sequence in columnwise fashion :

Vowels : a, ā, i, ī, u, ū, ṛ, ṛī, ḷri, ḷrī

Diphthongs : e, ai, o, au, Anusvāra: aṁ, and Visarga : ah

Columns :	**1.**	**2.**	**3.**	**4.**	**5.**	**6.**	**7.**	**8.**
Gutteral :	ka	kha	ga	gha	ṅa	ha	ah	(a)
Palatal :	ca	cha	ja	jha	ña	ya	śa	(i)
Cerebral :	ṭa	ṭha	ḍa	ḍha	ṇa	ra	ṣa	(ṛi)
Dental :	ta	tha	da	dha	na	la	sa	(ḷṛi)
Labial :	pa	pha	ba	bha	ma	va	aḥ	(u)

Special Notes to Remember : diacritical marks are very important :

do not confuse "e" with English "A"

do not confuse "ī" with English "E"

do not confuse "ṛ" or "ṛī" with semi-vowel "ra"

SPECIAL NOTE :

Columns one, two and seven are hard consonants.

Columns three, four, five and six are soft consonants.

Column eight represents vowel affinity to pronunciation.

Cerebral letters are sometimes called linguals or retroflexive letters in some texts.

In international transliterations there are the following variances:

ca = cha = cha = chha, ṣa = sha

ṛi is sometimes written as just ṛ

(as in ṛg - veda)

and also the palatal sibilant śa = sa

Here are some words for practice in correct pronunciation. Try to read aloud and do not concern yourself with memorization of these words, as in the process of learning Sanskṛit you will learn the inner full non-verbal meanings of the words rather than the traditional or sectarian translations. In the following chapter these same words will be set into Devanāgarī script.

1. ṛiṣi = sage
2. avatāra = Divine Incarnation
3. guṇa = a quality
4. gītā = Celestial Song
5. bhūta = a being or element
6. taijasa = shining, fiery
7. pṛthivī = earth
8. śarīra = form
9. puruṣa = man, spirit

10. veda = wisdom, Ancient scriptures
11. loka = world
12. bīja = seed
13. samādhi = spiritual state
14. nīla = blue
15. kośa = sheath
16. sutra = aphorism
17. nirvāṇa = liberation of spirit
18. Sāvitrī = Goddess of the sun
19. trimūrti = Trinity of Gods
20. prakriti = Nature
21. ācārya = teacher
22. prāna = life energy, breath
23. arhat = spiritually worthy one
24. jāgrat = waking state of consciousness
25. mārga = pathway for devotion
26. paramārtha = highest truth
27. ātman = the self
28. vidyā = knowledge
29. buddhi = understanding
30. kṛṣṇa = name of a Great Sage
31. Śambhala = sacred land
32. śāstra = scripture
33. śūnyatā = void, emptiness
34. kuṇḍalinī = serpent, spiral energy
35. śabda = sound
36. satya = truth
37. svapna = sleep state of consciousness
38. suṣupti = deep sleep consciousness
39. kleśa = pain
40. āśrama = Holy learning place
41. śloka = verse
42. krodha = anger

43. śiṣya	=	a disciple
44. bhakta	=	a devotee
45. nara	=	man
46. sarpa	=	snake
47. ānanda	=	bliss
48. candra	=	moon
49. junana	=	knowledge
50. amṛta	=	immortality
51. danta	=	tooth
52. vacana	=	speech
53. phala	=	fruit
54. dhana	=	wealth
55. annam	=	food
56. cakra	=	wheel, center
57. duḥkha	=	pain
58. sukha	=	happiness
59. iccha	=	wish
60. pūja	=	worship
61. sradhā	=	faith
62. tārā	=	a star
63. kṛyā	=	spiritual action
64. agni	=	fire
65. pitā	=	father
66. mātā	=	mother.

Mantram :

Satyān nāsti paro dharmaḥ	=	There is no religion higher than truth.
Brahmaivedaṁ sarvaṁ	=	All the Universe is Brahman!!
AUM, tat, sat	=	OM, That boundless Reality.

CHAPTER II

The Devanāgarī Script, Vowel Interpolation and Compound and Special Conjuct Consonants

The Sanskrit Devanāgarī script is an art form which permits the writer a great deal of leadway, but particular markings are very essential for reading recognition. There is only one design for each syllable, and all the consonants have an inherent short "a" sound like in the word Americ*a*. You can learn to write all the letters very quickly ultilization of the arabic numbers zero-five. Most important is the ligature's reference to the basic down-stroke! Practice this format, and then we will place them in the correct order.

० = व - ब - क - च - ञ

१ = र - ख - म - स ण[(b)] - न - ए - ऐ - ग

२ = श - थ

३ = अ - आ - ओ - औ - ड - ङ - इ - ई - उ - ऊ

धघ ल - ऌ - ॡ - छ

४ = झ - फ - भ - प - ष - त - ण[(b)]

(अ - आ - ओ - औ)[(a)] य

५ = ट - ठ - ढ - द - ज - ऋ - ॠ - ह

(a) (b) alternative forms

० व ब क च ञ
(Va or Wa) Ba Ka Ca ña
(Diphthongs)

(a)

१ र ख म स ण न ए ऐ ग
Ra Kha Ma Sa ṇa na e ai ga
(dental)

२ श थ झ
Śa (Palatal) Tha Jha
(b)

३ अ आ ओ औ ड ङ
a ā o au ḍa ṅa

३ इ ई उ ऊ ध घ झ
i ī u ū dha gha jha

३ ल लृ छ
la ṛi cha
(c)

४ फ झ भ प ष त ण
pha jha bha pa ṣa ta ṇa
(b)

४ अ आ ओ औ य
a ā o au ya

५ ट ठ ढ द ज ऋ ॠ
ṭa ṭha ḍha da ja ṛi ṛī

५ ह
ha

---

a =
b = } alternate forms.
c =

Vowels—Alphabetical order

अ	आ	इ	ई	उ	ऊ	ऋ
a	ā	i	ī	u	ū	ṛi
ॠ	लृ	ॡ	ए	ऐ	ओ	औ
ṛī	ḷri	ḷrī	e	ai	o	au

(.... diphthongs.......)

CONSONANTS, NASALS, SEMI-VOWELS, ASPIRANTS, SIBILANTS, Alphabetical Order

	1.	2.	3.	4.	5. Nasals	6. Aspirant / Semi-Vowels	7. Visarga / Sibilants......
Gutteral	क	ख	ग	घ	ङ	ह	:
	ka	kha	ga	gha	ṅa	ha	aḥ
Palatal	च	छ	ज	झ	ञ	य	श
	ca	cha	ja	jha	na	ya	sa
Cerebral	ट	ठ	ड	ढ	ण	र	ष
	ṭa	ṭha	ḍa	ḍha	ṇa	ra	śa
Dental	त	थ	द	धा	न	ल	स
	ta	tha	da	dha	na	la	sa
Lebial	प	फ	ब	भ	म	व	:
	pa	pha	ba	bha	ma	va	aḥ

Hard Consonants = Columns 1 , 2 , 7

Soft Consonants = Column 3 , 4 , 5 , 6

Alternate Forms :

अ	आ	ओ	औ	झ	झ	ण
a	ā	o	au	jha	jha	ṇa

Vowel Interpolatiion :

In Sanskrit all consonants have an inherent short "a". Vowels and all the diphthongs have a special manner of placement within a word, called medial form. Ṛi or ṛī are the exceptions which can occur in their initial form. Placement of these medial forms must be very accurate when joined to the original ligature.

a being inherent, has no medial form. To delete the "a" an oblique stroke is placed under the basic downstroke of the consonant, slanting to the right. It is called a virāma or halanta. \

ā an additional downstroke next to the consonant.

i a down stroke *preceding the consonant*, with a hook going to basic downstroke.ा

ī a down stroke *following the consonant*, with a hook going to basic downstroke.ि

u like a comma under the basic downstroke, sweeping in from right side. The nub is under the downstroke.ु

ū like a comma with the nub underneath the basic downstroke, sweeping to the right.

ṛi a sickle-like mark placed *under* basic downstroke.ट

ṛī a tiny bac wards 3 placed *under* the basic downstroke.ह

ḷṛ the same as the initial symbol placed *under* the basic downstroke.ॢ

ḷṛi the same as the initial symbol placed *under* the basic downstroke.ॣ

e a feather-like stroke over the consonant's basic downstroke.

ai two feather-like strokes *over* the consonant's basic downstroke.

o an additional downstroke after the consonant with one feather above the matra.ो

au an additional downstroke next to the consonant with two feathers above matra.ौ

aṁ the anusvāra, a nub placed over the basic downstroke to the right * ं

aḥ the visarga, a colon mark. It is a reflected vowel sound, most commonly aḥ * :

*- Note : The visarga and anusvāra are not letters of the alphabet, but grammatical symbols.

Compound Consonants :

In Sanskrit when two or more consonants have to be written without an intervening vowel, the following general principle is followed : all consonants, except the last of the group drop their basic downstroke.

g + dha = ग + ध = ग्ध

n + ya = न + य = न्य

m + pa = म + प = म्प

These compounds are endless, Great care must be taken to write these compounded consonants accurately.

n + t + ya = न + त + य = न्त्य

s + dh + ra = स + ध + र = स्ध्र

Most compound consonants are easily deciphered. However, the printing is subjected to the artistry of the writer, and even in print there are no standard type fonts. The following is a list of conjunct consonants which look totally different and must be memorized. They are not new letters of the alphabet : They are, however, very common for grammatical contruction and they must be memorized.

Special Note Concerning "r"

If it is first of two consonants it is a half-moon above syllable.

If it is the second of two consonants it is an oblique stroke at bottom of basic downstroke, veering to the left :

rgā र् + ग = र्ग grā ग् + र = ग्र

SPECIAL CONJUNCTED CONSONANTS : (can also use vowel interpolation)

क्त	क्ष	क्ष	ज्ञ	त्र	त्त
kta	kṣa	kṣa	jña	tra	tta

रु	रू		
ru	rū		
दृ	द्द	द्ध	द्भ
dṛi	dda	ddha	dbha
श	ह्म		
śa	hma		

COMPOUNDED CONSONANTS COMMONLY USED : Remember, when you forget how to compound consonants, the virama will negate the previous inherent "a"...

ष्ट	ष्ठ	ङ्ग	क्र
ṣṭa	ṣṭha	Ṅga	Kra
ल्प	क्ष्य	भ्य	च्छ
Lpa	Kṣya	bhya	ccha
ध्य	हृ	ण्ड	राड
dhya	Hṛi	ṇḍa	Ṇḍa
ष्ण	ब्र	र्क	न्न
ṣṇa	BRA	RKA	NNA
न्द	म्द	स्त्र	ब्म
NDA	Mda	STRA	BMA

A preview of the type fonts that I will use later in this text. First the entire alphabet, and then a duplication of the previous page of conjuncted and compounded consonants.

अ	आ	इ	ई	उ	ऊ	ऋ	ॠ
a	ā	i	ī	u	ū	ṛi	ṛī
ऌ	ॡ	ए	ऐ	ओ	औ	ं	:
ḷri	ḷrī	e	ai	o	au	aṁ	aḥ
क	ख	ग	घ	ङ	ह	:	
ka	kha	ga	gha	ṅa	ha	ah	
च	छ	ज	झ	ञ	य	श	
ca	cha	ja	jha	ña	ya	śa	

ट	ठ	ड	ढ	ण	र	ष
ṭa	ṭha	ḍa	ḍha	ṇa	ra	ṣa
त	थ	द	ध	न	ल	स
ta	tha	da	dha	na	la	sa
प	फ	ब	भ	म	व	:
ph	pha	ba	bha	ma	va	aḥ

SPECIAL CONJUNCTED CONSONANTS : (Can also use vowel interpolation).

क्त	क्ष	ज्ञ	त्र	त्त	रु	रू
kta	kṣa	jña	tra	tta	ru	rū
दृ	द्द	द्भ	द्ध	श्र	ख्य	
dṛ	ddā	dbha	ddha	śra	khya	

COMPOUNDED CONSONANTS COMMONLY USED : (Remember, when you forget how to compound consonants, the virama will negate the previous inherent "a" ....

ष्ट	ष्ठ	क्र	ल्प	क्ष्य	भ्य	च्छ	ध्म	द्य	
ṣṭa	ṣṭha	kra	lpa	kṣya	bhya	ccha	dhma	dya	
हृ	ण्ड	ष्ण	ब्र	र्क	न्न	न्द	म्द	स्त्र	ब्म
hṛ	ṇḍa	ṣṇa	bra	rka	nna	nda	mda	stra	bma

[For all other look for the basic down stroke, medial vowel signs, etc.] On my typewriter the numbers look like this:-

१	२	३	४	५	६	७	८	९	१०
1	2	3	4	5	6	7	8	9	10

For practice a list of words in correct transliterated form is give, and its correct form in Devanāgarī script is given on the following pages.

1. arth
2. Sannyās
3. Vānaprasth
4. Grihastha
5. Brahmacarya
6. Āśrama
7. Upniṣad
8. Śūdra
9. Bhuṣaṇaṁ
10. Ratnaṁ
11. Haṁsah
12. Jīvanaṁ
13. Vanaṁ
14. Kupaḥ
15. Srī Aurobindo
16. Buddha Siddhārtha
17. Mahātmā Gandhi
18. Śri Kṛṣṇa
19. Patañjali
20. Rāmakṛṣṇa
21. Śaṅkarācārya
22. Vivekānanda
23. Īśvara
24. Brāhamaṅa
25. Kāma
26. Mokṣa
27. Aśvaḥ
28. Deśah
29. Gajaḥ
30. Jalaṁ
31. Śīlaṁ
32. Palṛaṁ
33. Kamalaṁ
34. Kanakaṁ
35. Annaṁ
36. Meghaḥ
37. Vṅkṣaḥ
38 Hatha yoga
39. Chatur varṇa
40. Kṣatriya
41. Dāsaḥ
42. Vaiśya

१ अर्थ
२ संन्यास
३ वानप्रस्थ
४ गृहस्थ
५ ब्रह्मचर्य
६ आश्रम
७ उपनिषद्
८ शूद्र
९ मषनं
१० रत्नं
११ हंस:
१२ जीवनं
१३ वनं
१४ कुप:
१५ श्री औरोबिन्दो
१६ बुद्ध सिद्धार्थ

१७	महात्मा गाँधी	३०	जलं
१८	श्री कृष्ण	३१	शीलं
१९	पतञ्जली	३२	पत्रं
२०	रामकृष्ण	३३	कमलं
२१	शंकराचार्य	३४	कनकं
२२	विवेकानन्द	३५	अन्नं
२३	ईश्वर	३६	मेघः
२४	ब्राह्मण	३७	वृक्षः
२५	काम	३८	हठयोग
२६	मोक्ष	३९	चतुरवर्ण
२७	अश्वः	४०	क्षत्रिय
२८	देशः	४१	दासः
२९	गजः	४२	वैश्य

Vowel Interpolation :

K	Ka	Kā	Ki	Kī	Ku	Kū	Kṛi	Kṛī	Kḷri	Kḷrī	Ke	Kai	Ko	Kau	Kaṁ	Kaḥ)
क्	क	का	कि	की	कु	कू	कृ	कॄ	क्लृ	क्लॄ	के	कै	को	कौ	कं	कः
ख्	ख	खा	खि	खी	खु	खू	खृ	खॄ	ख्लृ	ख्लॄ	खे	खै	खो	खौ	खं	खः
ग्	ग	गा	गि	गी	गु	गू	गृ	गॄ	ग्लृ	ग्लॄ	गे	गै	गो	गौ	गं	गः
घ्	घ	घा	घि	घी	घु	घू	घृ	घॄ	घ्लृ	घ्लॄ	घे	घै	घो	घौ	घं	घः
ङ्	ङ	ङा	ङि	ङी	ङु	ङू	ङृ	ङॄ	ङ्लृ	ङ्लॄ	ङे	ङै	ङो	ङौ	ङं	ङः
च्	च	चा	चि	ची	चु	चू	चृ	चॄ	च्लृ	च्लॄ	चे	चै	चो	चौ	चं	चः
छ्	छ	छा	छि	छी	छु	छू	छृ	छॄ	छ्लृ	छ्लॄ	छे	छै	छो	छौ	छं	छः
ज्	ज	जा	जि	जी	जु	जू	जृ	जॄ	ज्लृ	ज्लॄ	जे	जै	जो	जौ	जं	जः
झ्	झ	झा	झि	झी	झु	झू	झृ	झॄ	झ्लृ	झ्लॄ	झे	झै	झो	झौ	झं	झः
ञ्	ञ	ञा	ञि	ञी	ञु	ञू	ञृ	ञॄ	ञ्लृ	ञ्लॄ	ञे	ञै	ञो	ञौ	ञं	ञः
ट्	ट	टा	टि	टी	टु	टू	टृ	टॄ	ट्लृ	ट्लॄ	टे	टै	टो	टौ	टं	टः

ट् ठ ठा ठि ठी ठु ठू ठृ ठॄ ठ्लृ ठ्लॄ ठे ठै ठो ठौ ठं ठः
ड् ड डा डि डी डु डू डृ डॄ ड्लृ ड्लॄ डे डै डो डौ डं डः
ढ् ढ ढा ढि ढी ढु ढू ढृ ढॄ ढ्लृ ढ्लॄ ढे ढै ढो ढौ ढं ढः
ण् ण णा णि णी णु णू णृ णॄ ण्लृ ण्लॄ णे णै णो णौ णं णः
त् त ता ति ती तु तू तृ तॄ त्लृ त्लॄ ते तै तो तौ तं तः
थ् थ था थि थी थु थू थृ थॄ थ्लृ थ्लॄ थे थै थो थौ थं थः
द् द दा दि दी दु दू दृ दॄ द्लृ द्लॄ दे दै दो दौ दं दः
ध् ध धा धि धी धु धू धृ धॄ ध्लृ ध्लॄ धे धै धो धौ धं धः
न् न ना नि नी नु नू नृ नॄ न्लृ न्लॄ ने नै नो नौ नं नः
प् प पा पि पी पु पू पृ पॄ प्लृ प्लॄ पे पै पो पौ पं पः
फ् फ फा फि फी फु फू फृ फॄ फ्लृ फ्लॄ फे फै फो फौ फं फः
ब् ब बा बि बी बु बू बृ बॄ ब्लृ ब्लॄ बे बै बो बौ बं बः
भ् भ भा भि भी भु भू भृ भॄ भ्लृ भ्लॄ भे भै भो भौ भं भः
म् म मा मि मी मु मू मृ मॄ म्लृ म्लॄ मे मै मो मौ मं मः
य् य या यि यी यु यू यृ यॄ टलृ टलॄ ये यै यो यौ यं यः
र् र रा रि री रु रू - - - - रे रै रो रौ रं रः
ल् ल ला लि ली लु लू - - - - ले लै लो लौ लं लः
व् व वा वि वी वु वू वृ वॄ व्लृ व्लॄ वे वै वो वौ वं वः
श् श शा शि शी शु शू शृ शॄ श्लृ श्लॄ शे शै शो शौ शं शः
ष् ष षा षि षी षु षू षृ षॄ ष्लृ ष्लॄ षे षै षो षौ षं षः
स् स सा सि सी सु सू सृ सॄ स्लृ स्लॄ से सै सो सौ सं सः
ह् ह हा हि ही हु हू हृ हॄ ह्लृ ह्लॄ हे है हो हौ हं हः

Overall review of Chapter II :

1. In correct order write the vowels and diphthongs.
2. In Devanāgarī script write the five categories of consonants, including the nasals.
3. Write the semi-vowels, sibilants and final aspirant.
4. In chart fashion write the seven columns of letters.
5. Write the full vowel interpolations of : “ja, bha, la.”

6. Set into Devanāgarī the following passage from the Gītā.

   budhirjṅānanasammoḥ kṣamā satyaṁ damaḥ śamaḥ sukhaṁ duḥkhaṁ bhavobhāvo bhayaṁ cābhayameva ca,

   Gītā X,4.

   na hi jṅānena sadṛśaṁ pavitramiha vidyate
   tatsvayaṁ yogasaṁsiddhaḥ kālenātmani vindati

   Gītā IV, 38

   बुद्धिर्ज्ञानम सम्मोहः क्षमा सत्यं दमः शमः।
   सुखं दुःखं भवोऽभावो भयं चाभयमेव च।

   गीता १०, ४

   न हि ज्ञानेन सदृशं पवित्रमिह विद्यते।
   तत्स्वयं योगसंसिद्ध : कालेनात्मनि विन्दति।

   गीता ४, ३८

Now : Try to read these Devanāgarī words with or without the help of the reading list in the previous chapter. For practice also copy them. Consult next page for Roman transliterations.

ज्ञान । चन्द्र । आनंद । सर्प । नर । भक्त ।

पृथ्वी । शरीर । पुरुष । वेद । लोक ।

समाधि । नील । कोश । सूत्र ।

सावित्री । त्रिमुर्ति । प्रकृति । आचार्य ।

विद्या । बुद्धि । कृष्ण । शम्भल ।

शून्यता । कुण्डलिनी । शब्द । सत्य । स्वप्न ।

सुषुप्ति । क्लेश । आश्रम । श्लोक । क्रोध । शिष्य ।

तैजस । भुत । गीता । गुण । अवतार। ऋषि ।

अमृत । दन्त । वचन । फल । धन । अन्नम्

चक्र । दुःख । सुख । इच्छ । पुज । श्रद्ध ।

बीज । निर्वाण । प्राण । आत्मन् । शास्त्र । क्रिया ।

(मन्त्र)–

सत्यान् नास्ति परो धर्म

ब्रह्मैवेदं अर्वं

ॐ तत् सत्

After having read the previous page, you may consult this transliterated roman script page for any problems that you may have had.

jñāna	chandra	ānanda	sarpa	nara	bhakta
pṛthivī	śarīra	puruṣa	veda	loka	
samādhi	nīla	koṣa	sutra		
sāvitrī	trimurti	prakṛti	acarya		
arhat	jāgrat	mārga	paramārtha		
vidhyā	buddhi	kṛṣṇa	sambhala		
śunyatā	kuṇḍalini	śabda	satya	svapna	
suṣupti	kleśa	āṣrama	ṣloka	krodha	śi¨ya
taijāsa	bhuta	gītā	guṇa	avatāra	ṛiṣi
amṛta	danta	vacana	phala	dhana	annam
cakra	duḥkhaṁ	sukha	iccha	puja	śraddha
tārā	kriyā	agni	pitā	mātā	

mantraṁ

satyān nāsti paro dharmaḥ
brahmaivedaṁ sarvaṁ
Aum tat sat

The purpose of your dedication to learn this Divine language is to feel the non-verbal energy and power it communicates. I hope that you will bear in mind the discipline, dedication and devotion to organically grow with each step of your learning.

"The complete vowel interpolation of all of the letters of the alphabet has been given earlier in this book."

Each letter has a numeric basis correlated to the molecular structure of the physical and psychic body. The word "mantra" literally means thinking, by knowing in feeling, in order to transcend to altered states of consciousness and Divine Communion known as meditation.

Meditation requires a quiet place and an uninterrupted

time span. If you can sit in the lotus posture, this is good, but not required. One should sit comfortably, and breathe deeply, utilizing the full power of the diaphragm to empty the lungs, and then refill them. When you empty the lungs, wait a few seconds to activate the Kumbha (Divine-Fire), and again after you fill the lungs also wait for the Khumba to activate.

Doing the entire vowel interpolation is the longest form of meditation and is sometimes referred to as śabda-Brahma-Mantra, or receiving the non-verbal transcendental Divine inflow of both ascension and descension of Energy. I encourage you to do this not only for meditation, but also for memorization of the syllabic construes for further grammatical growth.

The Cakras are the energy-centers deep within the physical body and the psychic being. Study their locations, and note that each has a seed in the center, the "bija-letter," and around are the lotus petals each having a letter also. Just as sound vibrates at lower frequencies, at higher frequencies colours vibrate as well. Each cakra has a colour attached springing from the spectrum of the 'rainbow-prism'.

For this form of meditation there are two methods that can be used:

1. Seated comfortably, quietly repeat the bīja of a particular mantra of your own choosing. Try not to think; try to imagine the colour of the Energy-Center, with no other thoughts in your mind. Repeat the bija with your own body sound first outwardly and then inwardly. Use the fullest praṇic breathing (as taught in the techniques of yoga) as you can, and open up to receive the Divine Inflow of Energy.
2. If you have more time to meditate with this form of meditation, you can do the vowel interpolation of each of the letters of the cakra. Our life is a 'continuum', as opposed to a straight-line of being born and waiting to die. When we are born we appear as a point on this circle and bring with us a great deal of praṇic life-force. In this bija-mantra meditation we open up to receive the inflow through the 'top-knot' for self-Realization. Do not ask or expect anything, and just let the state of consciousness fill with Divine Energy.

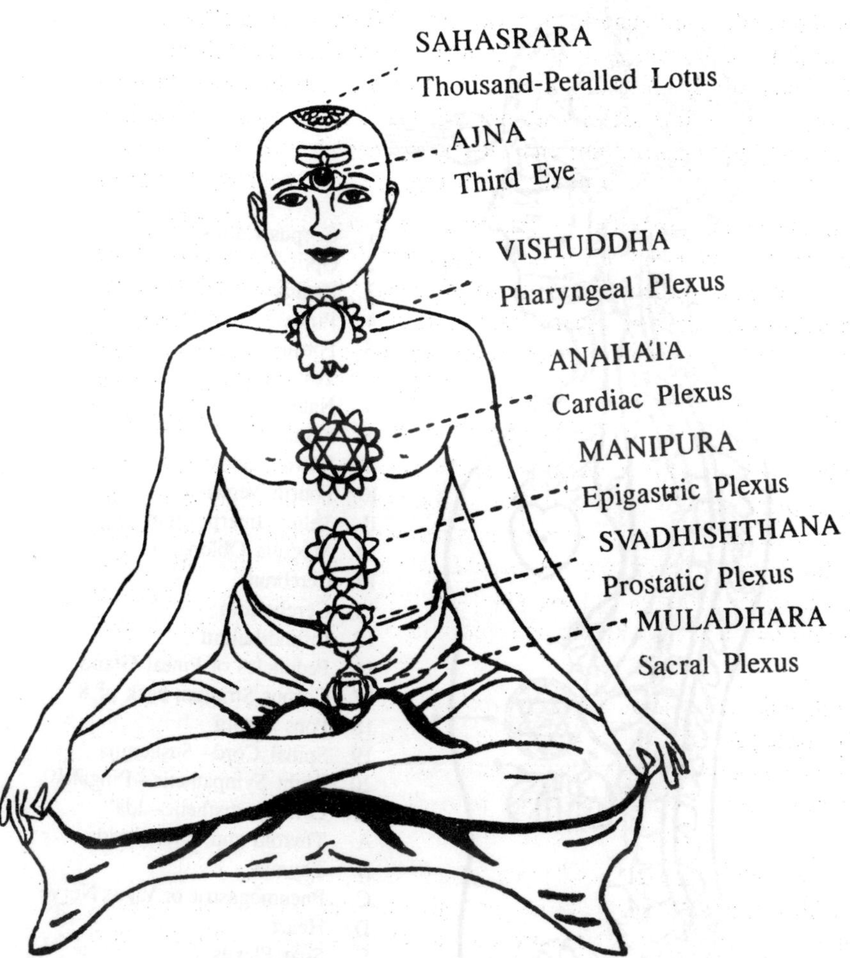

SEVEN LOTUS CHAKRAS

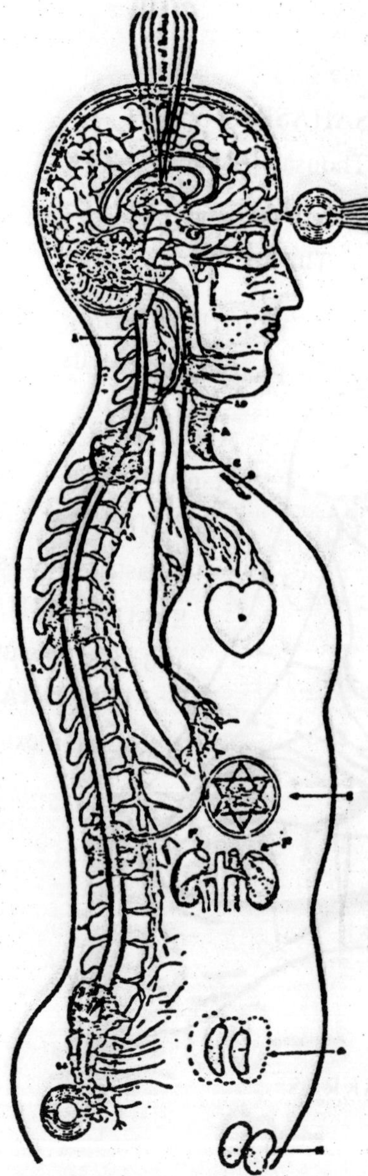

1. Corpus Callosum
2. Optic Thalamus
3. Pituitarty
4. Pineal
5. Formix
6. Testes }
7. Nates } Corporaquadrigemina
8. Septum Lucidum
9. Third Ventricle
10. Fourth Ventricle
11. Velum Interpositum
12. Medulla Oblongata
13. Cerebrum
14. Cerebellum
15. Infundibulum
16. Peduncles of Pineal Gland
17. Corpus Striatum back of 8
18. Pons Varolii
19. Spinal Cord—Sushumna
20. Right Sympathetic—Pingala
21. Left Sympathetic—Ida

A. Thyroid and Parathyroids
B. Thymus
C. Pneumogastric or Vagus Nerve
D. Heart
E. Soar Plexus
F. Adrenals
G. Gonads—Female Ovaries
H. Gonads—Male Testes

VITAL CENTERS OF CONSCIOUSNESS

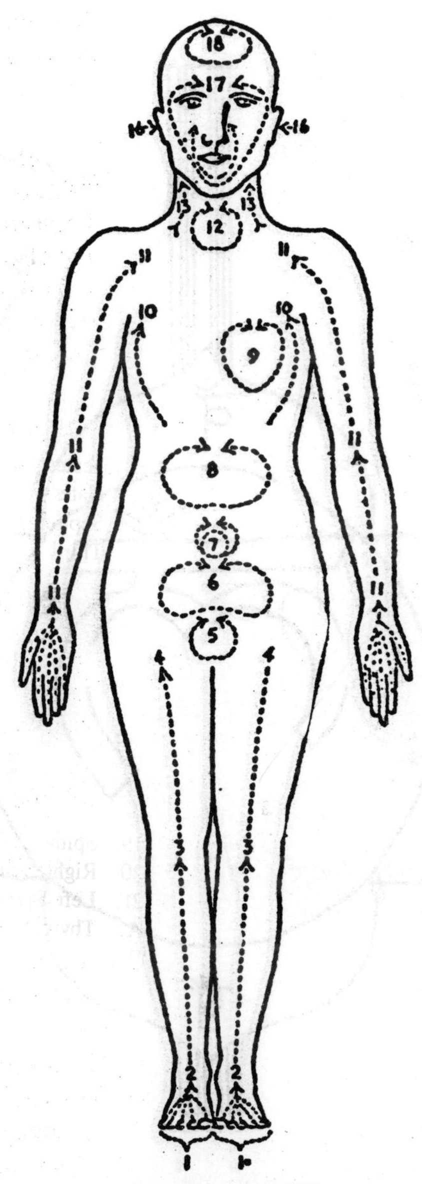

BODY CHART
(For Relaxation and Charging)

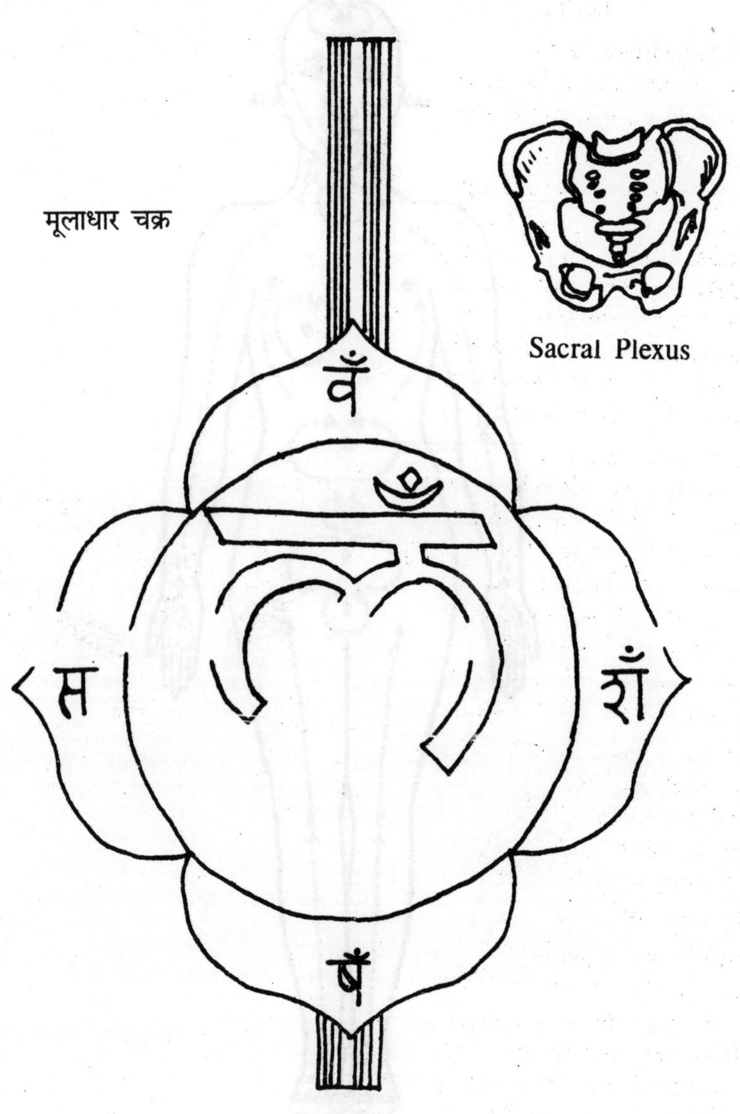

MŪLĀDHĀRA CHAKRA

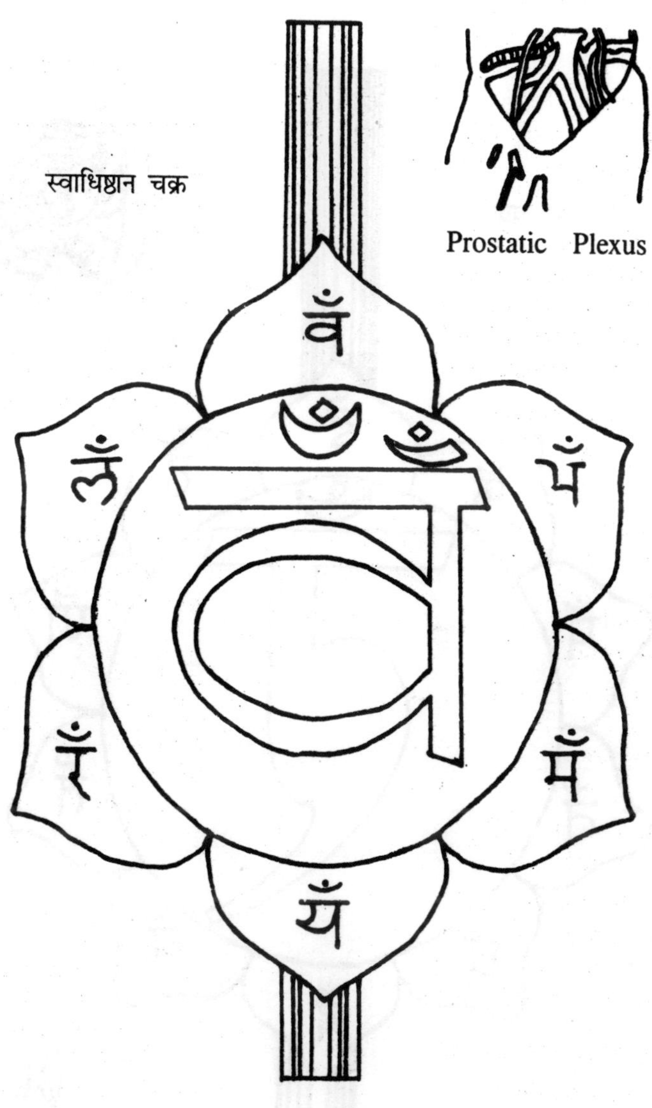

SVĀDHIṢṬHĀNA CHAKRA

MAṆIPŪRA CHAKRA

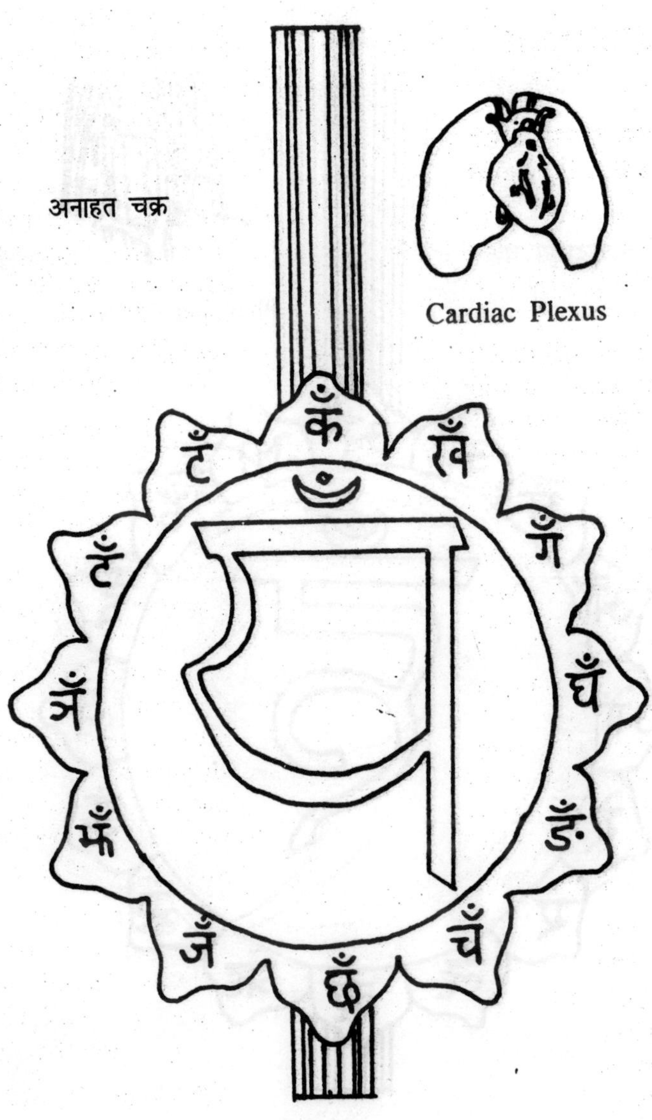

ANĀHATA CHAKRA

VIŚUDDHA CHAKRA

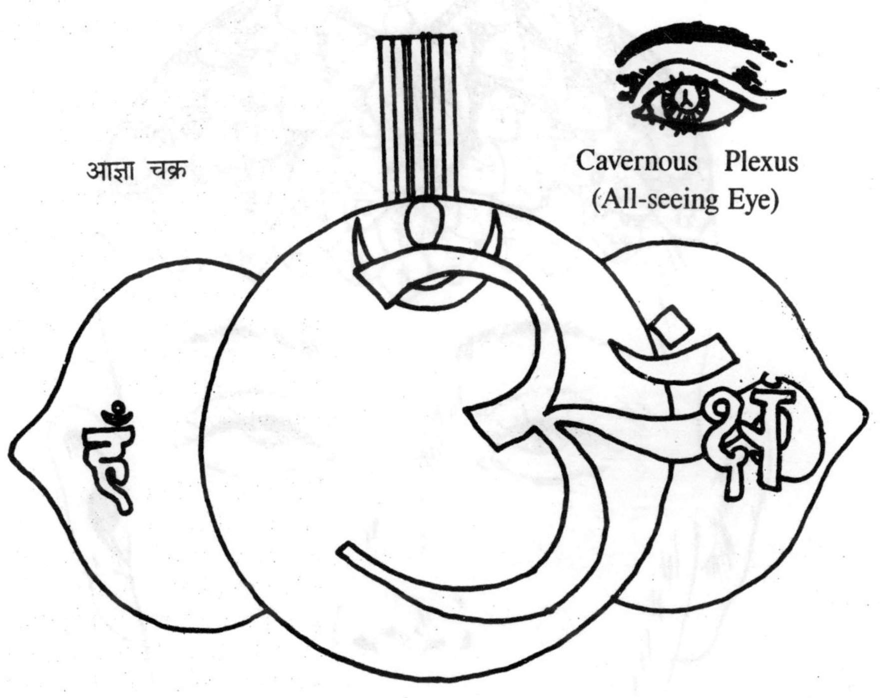

ĀJÑĀ CHAKRA

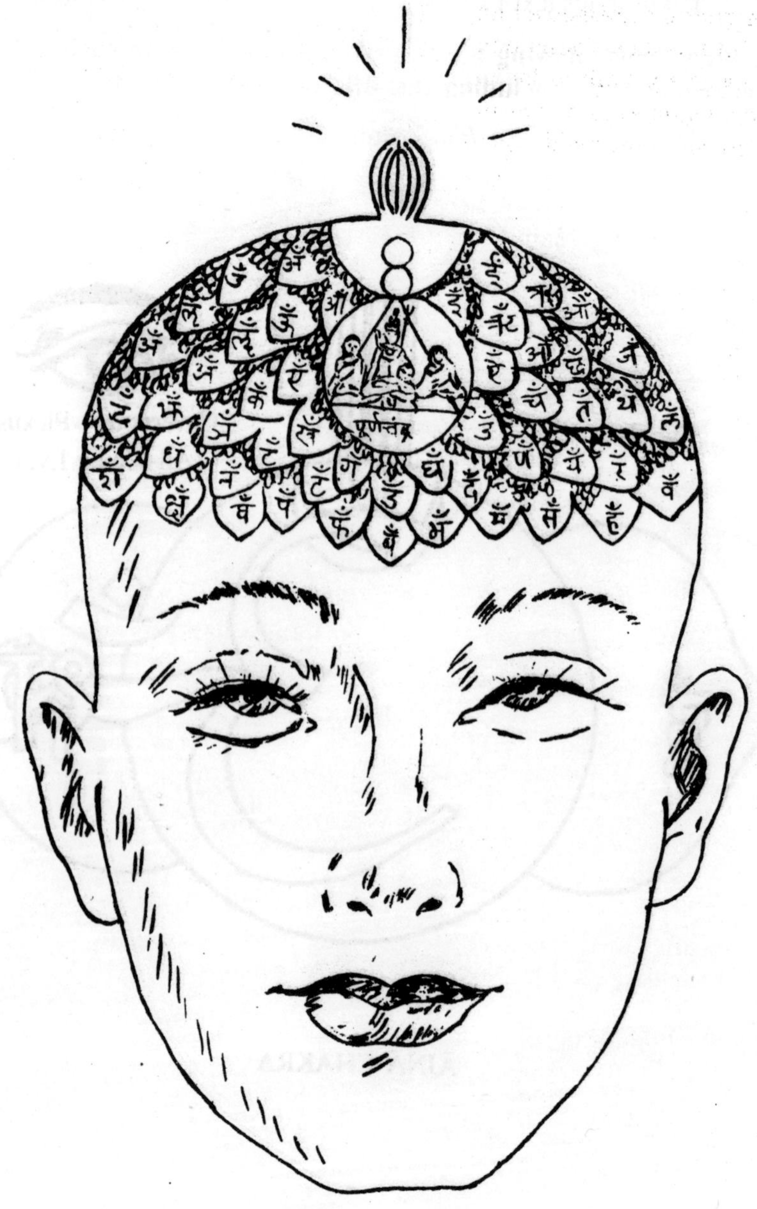

SAHASRARA CHAKRA

Later in this text I will introduce other forms of meditation.

Cakra Chart showing the letters of the alphabet in each 'energy-centre', including the Bija or seed letter.

Mūlādhāracakra : Bija =laṁ लँ

वँ शँ षँ सँ

vam śam ṣam sam

Svadhiṣṭhānacakra : Bija = Vaṁ वँ

Yaṁ raṁ laṁ vaṁ bhaṁ maṁ

यँ रँ लँ वँ भँ मँ

Maṇipūracakra : Bija = raṁ रँ

taṁ thaṁ daṁ dhaṁ naṁ paṁ phaṁ ḍaṁ ḍhaṁ ṇaṁ

तँ थँ दँ धँ नँ पँ फँ डँ ढँ णँ

Anāhatacakra : Bija = yaṁ यँ

kaṁ khaṁ gaṁ ghaṁ ṅaṁ caṁ chaṁ jaṁ

कँ खँ गँ घँ ङँ चँ छँ जँ

jhaṁ ñaṁ ṭaṁ ṭhaṁ

झँ अँ टँ ठँ

Viśudhākhyacakra: Bija =haṁ हँ

अँ आँ इँ ईं उँ ऊँ ऋँ ॠँ लृँ

aṁ āṁ iṁ īṁ uṁ ūṁ ṛiṁ ṛīṁ ḷriṁ

लॄँ एँ ऐं ओं औं :

ḷrīṁ eṁ aiṁ oṁ auṁ am (anusvara) aḥ (visarga)

Ājñācakra : Bija - AUM ॐ

haṁ kṣaṁ

हँ क्षँ

Ṣahasraracakra : The entire Devanāgarī alphabet with all vowels interpolated.

CHAPTER III

INTRODUCTION TO THE FIRST CONJUGATION ETC.

Lesson One : Cursory over-view of conjugations and grammatical terminology, vowel strenghthening clarification.

Lesson Two : First conjugation :

Step One : Roots with no changes.

Step Two : Roots with medial vowel change.

Step Three : Roots with final vowel change.

Step Four : Irregular roots of First conjugation.

Lesson Three : Introduction to the Nominative and Accusative Cases.

Step One : Vocabulary of Masc. and Neuter Nouns in अ

Step Two : Prepositions governing Accusative Case.

Step Three : Exercises using transitive sentence structures. Sandhi rules for visarga, and final.म्.

Lesson Four : Total review to this point.

LESSON ONE : CURSORY OVER-VIEW OF CONJUGATIONS AND GRAMMATICAL TERMINOLOGY AND VOWEL STRENGHTHENING.

"Now we will review all of the grammatical terminology which we will jenerals all ready discured in chapter one".

—Vowels, letters representing a free flowing sound in sets of cannot be used within a word, so remember the medial forms from the earlier vowel interpolation exercises.

अ a — ā आ (ा)

इ i (ि) ī ई (ी)

उ u (ु) ū ऊ (ू)

ऋ ṛ (ृ) rī ॠ (ॄ)

लृ ṛi (लृ) ḷṛī लॄ (लॄ)

—Diphthongs, a double vowel sound showing its component parts in pronunciation, and corresponding semivowel (alternative form) shown.

Remember the medial forms too!

ए e (े) = अ+इ corresponding semivowel is य

ऐ ai (ै) = आ+ई corresponding semivowel is य

ओ o (ो) = अ+उ corresponding semivowel is व

औ au (ौ) = आ+ऊ corresponding semivowel is व

Simple Vowels अ–आ	इ–ई	उ–ऊ	ऋ–ॠ	लृ–लॄ
Guna strenghthening अ	ए (े)	ओ (ो)	अर्	अल्
Vriddhi strenghthening आ	ऐ (ै)	औ (ौ)	आर्	आल्

—Special note! The anusvāra is not a letter of the alphabet, but merely a special grammatical usage. aṁ.

The visārga is not a letter of the alphabet, but merely a special grammatical usage.: aḥ

—Semivowels, sounds which partake of the nature of a vowel and of a consonant. Study the following triangles showing inter-relationships of vowels, diphthongs and semivowels. This is called samprasaraṇa, and can be used for meditation, perhaps referred to bijam (seed) mantras.

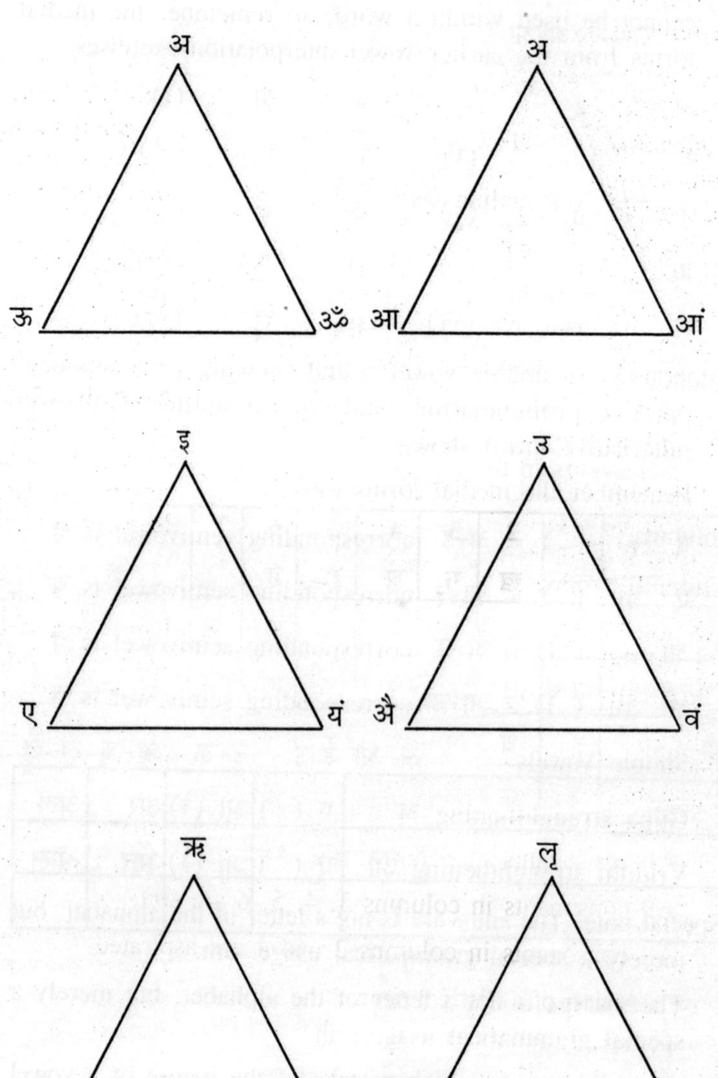
अ
ऊ
ॐ
अ
आ
आं
इ
ए
यं
उ
औ
वं
ऋ
अर्
रं
ऌ
अल्
लं

Simple Vowels	अ-आ	इ-ई(य)*	उ-ऊ(व)*	ऋ-ॠ(र)*	ऌ-ॡ(ल)*
guṇa form	अ	ए (े)	ओ (ो)	अर्	अल्
vṛddhi form	आ	ऐ (ै)	औ (ौ)	आर्	आल्

* = corresponding semivowel!

—Consonant, any sound where the tongue, lips, teeth or glottis block the air in pronunciation. In Sanskrit all are classified according to where the sound comes from. Each consonant is oramented with and aspirant forming a single phoneme as indicated in columns two and four. Each classification of consonants has its own nasal, and a sibilant occurs in the palatal, cerebral and dental as well :—

Columns :	1	2	3	4	5	6	7	Related Vowels
Gutteral	क	ख	ग	घ	ङ	ह	:	अ - आ
Palatal	च	छ	ज	झ	ञ	य	श	इ - ई
Cerebral	ट	ठ	ड	ढ	ण	र	ष	ऋ - ॠ
Dental	त	थ	द	ध	न	ल	स	ऌ - ॡ
Labial	प	फ	ब	भ	म	व	:	उ - ऊ

All consonants in columns 1,2,7 are hard.

All consonants in columns 3, 4, 5, 6 are soft.

All consonants in columns 2 and 4 are aspirated.

Tense : Action of a distinct time.

I. Present

II. Imperfect

III. Future

IV. Perfect

V. Infinitive

VI. Aorist : denoting that action of the verb which took

place in an unspecified past time without implication of continuance or of repetition.

VII. The usage of particles or auxiliaries instead of inflection.

Mood : To express a manner in which the verbal action or state was conceived; whether as a fact, a supposal, wish, benediction or possibility.

I. Imperative

II. Potential or optative

III. Causative

IV. Desiderative

V. Frequentative

VI. Conditional

Participle : Forms of the verbs used as an adjective in all voices and for very special tense constructions. Unlike the Verbosity of English, in Sanskrit one constantly combines constures into more compact units.

Inflection : The change of form in which words undergo a distinction of case, gender, tense, person, mood, voice, etc. by prefixes affixes and infix particles or letters.

Indeclinables : Parts of speech not subject to inflectional termination.

—Sibilants, the various sounds of s's. Note column 7 where each is specifically classified, i.e. palatal, cerebral and dental. Also remember they are *hard* consonants.

—Aspirant, a diaphragmatic rushing of air, the letter "ha."

Conjugation, a schematic arrangement of the inflectional forms expanded from the basic root form. The endings attached to the root clarify person, "I, you, he, she to it, etc. The gender (masculine, feminine, neuter) and the number (singular, dual or plural,)

Declension, a schematic arrangement of the inflectional forms expanded from the nouns, adjectives, substantives, etc.

derived from the verbal original root forms.

Voice : Form of the verb which indicates the relation of the subject of the verb to the action which it expresses:-

1. Active Voice—You are eating bread. (Can include an object)
2. Passive Voice - Bread is eaten by me.
3. Intransitive- He is eating (no object).
4. Parasmaipada - I build house for others.
5. Atmanepada - I build house for myself.
6. Impersonal Voice: It is done by me.
7. Ubhaypada—Verbs used either parasmai or atmane-pada.

Agglutination : A running together of primitive words into compounds, in which the form and meaning of the constituent parts undergo little or no change.

Particle : A unit of speech used as an uninflected word but serving as a loose affix expressing some general aspect of meaning or some connective or other junction. i.e. prepositions, conjunctions, prenominal adverbs, etc.

Hiatus : A gap in the sound

Coalescence : Combining into one unit of pronunciation.

Sandhi : Assimilation resulting when words are pronounced without a pause inbetween them. Saṁ = putting together, and dhi = in orde to hold. Special rules for vowels, consonants, and the visarg constructions.

VERBAL ROOTS

In addition to vowel strenghthening verbal roots can be subjected to :

a. a prepostional prefix, altering the intent
b. 10 tenses
c. 4 moods
d. various forms of Sandhi
e. in noun forms, 8 cases.

Grammatical construction in Sanskrit is more concerned with inner vibration and poetical metre, hence a rigid word order guided by a continuous flow of energy brought about by internal and external Sandhi rules. The following is an example of the multiplicity of constructions from a simple root "budh, to understand, to know."

bodhati, he, she or it knows or understands (present tense)

abodhat, he, she or it knew or understood (imperfect tense)

bodhate, he, she or it knows or understands for himself (Atmanepada)

Parasmaipada infers an action for someone else, and Atmanepada infers an action for one's self. Some roots belong to either P. or A., and some can be used both ways, and are called Ubhayapada.

Now this same verbal root prefixed with a preposition : note new meanings

*anu*bodhyate = to think of internally

*ava*bodhyate = to perceive internally

*ud*bodhyate = to awaken internally

*pra*bodhyate = to awaken internally, a different inner vibration number.

*prati*bodhyate = to observe internally

*vi*bodhyate = to learn and understand internally

sambodhyate = to recognize internally

(Now shown in noun and adjectival forms) :

bodha, bodhana = knowledge

buddhi = intellect

bodhaka = informer

baudha = wise

buddhimat = intellectual

budhyate = it is know by him

bubhudtsate/bubhudiṣate = he wishes to know

bobudhyate = he knows well!

bodhidharma = he knows a right action

bodhisatva = one who feels the duality of truth

budhaḥ = a Sage, the planet Mercury

Yet one more example of verbal root construes, bearing in mind that each incorporates the first, second and third person, singular or dual or plural :-

nī = to lead, Conjugation I, guṇa change to redical naya (P. & A.)

nayati, present tense, he leads, etc.

anayat, imperfect tense, he led, etc.

nayatu, imperative mood, 'let him lead'

nayet, potential mood, 'May he lead'

niṇāya, perfect tense, 'he led'

anaisīt, Aorist tense, 'he led'

neṣyati, future tense, 'he will lead'

aneṣyat, conditional mood, 'he would have led'

nīyate, passive construction, 'he is led'

nāyayati, causative mood, 'he causes to lead'

anāyayat, imperfect causative mood, 'he caused to lead'

nayayatu, imperative causative, 'let him cause to lead'

nananet, optative causative mood, 'he may cause to lead'

nināyayiṣati, desiderative causative mood, 'he wants to ċause to lead'

ninīsu, adjectival form, wanting to lead

ninīṣā, substantive form, the wish to lead

nenīyate, Intensive form, 'he leads forcibly'

(Now with prefixing root with a propositioṇ)

*anu*nayati = to request

*apa*nayati = to carry away

*abhi*nayati = to act on the stage

ānayati = to fetch or bring

*ud*nayati	=	to raise
*upa*nayati	=	to offer
*nir*nayati	=	to decide
*pari*ṇīyati	=	to marry
*vi*nayati	=	to dispel
saṁmayati	=	to unite

An astounding array of constructions from a simple verbal root!

There are approximately 2200 primitive verbal energy root forms. These are divided into two basic classifications; those that are conjugated in the same manner, and those that are conjugated irregularly with special letter inserts, or various other devises. The following is a tabulation showing approximate amounts of roots, noting that in the early stages of mastering their usage we will be using only the regular (conjugational) ones which will comprise most of the language:-

CONJUGATIONAL ROOTS :

I	=	1079 roots
IV	=	140 roots
VI	=	157 roots
X	=	598 roots
		1974 roots (A majority of forms)
II	=	72 roots
III	=	24 roots
V	=	34 roots
VII	=	25 roots
VIII	=	10 roots
IX	=	61 roots
		226 roots (Highly irregular reserved for more advanced studies)

Special Note : The verbs in their primitive form are the energy out of which nouns, substantives, adjectives and further forms are created. Every letter of the alphabet contains a numeric vibration which internalizes in meditation, hence the "inner-implosive" meanings which brings about a non-verbal understanding of intense spiritual communion. Most of the roots are monosyllabic and subject to vowel strengh-thening and orthographic changes to enable the philosophical under-standing to become internalized. Vowel changes can alter the entire meaning of the various construes, i.e.

Verb root	Noun	Adjective
man=to think	manas=the mind	mānasa=mental
div=to shine	deva=god	daiva=divine
budh=to understand	bodha=knowledge	baudha=wise
dṛi=to hold	dharm=a way	
dhārmika=righteous		
kḷrip=to be in order	kalpa=time	kālpa=cyclic

Slowly grow with the practice both written and sounded out orally. Be patient as Sanskrit has been here for over 6,000 years, and don't rush ahead until each step is mastered using the 3 d's mentioned in an earlier chapter.

THE CONSTRUCTION OF VERBAL ROOTS OF CONJUGATION

Step One :—Present tense, active voice, intransitive constructions. Study following paradigms :

PERSON:	*SINGULAR*	*DUAL*	*PLURAL*
1	I	We two	We
2	(thou) you	you two	you
3*	he, she, it	they two	they

Sanskrit endings preceded by short अ, excepting in 1st pers. S, D, Pl. Where म् and व् is preceded by long आ, remembering अ is inherent in all consonants, and long आ uses medial form within words : (ा)

1	āmi ामि	āvaḥ ाव:	āmaḥ ाम:
2	asi सि	athaḥ थ:	atha थ
3*	ati ति	ataḥ त:	anti अन्ति

* In vocabulary lists, verbs are shown in 3rd per. sing. including changes needed for each conjugation. In the philosophy the ego is subdued, hence he, she or it is emphasized!

LESSON TWO : FIRST CONJUGATION

The first conjugation will be approached by steps which should be mastered and organically memorized by both sounding out each example and mentally drilling the exercises. First will be an exercise of Sanskrit to English, and then English to Sanskrit, The answers will be given in a special appendix.

STEP ONE :—The verbal root requires guṇa for medial vowel. (remember अ is its own guṇa form, hence no change)

Vocabulary list :—Included will be synonyms, however the most common usage will be underscored.

Vocabulary list

Sanskrit

Root	**3rd. per. sing.**	**English**
पठ्	पठति	to study, learn, read.
चिन्त	चिन्तति	to think over, reflect, consider.
जल्प	जल्पति	to prattle.
वद्	वदति	to speak.
पत्	पतति	to fall, fly.
रक्ष्	रक्षति	to protect, to take care of.
वस्	वसति	to dwell.
पच्	पचति	to cook.
खन्	खनति	to dig.
जीव्	जीवति	to be alive, live.
धाव	धावति	to run.
ईर्ष्य्	इर्ष्यति	to enevy, be jealous of.

Exercise *1*. Translate following into Sanskrit consult Answer given below.

१. रक्षत:	२. वदन्ति	३. चलत:
४. वपति	५. वसाम:	६. चिन्तामि
७. पतति	८. पठामि	९. हसामि
१०. क्रीडति:	११. जीवथ	१२. निन्दय:
१३. वदन्ति	१४. नमाव:	१५. खादाम:

Answer :

1. They two protect.
2. They speak.
3. They two move.
4. He/she/it rours.
5. We dwell.
6. I reflect.
7. He/she/it falls.
8. I study.
9. I laugh.
10. You two play.
11. You live.
12. You two blame.
13. They speak.
14. We two reverse.
15. We eat.

Exercise *2 :* English/ Sanskrit

Set the following sentences into Sanskrit from the English. Check the appendix after you have done them.

1. They two are alive.
2. We are studing.
3. You two protect.
4. They are worthy.
5. She is delighted.
6. We two are running.
7. We are worshiping.
8. He goes astreay.
9. They are speaking.
10. You are playing.
11. They two are eating.
12. We two rove.
13. He protects.
14. She is laughing.
15. I am playing.
16. They are jealous.
17. We are reflecting.
18. You (Pl) run.
19. It falls.
20. I speak.

Following be appended in the last.

Answer :

१. जीवत:	२. पठाम:
३. रक्षय:	४. अर्हन्ति
५. नन्दति	६. धावाव:
७. यजाम:	८. चलति
९. वदन्ति	१०. क्रीडय:
११. खादत:	१२. अटाव:
१३. रक्षति	१४. हसति
१५. क्रीडामि	१६. इर्ष्यन्ति
१७. चिन्ताम:	१८. धावय
१९. पतति	२०. वदामि।

INDECIBLES : INTRANSITIVE SENTENCE CONSTRUCTIONS :-

1. च – Particle, meaning "and" "or" "both".

   Example - धावन्ति क्रीडन्ति च (They run and play. or, they are both running and playing.)

2. न – Particle, denoting negation of action.

   Example - न धावन्ति (They are not running.)

3. अत्र – meaning "here".

   Example - अत्र धावन्ति (Here they are running.)

4. तत्र – meaning "there".

   Example - तत्र धावन्ति (There they are running.)

5. अधुना – meaning "now".

   Example - अधुना धावन्ति (Now they are running.)

6. अद्य – meaning "today".

   Example - अद्य धावन्ति (Today they are running.)

7. सर्वत्र – meaning "everywhere".

   Example - सर्वत्र धावन्ति (They are running everywhere.)

8. तथा – meaning "in that manner".

   Example - तथा धावन्ति (In this manner, they are running.)

9. स्म – Particle which converts present tense to simple past tense.

   Example- धावन्ति स्म (They ran.).

STEP TWO :- The medial vowel takes the guṇa strengthening unless it meets a compounded consonant. Note very carefully the parenthetical construes for each of the new roots given.

कृष् (कर्षति)
to draw, pull a cart

क्लृप् (कल्पति)
to be in order

कृष् (क्रोधति)
to be angry

घृष् (घर्षति)
to rub

चित् (चेतति)
to notice

च्युत् (च्योतति)
to drop

द्युत् (द्योतति)
to shine.

बुध् (बोधति)
to *know,* understand

मृष् (मर्षति)
to sprinkle

रुह् (रोहन्ति)
to grow

शुच् (शोचति)
to *grieve,* sorrow for

शुभ् (शोभति)
to shine

सृप् (सर्पति)
to *creep,* crawl

Exercise 3

Sanskrit to English Exercise. Copy over in your own (Sanskrit) script and translate.

१. बोधामि २. रोहति

३. शोभति च न दहति ४. तत्र द्योतति

५. अधुना कल्पति ६. अद्य कषमि:

७. च्योतति स्म ८. शोचति च चिन्तति च

९. शोचथ: १०. रोहसि

११. घर्षामि १२. न द्योतति।

Answer :

1. I understand (or know). 2. It is growing.

3. It shines and does not brun. 4. There it shine.

5. Now it is in order. 6. Today we draw (a cart).

7. It dropped. 8. She both sorrows and reflect.

9. You two grieve. 10. You grow.

11. I rub. 12. It does not shine.

Exercise 4

Set the following English sentences into Sanskrit.

1. Here it creeps.
2. You two sorrow.
3. We to crowled.
4. Today it is growing.
5. Everywhere they pull a cart.
6. I notice and understand.
7. It shines and does not burn.
8. There it shines.
9. In that manner you rub and notice.
10. It sprinkled everywhere.
11. It is not shining.
12. She/he/it rubs.

Answer

१. अत्र सर्पति २. शोचम:

३. सर्पाव:	४. अद्य रोहति
५. सर्वत्र कुर्वन्ति	६. चेतामि च बोधामि
७. शोभति च न दहति	८. तत्र द्योतति
९. तथा घर्षम चेतथ च	१०. सर्वत्र मर्षति स्म
११. न शोभति	१२. घर्षति।

STEP THREE : Final vowel or root takes guṇa vowel strenghthening. Two vowels in a row are not permitted so in some cases the semivowel is used before the personal endings. Examine each root carefully as shown in parenthesis.

Roots of First Conjugation continued :-

क्षि (क्षयति)	to decay	श्रि (श्रयति)	to reach
गै (गायति)	to sing*	श्वि (श्वयति)	to swell
ग्लै (ग्लायति)	to be weary*	सृ (सरति)	to go
जि (जयति)	to conquer	स्मृ (स्मरति)	to remember
डी (डयति)	to fly	हृ (हरति)	to take
तॄ (तरति)	to cross over / to transcend	ह्वे (ह्वयति)	to call
द्रु (द्रवति)	melt, flow, ooze		
धृ (धरति)	to hold		
नी (नयति)	to lead		
प्लु (प्लवति)	to float		
भू (भवति)	to be, to exist		
म्लै (म्लायति)	to fade*		
वे (वयति)	to weave		

Note :- The diphthongs retain the strength of the medial vowel before the corresponding semi-vowel.

Exercise 5 : Translate into English. Answer given below :—

१. श्रयसि	२. न श्वयन्ति
३. तथा हरति	४. क्षयन्ति
५. अधुना ग्लायत:	६. तत्र स्मराम:
७. वयथ:	८. सर्वत्र ह्याव:
९. अद्य खादाम: च नन्दाम:	१०. न प्लवति
११. धरामि	१२. डयति स्म
१३. अद्य गायाम:	१४. न जयसि
१५. द्रवति	१६. तथा तरथ।

Answer :

1. You reach.
2. They do not swell.
3. In that manner she/he lakes.
4. They delay.
5. Now they two are weary.
6. There we remember.
7. You two weave.
8. Everywhere we two call.
9. Today we eat and satisfied.
10. It does not float.
11. I hold.
12. She/he/it flew.
13. Today we sing.
14. You do not conquer.
15. It melts.
16. In the manner we cross over.

STEP FOUR : First conjugation continued introducing verbal roots which have irregular forms due to various Sandhi rules. Study each carefully and slowly memorize them.

Vocabulary list of these verbs :—

उष् (ओषति)	दृश् (पश्यति)
to burn	to see (visionary)
चित् (चिकित्सति)	ध्मा (धमति)
to describe, express, listen to	to blow (like elephant)
क्रम् (क्रामति)	पा (पिबति)
to walk, go	to drink
गम् (गच्छति)	म्न (मनति)
to go	to think
गुप् (गोपायति)	यम् (यच्छति)
to protect	to restrain, check
गुह् (गूहति)	सद् (सीदति)
to hide	to sit
घ्रा (जिघ्रति)	सस्ज् (सज्जति)
to smell	to get ready
दा (यच्छति)	स्था (तिष्ठति)
to give	to stand, halt
दश (दशति)	
to bite	

Exercise 6 *:* Translate into English. Answer is given below

१. अधुना गच्छथ:	२. धमति स्म
३. तथा पश्यन्ति	४. सर्वत्र यच्छत: च सज्जत:
५. अधुना धमति	६. अद्य तत्र क्रमाम:
७. चिकित्यत:	८. सीदति च स्वेदति
९. तथा गोपयन्ति	१०. न गुहामि।

Answer :

1. You two go now.
2. It blew.

3. They see in that manner.
4. They two restrain and get ready everywhere.
5. Now it blow.
6. Today we walk there.
7. They two describe.
8. He/she/it sits and perspires.
9. The protect in that manner.
10. I am not hiding.

Exercise 7 : Translate into Sanskrit (Answer given below)

1. We do not drink.
2. You smell and drink.
3. We stopped and revered.
4. It does not bite.
5. Now we stop and get ready.
6. We two restrained.
7. I perspired.
8. Today it burn and smell.
9. You two discribe and see.
10. You both think and protect.

Answer :

१. न पिबाम २. जिघ्रथ च मनथ

३. तिष्ठताम च न वयामः च ४. न दशति

५. अधुना तिष्ठामः च सज्जामः ६. यच्छावः स्म

७. स्वेदामि स्म ८. अद्य ओषति जिव्रतिः च

९. चिकित्सयः पस्ययः च १०. मनथ गोपायथ च।

LESSON 3 : INTRODUCTION TO SANDHI

Till now we have been discussing construction of intransitive sentences with or without an indeclinable or particle.

Not it intransitive sentences have no object or personal pronoun. Also the word order in Sanskrit is not strict as in English and word order is governed by concordance.

Before starting Sandhi we must know the following.

Kridant—It means adding certain affixes to the root, the vowel of which is liable to some form of vowel drengthening (guṇa or vṅddhi). Crude base of noun are made by Kridant.

"Taddhita" —means adding certain affixes to bases of nouns already formed.

Dhātu (root) —these are elementary sounds and mostly monosyllabic, which forms other words (adjectives, nouns, substantive etc.) in Sanskrit.

Following is list of Dhātu (roots) with its meaning—

kṣip = throwing
kṛ = doing, making spiritually
krī = buying
hṛi = seizing, taking
yuj = joining
as, vṛit = being
bhū = being, becoming
jīv = living
nī = leading
ji = conquering
gam, yā, car, kram, i, sṛ, skand } = going
vad, vac, brū = speaking
budh, jñā = knowing
dṛiś = seeing, visionary
iṣ, kam = wishing
mṛi = dying
dā = giving
jan = producing
dhā = placing
ad, bhuj, bhakṣ = eating
ap, labh = obtaining
stu, śaṁs = praising

han = killing
pat = falling, flying
vas = dwelling
viś = entering
sthā = standing
śru = hearing
spriś = touching
sidh, sādh = accomplishing
kup, krudh = being angry
ci = collecting
snā = bathing
ghrā = smelling
khyā = relating, enumerating
tyaj, rah = quitting, abandoning
dviṣ = hating, dividing
nind = blaming
dru = running, flowing, melting
dyut, dīp, bhā, śubh = shining
pū = purifying
pracch = asking
tap = heating
dah = burning

yat = striving
yam = restraining
sak = being able
pā = drinking
pac = cooking

muc = liberating
muh = being foolish
yudh = fighting
ruh = growing
has = laughing
svap = sleeping
sna = bathing

SANDHI

The object of Sandhi is to avoid a break in the sound and to expend the compounded meaning of a sentence.

The word Sandhi is a compound of som- to hold together = dhi—to make firm (to stand). The meeting of final letter of a word with the initial letter of the next word is subject to "Sandhi".

There are two types, external as described earlier and internal which refers to alterṅating a verbal root to creat, an adjective, noun, substantive etc.

Vowel Sandhi—When a vowel meets another vowel.

Rules I.—When similar vowels meet it takes the long form.

a + a = ā, ā + ā = ā

i + i =i, ī + ī = ī

u + u = ū, ū + ū = ū.

II.—When dissimilar vowels meet, either guṇa or vṛiddhi takes place.

a + i = e (Corresponding semivowel "va").

a + ī = ai,

a + u = o (Corresponding semivowel "ya").

ā + ū = au

Example

na + arhati = nārhati (not worthy)

na + aṭate = nāṭati not (roaming)

Vowel Sandhi Chart :

VOWEL STRENGHTHENING CHART :—

Simple Vowels	a ā	i ī	u ū	ṛi ṛī	ḷri ḷrī
Guṇa	a	e े (य)*	# o ो (व)	ar (र्)$	al (ल)
Vriddhi	ā	ai ै (य)	au ौ (व)	ār (र्)	āl (ल)

Sandhi Chart for Dis-similar Vowels

following vowel :

initial vowels	a or ā	i or ī	u or ū	ṛi or ṛī	e	ai	o	au
a or ā	ā	e ai	o au	ar ar	ai	ai	au	au
i or ī	ya or yā	ī ī	yu or yū	yṛi or yṛi	ye	yai	yo	yau
u or ū	va or vā	vi or vī	ū ū	vṛi or vṛi	ve	vai	vo	vau
ṛi or ṛī	ra or rā	ri or rī	ru or rū	ṛī or ṛī	re	rai	ro	rau

Example " ā +ū (triangulate) = au

Bear in mind the samprasaraṇa of the relationship of : Initial vowel forms not used within a word, or blended forms.

* i = yइ - य

\# u = v उ - व

$ ṛ = rऋ - अर्

LESSON FOUR : INTRODUCTION TO THE NOMINATIVE AND ACCUSATIVE CASES.

Step One : Vocabulary of Masculine and Neuter Nouns in अ.

Step Two : Prepositions governing Accusative Case.

Step Three : Exercises using transitive sentences and Sandhi rules for the visarga and final म्.

Thus far we have been constructing intransitive sentences (no object), and now we progress to the transitive type (with an object).

Nominative Case : This case is used for :

—The subject :

The man is eating. नरः खादति।

—The subjective complement :

The men are heroes. नराः वीराः भवन्ति।

—To indicate a noun in apposition to the subject:

The man, the hero is eating. नरः खादति वीरः।

Accusative Case : This case indicates the direct object of a transitive.

Verb: The man is eating food. नरः खादति अन्नम्।

—Used to indicate the objective complement:

We know the man to be a hero. नरः भवति वीरम्।

—Used after verbs indicating movement :

The man goes to the forest. नरः वनम् व्रजति।

Prepositions governing the Accusative Case:—

near, in front अभितः	near समया or निकषा
around परितः	without विना or अन्तरेण
on all sides सर्वतः	above अति

on both sides near-उभयत:	after, according to, along अनु
to, towards प्रति	between अन्तरा near, below उप

	Singular	(English)	Dual	Plural
Nom	देव:	(the God)	देवौ	देवा:
Acc	देवम्	(to the God)	देवौ	देवान्
Inster	देवेन	(with the God)	देवाभ्याम्	देवै:
Dative	देवाय	(Ind. obj. to the God)	देवाभ्याम्	देवेभ्य:
Ablative	देवात्	(from the God)	देवाभ्याम्	देवेभ्य:
Genitive	देवस्य	(God's)	देवयो:	देवानाम्
Locative	देवे	(In the God)	देवयो:	देवेषु
Vocative	हे देव	(Oh! God)	हे देवौ	हे देवा:
Nom	रूप		रूपे	रूपति
Acc	रूप		रूपे	रूपति
Voc	हे रूप		हे रूप	हे रूपति

"देव = Masc. noun (अ) God."

रूप = NEUTER FORM, BODY, SHAPE

Masculine Nouns-Substantives in अ–

अश्व: Horse	नर: Man	लोक: World people
आनन्द: Bliss	पर्वत: Mountain	वृक्ष: Tree
आचार: Conduct	पान्थ: Traveller	व्याघ्र: Tiger
आराम: Garden	पुत्र: Son	शिष्य: Disciple
कपोत: Dove, Pigeon	बक: Crane	श्रृगाल: Jackal
कर: Hand	बाल: Boy	सर्प: Snake
क्रोध: Anger	ब्राह्मण: Brahmin	समुद्र: Ocean
गुण: Quality	भक्त: Devotee	हस्त: Hand

ग्राम: Village मनुष्य: Man

चन्द्र: Moon मालिक: Gardener

चौर: Thief मृग: Deer

जन: Person,People मेघ: Cloud

दास: Servant मूषिक: Mouse

देश: Country योग: Union

देव: God रावण: Ravana

धर्म: Merit राम: Rama

नृप: King रथ: Chariot, Wheel.

Neuter Nouns in अ

अन्नं	Food	पातकं	Sin
अमृतं	Immortality	पुष्पं	Flower
आसनं	Seat, Posture	पुस्तकं	Book
इन्धनं	Fuel	फलं	Fruit
कनकं	Gold	बीजं	Seed
कमलं	Lotus	भूतं	A Being
कुलं	Family	मस्तकं	Head
चक्रं	Wheel	मृतं	Death
जलं	Water	रूपं	Form, Body
ज्ञानं	Knowledge	वचं	Speech
तृणं	Grass	वनं	Forest, Wood
तीरं	Shore	शरीरं	Body
धनं	Wealth	शास्त्रं	Sacred Precepts
दु:खं	Pain, Misery	शीलं	Character
पत्रं	Page, Leaf	सत्यं	Truth
पात्रं	Jug, Vessel	सुखं	Happiness
हुतं	Sacrifice	स्थानं	Place

Agreement of endings is very exacting in both conjugations and declensions. There is no such verb in Sanskrit as "to have." The ending is governed by the genitive case. There is a constant compounding of words (Sandhi) to avoid a break in the sound (hiatus.)

Vowels are specially treated. A change —guṇa or vṛiddhi (01 vowel strengthening) can alter the entire meaning of the word :

Root,	*Verbal*	*Noun + Vowel Change*		*Adjective Derivative*	
man,	think	manas,	mind	mānasa,	mental
div,	shine	deva,	god	daiva,	divine
budh,	know	bodha,	knowledge	baudha,	wise
dhṛi,	hold	dharma,	duty, order	dhārmika,	righteous
kḷrip,	be in order	kalpa,	age, cycle	kālpa,	cyclic

The rules of Sandhi are continuous and should be learned organically so changes can be made directly during grammatical constructions. Refer to alphabet table on p. 80 for column and class designations.

Rule One : When any visarga meets a hard consonant from column I, II & VII, class 1 (gutteral), 5 (labial) or any VII sibilant, there is no change, words are not connected. Aḥ meeting a sibilant incurs an optional change. See example.

The boy falls. बालः पतति।

Ram reads. रामः पठति।

Optional Change

The boy remembers. बालः स्मरति। बालस्स्मरति।

The snake creep. सर्पः सर्पति। सर्पस्सर्पति।

Rule Two : When a visarga (aḥ) meets a soft consonant from columns III, IV, V, VI of all classes it is changed to ओ (ो) (o), and words not combined.

The boy conquers = बालः जयति।

: (aḥ) + ja = o बालो जयति।

The boy runs = बालः धावति = बालो धावति।

: (aḥ) + ḍha = बालो धावति।

Rule Three : When a visarga (aḥ) meets any vowel except अ the visarga (aḥ) is dropped, and words are not connected, hiatus (break in sound) remains.

The boy wishes - बालः इच्छति = : (aḥ) + i = : (aḥ) dropped. = बाल इच्छति।

The son wishes = पुत्रः इच्छति = : (aḥ) + i = : (aḥ) dropped. = पुत्र इच्छति।

Rule Four : When a visarga (aḥ) meets अ, it is changed to ो (o) and an avagraha ऽ replaces the अ and the words are read with no break in the sound (no hiatus).

The boy is worthy = बालः अर्हति = : (aḥ) + a = ो ऽ = बालोऽर्हति!

The boy roves = बालः अटति = : (aḥ) = ो ऽ = बालोऽटति।

Rule Five : When visarga (āḥ) meets any soft consonant, colums III, IV, V, VI, and any vowel, it is dropped and the hiatus (break in sound) remains. The words are not connected.

The boys conquer = बालाः जयन्ति = बाला जयन्ति।

The trees burn = वृक्षाः दहन्ति = वृक्षा दहन्ति।

The boys know = बालाः बोधन्ति = बाला बोधन्ति।

The sons are worthy = पुत्राः अर्हन्ति = पुत्रा अर्हन्ति।

The tigers rove = व्याघ्राः अटान्त = व्याघ्रा अटन्ति।

Rule Six : When visargas are preceded by iḥ, uḥ, or any vowel excepting अ , convert the visarga to R and connect the words. The congluate (combined words) is pronounced with no break in the sound (hiatus.) If the following word begins with R, since a double "r" is never permitted, the preceding vowel, if short, is lengthened, and the visarga is dropped.

The sage knows = मुनि: बोधति = मुनि बोधति।

(: (aḥ) is preceded by i)

The teacher speaks = गुरु: वदति = गुरुर्वदति।

(:(aḥ) is preceded by u)

The fire grows = अग्नि: रोहति = अग्नी रोहति।

(:(aḥ) is preceded by i but followed by "r")

*Rule Seven :*When a visarga (aḥ) meets a hard consonant from column I & II class or category 2, palatal, 3, cerebral, 4, dental, the visarga is replaced with the corresponding sibilant of the specific class, and the words are combined (palatal "s" श् or श्र्), (Cerebral "s" ष्), or (Dental "s" स् .)

The boy goes = बाल: चरति = : (aḥ) + ca = śa (श्) = बालश्चरति।

The tree moves = बृक्ष: टीकते = : (aḥ) + ta = ṣa (ष्) = वृक्षष्टीकते।

The boy transcends = बाल+ तरति = : (aḥ + ta = s (स्) = बालस्तरति।

*Rules Eight :*A final म् when followed by any consonant, semivowel, sibilant or aspirate is changed to anusvara. (ं)

We know Rāma the hero. रामम् वीरम् बोधाम: = रामं वीरं बोधाम:।

Rule Nine : स् and र् are always changed to visarga when found at the end of a sentence or when standing alone. (See example a.) Punar, (meaning again,) when standing alone drops R for a visarga. (See example b.) Punar before hard consonants from Column I & II, class 1, 2, 3, 4, 5 and sibilants becomes a visarga. Final "r" before hard consonants columns I & II, classes 2, 3, 4, optionally becomes the corresponding sibilant.

(a) बालस् = बाल:

(b) पुनर् = पुन:

(c) Again he falls = पुनर् पतति = पुन: पतति।

(d) Again they transcend. पुनर् तरन्ति = पुनस्तरन्ति।

Rule Ten : Final म् remains the same at the end of a sentence and before vowels. It is usually combined with the following vowel.

पुत्रम् अर्हति The son is worthy.

= पुत्रमर्हति If word order reversed.

= अर्हति पुत्रम्।

Rule Eleven : Final म् before all consonants becomes anusvara or may be joined by using the corresponding nasal.

He cooks the food. अन्नं पचति या अन्नम्पचति।

He conquers the man. नरं जयति या नरञ्जयति।

He digs the Ground . भूमिं खनति या भूमिङ्खनति।

He abandons the house. गृहं त्यजति या गृहन्त्यजति।

The use of the conjunction " and च " can be constructed in several ways :

1. It can appear immediately after multiple subjects or objects. Keep in mind the Sandhi rules which are applicable, or,
2. It can be added to the last of the multiple subjects or objects. See examples.

नरश्च बालाश्च ग्रामं गच्छन्ति, The man and the boys go to the village—or—नरोबालाश्च ग्रामं गच्छन्ति।

To negate a verb, it is preceded by न, and again keep in mind applicable Sandhi rules.

The boys eat the food. अन्नं बाला: खादन्ति।

The boys *do not eat* the food. अन्नं बाला न खादन्ति।

The tree burns. वृक्षो दहति।

The tree *does not* burn. वृक्षो न दहति।

Before commencing the excrcises summarizing the last three lessons of this chapter check back and review the following :

I. Personal endings for the verbal roots —

	Singular No.	Dual No.	Plural No.
Ist Person	ामि (I)	ाव: (We two)	ाम: (We)
IInd Person	सि (You)	थ: (You two)	थ (You)
IIIrd Person	ति (He, She, It)	त: (They two)	अन्ति (They)

II. The declension endings for masculine and neuter nouns ending in अ

Masculine Nouns

	Sing. No.	Dual No.	Plural No.
Nominative (Subject)	aḥ	au	āh
Accusative (direct object)	am	au	āh
Vocative (to evoke)	a	au	āḥ

Neuter Nouns

	Sing. No.	Dual No.	Plural No.
Nominative (Subject)	am	e	āhi
Accusative (direct object)	am	e	āhi
Vocative (to evoke)	a	e	āhi

Note—In the vocative case the noun is preceded by हे= oh! o!

Summarizing exercises for Chapter III

(1) Copy Sanskrit and translate. Then copy English and set into Sanskrit .... Intransitive Sentences.

धावति	I eat.
यजति	We become.
वदाव:	You two protect.
त्यजसि	They abandon.
पतत:	He speaks.

स्मराम:	We know.
पचथ:	They two dwell.
बोधामि	We rove.
द्रवति	She grieves.
जयथ	He is worthy.
नमन्ति	We two play.

(2) Again , copy Sanskrit and translate. Then copy the English and set into Sanskrit.

मूषिक: खनति।	The two horses run.
बाला: रोहन्ति।	The boys remember.
रामौ स्मरत:।	Rāvaṇa Conquers.
दास: पचति।	We two disciple learn.
अश्वा: धावन्ति।	The Jackals play.
नृप: वीर: वदति।	The cloud moves.
पान्थौ जल्पत:।	The sons become heros.
चन्द्र: रोहति।	The two people speak.
राम: नयति।	The servant is angry.
ग्राम: दहति।	We two snakes creep.
भक्तौ यजत:।	The trees burn.

(3) Write 10 sentences illustrating rule #2; then rewrite the sentences using the particle न also governed by this rule.

(4) Using the following verbal bases, write ten sentences illustrating Sandhi rule #3.

इच्छ	इर्ष्य	ईस्य	
to wish	to envy	to move	
इष्य	ओष्य	ऋष्य	उष्छ
to go	to burn	to prosper	to glean

(5) Using the following verb bases, write 10 sentences illustrating Sandhi rule #4.

अट	अर्ह	अञ्च
to rove, roam	to be worthy	to worship
अर्च	अर्ज	अव
to worship	to earn	to protect

(6) Using the nominative plural of masculine nouns, write ten sentences illustrating Sandhi rule #5. Consult the rule for a guide.

(7) Using the following Nouns that end in iḥ. and uḥ write ten sentences illustrating Rule #6. Be sure to include both parts of the rule.

अग्निः = Fire, Masc. Noun ending in इ

अरिः = Enemy, Masc. Noun ending in इ

कविः = Poet, Masc. Noun ending in इ

गिरिः = Mountain, Masc. Noun ending in इ

मुनिः = Sage, Masc. Noun ending in इ

उदधिः = Ocean, Masc. Noun ending in इ

इन्दुः = Moon गुरुः dispeller of darkness
तरुः = Tree शिशुः = baby.
इषुः = Arrow पशुः = beast
} Masc. Noun ending in उ

(8, 9, 10, 11, 12) Write ten sentences illustrating each of the remaining Sandhi rules. Use neuter nouns for final म.

CHAPTER IV

Introduction to Cardinal Numbers. Nominative and Accusative Cases Continued—Introduction to the Instrumental Case

LESSON 1 : INTRODUCTION TO CARDINAL NUMBERS

If you examine carefully the clock faces, you will recognize the cardinal numbers very quickly!

n.b. : There is no zero [0] in the Roman numerals, and during the 1300 years of Islamic occupation of India, the Muslims adopted the Sanskrit numbers, which include the zero, and this is what we use to the present day.

In the extensive appendix on numbers it would be worth your while to carefully compare the counting of one through ten, and you will find some exciting interesting comparisons. In India each of the Major Aryan, Dravidian and Arabic derived languages pronounce the numbers slightly different, but they all look like the original Sanskrit ones.

1	=	१	eka	एक
2	=	२	dvi	द्वि
3	=	३	tri	त्रि
4	=	४	catur	चतुर्
5	=	५	Pañca	पञ्च

6	=	६	ṣaṣ	षष्
7	=	७	sapta	सप्त
8	=	८	aṣṭa	अष्ट
9	=	९	nava	नव
10	=	१०	daśa	दश
11	=	११	ekādaśa	एकादश
12	=	१२	dvādaśa	द्वादश
13	=	१३	trayodaśa	त्रयोदश
14	=	१४	caturdaśa	चतुर्दश
15	=	१५	pañcadaśa	पञ्चदश
16	=	१६	ṣodaśa	षोडश
17	=	१७	saptadaśa	सप्तदश
18	=	१८	aṣṭādaśa	अष्टादश
19	=	१९	navadaśa	नवदश*
			or ekonaviṁsati	एकोनविंशति*
			ūnaviṁśati	ऊनविंशति*
20	=	२०	viṁśati	विंशति

* Navadasa is the most common, however, the other two stand for one-minus-twenty!

Memorize numbers one through twenty as all exercises henceforth will be designated in Sanskrit numbers. 1980 is written १९८०.

LESSON 2 : REVIEW OF NOMINATIVE AND ACCUSATIVE CASES.

Word order in Sanskrit is not as strict as in English. It is subject to the writers choice. A beginner can choose the order which mininizes the Sandhi change.

Here are a few illustrations to help you allocate the applicable cases and prepositions.

1. The boy plays near the shore.

   Nom. Sing. the boy बाल:

   Acc. Sing. shore तीरम्

   Preposition governing Acc.Near समया

   Verb Pres. Active, he plays क्रीडति।

   बाल: समया तीरं क्रीडति or समया तीरं बाल: क्रीडति।

2. The dove and the crane fly around the village.

   Nom. (double subject)

   Dove : कपोत:

   Crane : बक:

   Conjunction used two different ways : च

   Acc. village ग्रामम्

   Prep. governing acc. case. (optional choices.) परित:।

   Verb. pres. tense. 3rd. pers. plural. डयन्ति।

   १. कपोतो बकश्च परितो ग्रामं डयन्ति or

   २. कपोतश्च बकश्च परितो ग्रामं डयन्ति or

   ३. परितो ग्रामं कपोतो बकश्च डयन्ति etc.

3. The man is digging near the garden and the village.

   Nom. man नर:

   Double Accusative : the garden आरामम्

   the village ग्रामम्

   Preposition governing the acc. case. near निकषा

   Verb, pres. tense, 3rd. pers. sing. खनति।

   १. नरो निकषारामं ग्रामं च खनति or

   २. निकषा ग्रामं आरामं च नर: खनति।

4. The servant wanders around the place.

Nom. servant दासः

Acc. place स्थानम्

Prep. of Acc. around परितः

Verb. pres. tense, 3rd, pers. sing. अटति

दासः परितः स्थानं अटति।

परितः स्थानं दासोऽटति।

5. Everywhere people understand the truth.

Indeclinable. Everywhere सर्वत्र

Nom. pl. people जनाः

Acc. Truth सत्यम्

Verb. 3rd. pers. pl. pres. tense. They understand. बोधन्ति।

सर्वत्र जना सत्यं बोधन्ति।

सर्वत्र सत्यं जना बोधन्ति।

6. Today the men sprinkle water.

Nom. pl. Men नराः

Indeclinable. Today अद्य

Acc. water जलम्

Verb. pres. tense. 3rd pers. pl. they sprinkle मर्षन्ति।

अद्य नरा जलं मर्षन्ति।

7. Now the men perspire and plant seeds.

Indeclinable. Now अधुना

Nom. pl. Men जनाः

Acc. pl. बीजानि

Double verb: 3rd. pers. pl. they perspire, they plant : स्वेदन्ति वपन्ति।

अधुना जना स्वेदन्ति च बीजानि वपन्ति।

8. We two study the scriptures, conquer misery and salute the truth.

   Acc. pl. Scripturess शास्त्रानि

   Acc. Misery दु:खम् सत्यं

   Verbs: pres. Ist pers. dual पठाव: जयाव: नमाव:।

   Conjunction : च

   शास्त्रानि पठावश्च दु:खं जयावश्च सत्यं नमाव:।

9. The flowers floated near the water.

   Nom. pl. Flowers पुष्पननि

   Acc. Water जलम्

   Prep. gov. Acc. Near समया

   Verb. 3rd. pers. pl. + particle for simple past प्लवन्ति स्म।

   पुष्पानि समया जलं प्लवन्ति स्म।

10. The snake creeps in front of the house.

   Nom. Snake सर्प:

   Acc. House गृहम्

   Prep. gov. acc. In front of अभित:

   Verb, 3rd. per. sing. pres. It creeps सर्पति।

   सर्पोऽभितो गृहं सर्पति।

   Remember the various choices of prepositions that have similar meanings, and the Sandhi that ensues!

Exercise 1

Translate the following Sanskrit sentences into English. Check your answers with the appendix giving them.

१. नरान् गोपायन्ति।

२. तथा पर्वतं गच्छत:।

३. शिष्यो भक्तान् स्मरति।

४. नरा सुखं चिन्तन्ति।

५. अश्वा अभितो वृद्रान् धावन्ति।

६. भक्तः सत्यं मनति।

७. व्याघ्रोऽन्नं जिघ्रति

८. बाला जलं पिबन्ति च फलानि खादन्ति।

९. पान्थोऽमतो ग्रामं सीदति।

१०. बालं रामोवीरो यच्छति।

Exercise *2*

Translate the following English sentences into Sanskrit.

1. The horse runs near the forest.
2. The two doves drink water.
3. The mouse crawls on both sides of the village.
4. The boys worship the disciples.
5. Here, the dharma shines!
6. Rāma blames misery.
7. She restrains anger and is delighted.
8. Today the devotee does not eat.
9. You (sing.) sorunkle water near the garden.
10. You two did not speak the truth.
11. Now the king protects the servants.
12. Everywhere the people sing and are delighted.
13. The snake bites the boy.
14. The moon shines above the clouds.
15. In this manner we dig near the village.
16. The devotee does not grieve.
17. There the tree decays.
18. The brahman restrains misery.
19. We two stand near the garden.
20. Truth and happiness exist.

Refer to appendix for both Eng-Skṛt. and Skṛt.-Eng. exercises. (Bear in mind that there is a multiple choice of prepositions which govern the accusative case. Mine, might vary from yours.)

LESSON 3 : INTRODUCTION TO THE INSTRUMENTAL CASES.

The Nominative Case represents the 'subject', the Accusative Case represents the 'direct-object or where the action is carried to.' Take time to reflect the various prepositions which govern the accusative case. Your choice of preposition will be for rhythmic flow, etc. Here! study them again:—

अभित:	near, in front of
परित:	around
सर्वत:	on all sides of
उभयत:	on both sides of
समया, निकषा	near [two choices]
विना, अन्तरेण	without [two choices]
अति	above
अनु	after, according to, along
अभि, उप	near, below [two choices]
प्रति	to, towards
अन्तरा	between.

Remember word order is not strict but all the Sandhi rules must be observed. The indeclinables appear first, prepositions governing the accusative case precede the noun or substantive. The particle "sma स्म " which converts the present tense into simple past tense follows the verb.

The Instrumental Case infers 'by, with, for, on account of, because of, etc' and is used the following ways

(a) To indicate the instrument which is used to do the action.

ex. *with his two hands* the boy eats the food.

बालोऽन्नं कराभ्यां खादति।

- or -

बालोऽन्नं सह कराभ्यां खादति।

(b) To indicate the person or thing accompanying the action.

ex. I study *with the discipie.*

शिष्येन सह पठामि।

I go *with the men.*

जनैर्सह गच्छामि।

NOTE THE NEW CASE ENDINGS FOR THE MASC. & NEUTER NOUNS ENDING IN "a"

Singular	Dual	Plural
ena	ābhyām	aiḥ

(c) To indicate the cause or reason, i.e. 'owing to,' 'on account of,' 'out of,' 'because of,' etc.

ex. *Because of pain* I grieve.

दुःखेन शोचामि।

With happiness I sing.

सुखेन गायामि।

Owing to wealth the men win (conquer).

धनेन जना जयन्ति।

With food they worship.

अन्नेन यजन्ति।

(d) To translate expressions like 'by name, ' ' by nature,' 'by birth,' etc.

By conduct Rama is a hero.

आचारेन रामो वीरो भवति।

By bliss the devotee is delighted.

आनन्देन भक्तो नन्दति।

(e) With the prepositions:

सह with विना without

(f) With these particles :

अलम् or कृतम् = enough!

ex. अलं दुःखेन "Enough with misery!"

कृतं क्रोधेन "Enough with anger!"

For practice refer back to all the nouns presented thus far, and drill them orally and perhaps write out a few paradigms too.

	S.	D.	Pl.
ex.	अश्वेन	अश्वाभ्यां	अश्वैः
	आनन्देन	आनन्दाभ्यां	आनन्दैः
	भक्तेन	भक्ताभ्यां	भक्तैः

SPECIAL NOTE :Remember all the Sandhi rules introduced thus far, and dual endings are not subject to vowel Sandhi.

Exercise 3

Translate the following sentences into English.

१. नृपो ग्रामं दासैर्गच्छति।

२. कराभ्यां फलानि खादति।

३. सह सुखेन नन्दति।

४. सत्येन च शीलेम वृक्षा क्षयन्ति।

५. विना जलेन वृक्षाः क्षयन्ति।

६. दुःखेन बाला ग्लायन्ति।

७. सर्पः सह मृगेन देशं गच्छति।

८. रथो विना चक्रेनं चलति।

९. अमृतेन नरा रामां स्मरन्ति।

१०. पान्थेन गच्छथः or पान्थेन सह गच्छथः।

Exercise 4

Translate the following English Sentences into Sanskrit.

1. Because of sin the man reflects.
2. We plant seeds with water.
3. With two lotuses we honor the disciple.
4. Enough with sacrifice!

5. Sprinkle the flowers with water.
6. Union with God is noticed.
7. You two transcend with happiness.
8. Rāma the hero restrains Ravana with anger.
9. Because of death, the body decays.
10. The man was not happy without food.

REVIEW to this point. Freely refer to previous chapters when necessary.

1. The Sandhi rules involving the visarga.
2. Conjugate these verbs in present active tense :—
   (a) to learn (b) to grow (c) to weave (d) to restrain.
3. Write out the declensions of the following nouns in Nom. Acc. & Instr. Case, Singular, Dual and Plural.
   (a) merit (b) tree (c) scriptures (d) food.
4. Name the six Cakras and their seed Letters. (Bijam)
5. Interpolate the following special compound consonants :—
   (a) kta (b) jña (c) kṣa
6. Which columns contain the hard consonants, and which contain the soft?
7. From memory write the samprasaraṇa meditative triangles.
8. Write the vowel strengthening chart showing the medial forms in parenthesis.
9. What is the difference between a transitive and intransitive sentence?
10. On the next page is a complete cross-check of all of the Nouns, Verbs, Particles and Prepositions. How many can you identify before having to refer back. Keep in mind the original three "D's," for organic learning :—

Discipline

Detachment

Devotion

CHAPTER V

Introduction to the IV Conjugation, Introduction to the Future Tense. Introduction to the Imperative Mood. Introduction to Adjective (Karmadhāraya Compounds)

LESSON 1 : INTRODUCTION TO THE IV CONJUGATION

Before introducing the IV Conjugation, a reminder that in conjugations I, IV, VI and X the personal endings are all the same, being prefixed with अ excepting आ before either an म् or a व्. On the paradigm you will remember that this is in the first person singular, dual and plural. In the first conjugation either the medial or final vowel of the root took a guṇa vowel strengthening. *In the IV conjugation this does not take place.* The rule for this conjugation is to wedge a य् into the final consonant.

Regular Roots Stems			*Irregular Root Stems*		
अस्	= अस्य	to throw	दिव्	(दीव्य)	to play
तुष्	= तुष्य	to be pleased	शम्	(शाम्य)	to be quiet
नश्	= नस्य	to perish	श्रम्	(श्राम्य)	to forgive
नृत्	= नृत्य	to dance	मद्	(माद्य)	to be glad
पुष्	= पुष्य	to nourish	भ्रंश्	(भ्रस्य)	to fall
मुह्	= मुह्य	to faint	व्यध्	(विध्य)	to pierce
			क्षम्	(क्षाम्य)	to forgive
			भ्रम्	(भ्राम्य)	*to roam to err

* This verbal root is in both I & IV, but vowel is lengthened in IV.

अण् = अण्य	BREATH
इष् = इष्य	TO GO
ऋध् = ऋध्य	PROSPER
कुप् = कुप्य	BE ANGRY
क्रुध् = क्रुध्य	BE ANGRY
क्लिश् = क्लिश्य	BE AFFLICTED
क्षुध् = क्षुध्य	BE HUNGRY
क्षुभ् = क्षुभ्य	TREMBLE
तृष् = तृष्य	BE THIRSTY
दुष् = दुष्य	BE WRONG
दृप् = दृप्य	BE GLAD
द्रुह् = द्रुह्य	TO HATE
राध् = राध्य	TO GROW
सिव् = सीव्य	TO SEW
सो = स्य	TO DESTROY

Exercise 1 — Copy and Translate:

१. नरस्तुष्यति।

२. बाला ग्रामं समया नृत्यन्ति।

३. जनो गजं पष्यति।

४. नृपो दासं क्षाम्यति।

५. बालस्तृष्यति च जलं पिबति।

६. रामः क्षुध्यति च फलानि खादति।

७. मनुष्या[१] वृक्षान् स्यन्ति च दुष्यन्ति।

८. व्याघ्रा च गजा सर्वतो ग्रामं भ्राम्यन्ति।

९. पान्थस्तुष्यति।

१०. लोको दुःखेन सह क्लिस्यति च ज्ञानं शंसति।[२]

---

1. men; 2. praise

Exercise 2

Set the following sentences into Sanskrit, and be sure to bear in mind the Sandhi Rules.

1. The boy is afflicted with pain.
2. The people hate the snakes and tigers.
3. The Sage forgives the disciples.
4. Truth destroys ignorance.
5. The leaves perish and fall.
6. The disciple is wrong and speaks with anger.
7. Without water, the elephant faints and trembles.
8. The people dance in front of the king, and he is pleased.
9. A person prospers from knowledge and truth.
10. The Sage understands because of the sacred precepts, and I am glad.

I encourage you to utilize the additional lists of vocabulary resources to create sentences for further practice, especially utilizing the conjunctive particle च, and both the first and fourth conjugations.

LESSON 2 : AN INTRODUCTION TO THE FUTURE TENSE

In Sanskrit there are two future tenses —

1. An action which will occur in the far distant future, where the action may or may not see its fulfilment or "periphrastic".

2. Where the actor will possible see the fulfilment of the action. Either "Sya" or iṣya is appended to the root or radical stem of a verb to construct the future tense.

List of few irregular construction is given below.

Do mind it, although the word order of the sentence is arbitrary but generally the verb is at the end of the sentence. All Sandhi rules will stricktly be applied.

त्यज्+स्यति=त्यक्ष्यति Will abandon

दह्+स्यति=धक्ष्यति Will burn

वह्+स्यति=वक्ष्यति	Will carry
वस्+स्यति=वत्स्यति	Will dwell
पच्+स्यति=पक्ष्यति	Will cook
जि+स्यति=जेष्यति	Will conquer
द्रु+स्यति=द्रोष्यति	Will flow, melt, ooze.

Exercise *3 :*

Special Note : Consult verb appendix for correct future constructions.

Copy these sentences, and translate them.

१. गजो वत्स्यति।

२. चौरस्त्यक्ष्यति।

३. मृगोऽटष्यात।

४. शिष्योऽर्हिष्यति।

५. देवः स्मरिष्यति।

६. अन्नं धक्ष्यति।

७. सर्पः सर्प्स्यति।

८. ब्राह्मणो भ्रमिष्यति।

९. फलं क्षेष्यति।

Exercise 4 :

Set the following sentences into Sanskrit. Be certain of the future insert in each case, and of course, the Sandhi Rules:

1. The boys will go (gam) to the forest.
2. Rāma will drink water and will rejoice.
3. The people will be pleased.
4. The man will forgive the servants.
5. The Sage will sit near the village.
6. I shall restrain pain.
7. The deer will stand and will dwell in the forest.

8. The crane will smell the flowers.
9. The two lotuses will grow without water.
10. Knowledge will pierce ignorance.
11. I shall burn the trees.
12. With my two hands, I shall eat the food.
13. The man will become a sage.
14. We two shall remember the friends.
15. They will praise and speak.

LESSON 3 : AN INTRODUCTION TO THE 'IMPERATIVE MOOD'

To further enhance our ability to construct interesting sentences, thus far we have dealt with the present and future active tenses, and now an introduction to the "imperative mood."

(a) To express a command or an advice.

(b) To express a wish or a prayer.

(c) To express a possibility and a doubt.

(d) For prohibition the negative particle is मा, not न

For our purposes read carefully the next page of examples, and pay particular attention to the pronoun introduced plus extra words like "quickly," "immediately," "here," "there," and "one." Note that the second person singular is used minus the usual endings. Study the examples, and then with our expanded verbal vocabulary construct sentences of your own choice.

Imperative Mood— You Do—

कुरु	Do, Act, Perform	स्मर	Remember
भव	Be, Become	रक्ष	Give photection
धाव	Run	वद	Speak
नय	Lead, Takeaway	आनय	Bring
नृत्य	Dance	चल	Walk on
पश्य	See, Look	खेल	Play
गच्छ	Go	आगच्छ	Come

खाद्	Eat	क्रीड	Play
पठ	Read, Learn	लिख	Write
पिब	Drink	त्वं	You
मा	No-not, Do-not	एक	One
तत्र	There	अत्र	Here
शीघ्रं	Quickly	सत्वरम्	Immediate.

Model sentences using imperative form of verb.

1. त्वं पठ।	You read.
2. त्वं लिख।	You write.
3. त्वं वद।	You speak.
4. त्वं स्मर।	You remember.
5. तत्र क्रीड।	You play there.
6. त्वं अत्र खेल।	You play here
7. तत्र शीघ्रं गच्छ।	Go there quickly.
8. अत्र आगच्छ।	Come here.
9. पश्चात् भोजनं कुरु।	Take meal afterwards.
10. आरामं गच्छ।	You go to the garden.
11. गृहं सत्वरं आगच्छ।	You come home immediately.
12. अन्नं अपि खाद।	Also eat food.
13. त्वं एकं पत्रं लिख।	You write one page.
14. प्रथमं व्याकरणान् कुरु।	First you perform exercises.

Special notes :—

1. Sentence words order in Sanskrit arbitrary, governed by writer's artistry, and metrical ideas, etc.
2. Note : Verb generally at the end of the sentences.
3. The noun (object in accusative case) precedes verb.
4. Pronoun "you" inferred by verb ending itself.

LESSON 4 : AN INTRODUCTION TO THE USE OF ADJECTIVE AND KARMADHĀRAYA COMPOUNDS

Adjectives agree with the nouns that they modify in gender, number and case. They are declined like nouns when uncompounded. In this type of a compound they can be prefixed to the noun in the crude form, and as a prefix remain unchanged throughout the declension. Karmadhārāya compounds are known as descriptive compounds. Always bear in mind the case of the noun to which they are attached.

Examples :

A BLACK SNAKE	= कृष्णः + सर्पः	कृष्णसर्पः
A NEW TREE	= नवः + वृक्षः	नववृक्षः
AN OLD MAN	= वृद्धः + नरः	वृद्धनरः
By A BLUE LOTUS	= नीलं + कमलं	नीलकमलम्
A BELOVED MAN	= प्रियेण + नरेण	प्रियनरेण
A SHORT LESSON	= ह्रस्वः + पठः	ह्रस्वपठः
A BELOVED GIRL	= प्रिय + कन्या	प्रियकन्या

* Special Sandhi rule — refer to Chapter VII.

विश्व	ALL	ह्रस्व	SHORT
कृष्ण	BLACK	व्याकुल	PERPLEXED
शुक्ल	WHITE	स्थूल	BULKY
नील	BLUE	दूर	DISTANT
रक्त	RED	अन्धा	BLIND
महत	GREAT*	उदार	GENEROUS
संस्कृत	POLISHED	कुशल	SKILFULL
प्रिय	BELOVED	कृपण	WRETCHED
क्षुद्र	MEAN	खंज	LAME
अनन्त	ENDLESS	तीव्र	SHARP, ACUTE
चित्र	VARIEGATED	दुर्लभ	DIFFICULT TO GET

तुल्य	LIKE	नित्य	REGULAR OBLIGA-TORY
दीर्घ	LONG		
नव	NEW	पीन	FAT
* महात	GREAT = WHEN	व्याधित	SICK
	COMPOUNDED	दिव्य	DIVINE
बहु	MUCH	वृद्ध	OLD
अल्प	LITTLE	दक्षिण	SOUTHERN
शीघ्र	SWIFT	विस्मित	ASTONISHED
मन्द	SLOW	स्थिर	FIRM
साधु	GOOD	पुराण	OLD
शून्य	EMPTY	(**)उचित	PROPER
सुन्दर	BEAUTIFUL	स्मरणीय	PLEASANT
योग्य	SUITABLE	शोभन	SHINING, BRIGHT
		अद्भुत	EXTRA ORDINARY MARVELLOUS.

**NOTE : to reverse the meaning of any adjective, precede it with a negative particle : अ if the word starts with a consonant, or अन् if the word starts with a vowel.

Exercise 5 *:* —the Karmadhāraya Compunds.

Remember the agreement in gender, number and person.

1. We know *all the dharmas*.
2. *A black and white tiger* wanders in the forest.
3. *The blue vessel* (vase).
4. *A grest sage* speaks with the people. (Instr. case.)
5. *A beautiful girl* eats.
6. *A divine sacrifice.*
7. He reads a *suitable book*.
8. *Good food* will nourish the disciples. ["will nourish', irreg. future construction-- see answer page]

9. *Slow speech.*
10. *Improper speech.*
11. *Astonished sage.* (see glossary)
12. *Old scriptures.*
13. By a *good thought.* (Instr. case)
14. In a *beautiful house.* (Loc. case.)
15. From a *distant shore.* (Ablative case.)
16. She goes *firmly.* (as adverbial form)
17. He speaks *divinely.* (as adverbial form.)
18. Because of *endless pain.* (Instrumental case.)
19. With the *beautiful girl.* (Instrumental case.)
20. In the *southern forest.* (Loc. case.)

#'s 5 and 19 : "girl" either बालिका or कन्या (#5)
बालिकेना or कन्येना(#19)

Review of all materials presented to this point.

1. How does the first conjugation differ from the fourth?
2. How is the future tense constructed?
3. In adding the personal endings, when is आ (ा) inserted?
4. Which are the prepositions used in the instrumental case?
5. What is the rule for using the conjunction च ?
6. Which particles are used in the instrumental case?
7. How does the negative particle न differ in the imperative mood?
8. Practice conjugating the following irregular fourth conjugation verbs, both in present tense and in the future tense.
   (a) to forgive
   (b) to be glad
   (c) to pierce.
9. Looking through your verbal roots, how many Noun cognates can you find? i.e.

10. Combine the following with the Sandhi rules :—

१. नृपः जयति।

२. बालाः धावन्ति।

३. नरः त्यजति।

४. अश्व अन्नम् खादति।

५. बालैः धावति।

६. नरः बालाः ग्रामम् गच्छन्ति।

७. देवान् जयति।

८. अत्र मनस्।

९. पुनर पतति।

१०. पतिः जयति।

११. अग्निः रोहति।

१२. पुत्रः इच्छति।

CHAPTER VI

Introduction to Sixth Conjugation. Usage of the Past Passive Participle. Introduction to Interogatives. The Dative Case.

LESSON 1 : INTRODUCTION TO SIXTH CONJUGATION

Remember in conjugation I, the medial and final vowels take the guṇa vowel strengthening. In conjugation IV, *no guṇa change* and य is telescoped into the final consonant.

The VI conjugation is like the first conjugation excepting it does not take a guṇa change, nor add य.

Regular Roots		*Irregular Roots*	
कृष्	TO PLOUGH	इष् (इच्छ)	TO WISH
क्षिप्	TO THROW	कृत् (कृन्त)	TO CUT
तुद्	TO STRIKE	मुच् (मुञ्च)	TO RELEASE
दिश	TO SHOW	लुप् (लुम्प)	TO BREAK
लिख्	TO WRITE	लिप् (लिम्प)	TO ANOINT
विश्	TO ENTER	विद् (विन्द)	TO FIND
सृज्	TO CREATE	सिच् (सिञ्च)	TO SPRINKLE
स्पृश्	TO TOUCH	प्रच्छ् (पृच्छ)	TO ASK

As before, consult appendix E for additional roots belonging to this conjugation. Note in irregular, the corresponding nasal is inserted. To conjugate, merely add personal endings as before.

Exercise 1

Exercises : Copy and translate.

१. आरामं निकषा जनो कृषति।

२. रूपं बीजं मुञ्चति।

३. पुत्रा कुलं लिखन्ति।

४. हे बालौ शिष्यौ लिम्पथ:।

५. भूतानि सत्यं पृच्छन्ति।

६. सत्यं अज्ञानं मोक्ष्यति।

७. नर: सर्पं कराभ्यां तुदति।

८. दु:खं हुतं च सुखं विन्दन्ति।

९. माता पुत्रा न सुखेन लेखिष्यति।

१०. धर्म: क्रोधं कृन्तति।

Exercise 2

Set the following sentences into Sanskrit. Remember agreement of gender, person and number, and the Sandhi Rules. (Also tenses).

1. The boys will write and will study (their) lessons.

2. The *strong wind** will break the trees. (*wind = अनिल:; strong = great.)

3. Asanas will release pain.

4. Worship, man: (man = vocative case = नर)

5. The snakes do not find the food.

6. With (my) hands, I annoint the *beautiful girls**. (girls = कन्या)

7. The devotees will enter the house.

8. The *mean man* dances again and faints.

9. Knowledge will show the truth.

10. Īśvara creates man.

11. Because of wealth and gold people laugh.
12. Sacrifice and Asanas create Union.
13. The travelers touch the flowers and eat the fruits.
14. The jackal bites the boy and enters the village.
15. Do not write.
16. The *skillful disciple* will understand the Dharma.

LESSON 2 : INTRODUCTION TO PAST PASSIVE PARTICIPLE USAGE.

The past passive participle is a form of the verb generally ends in "J", which is treated as a adjective. It has three genders as an adjective and is declined like a noun. If must agree in gender, number and case with the noun or pronoun .

Ex उक्त: said or spoken.

	Masc.	Fem.	Neuter
Nom Sing.	उक्त:	उक्ता	उक्तम्
Acc Sing.	उक्तम्	उक्ताम्	उक्तम्
Nom. Pl.	उक्ता:	उक्ता:	उक्तानि

List of past passive participle construes :—

VERBAL ROOT P.P.P.

वच्	SPEAK	=	उक्त	SAID, SPOKEN
गम्	GO	=	गत	GONE
भू	TO BE	=	भूत	BEEN
स्मृ	REMEMBER	=	स्मृत	REMEMBERED
त्यय्	ABANDON	=	त्यक्त	ABANDONED
हृ	TO TAKE	=	हृक्त	TAKEN
जि	CONQUER	=	जित	CONQUERED
दा	GIVE	=	दत्त	GIVEN
लिख्	WRITE	=	लिखित	WRITTEN
खत्	DIG	=	खात	DUG
दृश्	SEE	=	दृष्ट	SEE

पत्	FALL	=	पतित	FALLEN
पा	DRINK	=	पीन	DRUNK
यम्	RETRAIN	=	यत	RESTRAINED
जत्	BORN, BE PRODUCED	=	जात:	BORN, BE PRODUCED
श्रु	HEAR	=	श्रुत	HEARD
म्ना	THINK	=	म्नात	THOUGHT
वह्	CARRY	=	ऊढ	CARRIED
बुध्	KNOW	=	बोधित	KNOWN
दह्	BURN	=	दग्ध	BURNED

Exercise 3

Exercises : Copy and translate. Note the Sandhi rules use:!*

1. सत्यं स्मृतं नरेण।
2. रामो जित: शत्रुणा।
3. व्याघ्रा द्रष्टा नरेण चरिष्यन्ति।
4. नरो ग्रामं गत:।
5. शास्त्रं ब्राह्मणेन स्मृतम्।
6. अन्नं हस्तेन हृतम्।
7. क्रोधो यत:।
8. क्रोधो भक्तेन जित:।

Exercise 4

Set these sentences into Sanskrit, and remember cases, gender, number and person involved as you write them.

1. Wealth (is) taken by the thief.
2. The pigeon, seen by the man, drinks water.
3. The scripture (is) heard by the devotees.
4. Knowledge (is) understood by the boys.
5. The food (is) seen by the people.

6. The lesson (is) studied by the pupils.
7. The fuel (is) burned.
8. The water (is) drunk.
9. Truth (is) abandoned.
10. The earth (is) dug. (Earth = खलं)

*Note : If म is at end of sentence, anusvara (ं) not permitted.

LESSON 3 : INTRODUCTION TO THE INTERROGATIVES.

All of the interrogatives start with the letter क् verbs like "to go," require the accusative case of the place which the motion is directed.

किम्	WHAT?	(occasionally : why?)
कुत्र	WHERE?	
कदा	WHEN?	
किमर्थम	WHY?	
	ON ACCOUNT OF WHAT?	
कथम्	HOW?	

Remind there is no punctuation marks as in English. But we will use question mark (?) for conuencince. Normally there is a single stroke (|) to show beginning of thought and double stroke (||) to show the ending of thought.

Exercise 5

Translate and copy the following exercises using the interrogative construction.

१. कुत्र बालो भवति ?
२. कदा वर्नगमिष्यामि ?
३. किं वदति ?
४. कुत्र वसति ?
५. किमर्थं कन्या बाल न स्मरति ?
६. कथं अन्नं पक्ष्यन्ति ?

७. किं माता शोचति ?

८. कदा पुत्रो मनुष्यात् पोषिष्यति ?

९. कुत्र मेघात् चलन्ति ?

१०. किं कवि* बोंधति ?

Set the following sentences into Sanskrit, and then create your own using present and future tenses, the P.P.P. construction, and the Karmadhāraya compounds.

Exercise 6

1. Why do I study the lessons ?
2. Where does the family live ?
3. Why does he not come ?
4. When will the trees grow ?
5. What is *good speech*?*
6. How will he remember the man ?
7. How is the *old elephant* ?
8. What will the men cook ?
9. How is the *beautiful girl* ?
10. Why doesn't the man return ?

*good speech =वचनम्

* कवि: = poet, sage

*return : prepositional prefix (back) प्रति + गम् = प्रतिगम्।

LESSION 4 : INTRODUCATION TO DATIVE CASE

Review.

1. *Nonivative case* — Represents the subject.
2. *Accusative Case* — Represents the direct object or where the action is transported.
3. *Instrumental Case* — Represent the instrumen vehicle) inbering "by, with, for, because, on, account of, etc".

DATIVE CASE :— The case used for indirect object and also for

"a. Verb meaning and to be angry with, to desire, to long for."

b. to express the purpose of the action or to indicate the person or thing for whom action is done.

Note : —Sandhi rules will be observed strictly.

Example

a. Indirect object

शिष्यांऽन्नं भक्तेभ्यों यच्छति।

(The disciple gives food *to the devotee.*)

b. Verbs meaning "to be angry with to desire, to long for" etc.

जनकः पुत्राय कुप्यति।

(The father is angry with **son**.)

c. To express purpose of action.

युध्याय गच्छति।

He goes **to war.**

d. To indicate person or thing for whom the act is done

कुपं पुत्रेभ्यः खनति।

He digs a well for **his son.**

e. With the following particles:

I. Salutation to नमः।

II. Hail to ! स्वस्ति।

N.B. : The new declension case endings are the same for both the masculine and neuter nouns ending in "a."

Dative Sing : āyea

Dative Dual : ābhyām

Dative Plural : ebhyah.

Exercise 7

Translate the following Sanskrit sentences into English.

१. बालाः पुष्पानि शिष्याय यच्छन्ति। *

२. कृष्णाय नमः।

३. नरः पुस्तकं भक्ताय वहति।

४. आरामं पुत्राय खनति।

५. पुत्राय कुप्यामि।

६. जनाय फलानि रोहन्ति।

७. अद्य ग्रामं शास्त्रैर्भक्तेभ्यो गच्छामि।

८. सत्याय स्वस्ति।

९. रामो ज्ञानं ब्राह्मणाय गायति।

१०. पापं युध्याय नयति।

Exercise 8

Set the following English sentences into Sanskrit. (Observe Sandhi rules)

1. Salutations to Śiva.
2. The girl (kanyā) gives the food to the boys.
3. I shall be angry with the boys.
4. The king gives the flowers to the hero.
5. They two show the moon to the two boys.
6. Enough with sin !
7. Hail to the king !
8. Here the boys will sing with happiness.
9. Where are the people going ?
10. I shall write to the boys.

[A review of the declension endings introduced thus far.]

(Masc.)	S.	D.	Pl.	(Neuter)	S.	D.	Pl.
Nom.	aḥ	au	āḥ		am	e	āni
Acc.	am	au	ān		am	e	ani
Instr.	ena	ābhyām	aiḥ		ena	ābhyām	aiḥ
Dat.	āya	ābhyām	ebhyaḥ		āya	ābhyām	cbhyaḥ

* Another irregular Conjugation I verb : "to give,: दा – यच्छति।

REVIEW AND RECAPITULATION OF VACABULARIES FOR CHECKING YOUR ORGANIC GROWTH.

1. What is the relationship between the construction of Conjugation I & VI ?
2. Review all of the irregular verbs of conjugations I, IV, & VI.

   Sepcial note : add to your list the verb (irr.) "to give"

   दा dā (yacchati)
3. Write out the numbers one through 20 with correct symbols, and names.
4. Translate the following verbs of Conj. IV :—

   अस् तुष् नश् नृत् पुष् मुह्

   दिव् शम् भ्रम् मद् भ्रशं

   व्यध् क्षम् भ्रम् अण् इष्

   ऋध् कुप् क्रोध क्लिश् क्षुध्

   तृष् तुष् दुष् दृप् द्रुह् राध् सिव् सो
5. In Devanāgarī script write out the radical forms of the Past Passive Participle construes of the following :—

   1. abandon, 2. burn, 3. carry, 4. dwell, 5. cook, 6. conquer, 7. flow.
6. Translate the following imperative mood forms :—

   कुरु धाव नृत्य गच्छ पठ

   स्मर वद चल आगच्छ लिख

   भव नय पश्य खाद पिब

   रक्ष आनय खेल क्रडि
7. In Davnāgarī script write the basic forms of these adjectives :—

   all/ great/ Diving/ proper/ improper/ black/ short/ much pleasant white/ perplexed/ little/ shining/ blue/ bulky/ Ranan/

swift/ marvelous/ red/ distant/ slow/ great/ blind/ good/ polished/ generous/ empty/ beloved/ skilfull/ beautiful/ mean/ wretched/ suitable/ unsuitable/ endless/ lame/ old/ variegated/ sharp/ southern/ like/ unlike/ long/ difficult to get to/ astonished/ fat/ firm/ new/ sick/ old.

8. How many of these verbs of Conj. VI have you memorized?

   कृश् क्षिप् तुद् दिश् लिख् विश् सृज् स्पृश् इष् कृत् मुच् लुप् लिप् विद् सिव् प्रच्छ्।

9. Review the Past Passive Participle constructions, expecially the irregular ones.

10. Translate the following interrogatives :—

    what "/ where?/ when?/ why?/ how?.

11. To which cases are these particles and prepositions attached to?

    अलम् कृतम् सह विना नमः स्वस्ति।

12. For practice purposes, write the following paradigms in Nom., Acc., Instr., and Dative cases. Singular-Dual-Plural :—

    (a) Moon, (b) scripture, (c) life, (d) food.

13. For practice purposes, conjugate the following verbs in present and future tenses.

    (a) lead, (b) see, (c) dwell, (d) abandon.

CHAPTER VII

Recapitulation of "Vowel-Sandhi", Complete analysis and exercises. Recapitulation and paradigms of Conjugations I, IV and VI. Introduction to Conjugation X. Introduction to prepositional prefixes for verbal roots.

LESSON 1 : RECAPITULATION OF "VOWEL-SANDHI", COMPLETE ANALYSIS AND EXERCISES.

I will again review the vowel-Sandhi chart that had been introduced in chapter three. As we increase our organic growth this is now of greater prominence :—

Simple Vowels	a or ā	i or ī	u or ū	ṛi or ṛī	ḷri or ḷrī
Guṇa	a	e	o	ar	al
Vṛiddhi	ā	ai	au	ār	āl

Dissimilar Vowel Sandhi Chart : (When a vowel at the end of one word [Column I] meets a vowel beginning the following word [Column A, across], then the vowels combine and become the respective vowels and semi-vowels in columns II, III, IV, V, VI, or VII within the box.

I	II	III	IV	V	VI	VII
A.	a or ā	i or ī	u or ū	ṛi or ṛī	e or ai	o or au
a or ā	ā	e	o	ar	ai	au
i or ī	ya or yā	ī	yu or yū	yṛi or yṛī	ye or yai	yo or yau
u or ū	va or vā	vi or vī	ū	vṛ or vṛī	ve or vai	vo or vau
ṛi or ṛī	ra or rā	ri or rī	ru or rū	ṛī	re or rai	ro or rau

Reflect upon the triangles of samprasaraṇa which showed the corresponding semi-vowel relationship to the simple vowel:—

i or ī is related to semi vowel "y"
u or ū is related to semi vowel "v"
ṛi or ṛī is related to semi vowel "r"
ḷri or ḷrī is related to semi vowel "I."

I. When similar simple vowels meet each other, they combine to the **long form.**

a or ā meets a or ā = ā मुनिना अटामि = मुनिनाटामि।

i or ī meets i or ī = ī नमसि ईश्चरम् = नमसीश्वरम्।

u or ū meets u or ū = ū किन्तु उवाच = किन्तूवाच।

ṛ or ṛī meets ṛi or ṛī = ṛī कर्तृ ऋजुः = कर्तृजुः।

II. Simple Vowels meet dissimilarVowels:-

a or ā meets i or ī = e नमथ ईश्वरम् = नमथेश्वरम्

a or ā meet u or ū = o गच्छथ उद्यानम् = गच्छयोद्यानम्

a or ā meet ṛi or ṛī = ar मुनिना ऋषिः = मुनिनर्षिः।

a or ā meet e = ai तिष्ठ एव = तिष्ठैव

a or ā meet o = au खादथ ओदनम् = खादथौदनम्

a or ā meet ai = ai इन्द्रः च ऐरावतः = इन्द्रश्चैरावतः

a or ā meet au = au पश्यथ औधम = पश्यथौधम्।

i or ī meeting a dissimilar vowel changes to corresponding semi-vowel "y."

धावति अश्वः धावत्यश्वः।

u or ū meeting a dissimilar vowel changes to corresponding semi-vowel "v."

ननु एव = नन्वेव।

ṛi or ṛī meeting a dissimilar vowel changes to corresponding semi-vowel "r."

कर्तृ इति = कर्त्रिति।

"e" or "o" followed by any vowel except "a" is changed to "ay" or "av".

"e" or "o" followed by "a" remains unchanged, while the "a" is dropped and replaced by an avagraha, but the construe is pronounced as a single unit.

मुनयै अन्नम् यच्छामि मुनयेऽन्नं यच्छामि।

प्रभो अधुना प्रभोऽधुना।

Before any vowel excepting "a". "ay", and "av", the corresponding semi vowel may be optionally dropped. The words are not joined.

कवे इच्छसि = कवयिच्छसि or कव = इच्छसि।

गुरो इति = गुरविति or गुर = इति।

"ai" and "au", followed by any vowel are changed to "āy" and "āv", but the corresponding semi-vowel may be optionally dropped. The words are not joined.

तस्मै इषुम् यच्छति = तस्मायिषुमं यच्छति or तस्मा इषुं यच्छति।

अग्नौ इन्द्रम् = अग्नाविन्द्रम् = अग्ना इन्द्रम्।

(When the semi-vowel is dropped, then all vowel Sandhi operations are finished.)

Interjections like "ā", "he", "aho," do not combine with following word.

"ī," "ū," and "e", when are *dual terminations remain unchanged* before vowels.

कवी इच्छत:।

वन्धु अतिथिम्।

Exercise 1

Correct the vowel Sandhi in the following exercises :

१. न अस्ति। २. जीव अन्त।

३. अधि ईश्वर। ४. ऋतु उत्सव।

५. पितृ ऋद्धि। ६. परम ईश्वर।

७. हित उपदेश।	८. गङ्गा उदक।
९. तव ऋद्धि।	१०. महा ऋषि।
११. पर एधित।	१२. विद्या एव।
१३. देव ऐश्वर्य।	१४. अल्प ओजस्।
१५. गङ्गा ओघ।	१६. ज्वर औषध।
१७. अग्नि अस्त्र।	१८. प्रति उवाच।
१९. तु इदनीम्।	२०. मातृ आनन्द।
२१. ते अपि।	२२. सो अपि।
२३. ते आगता:।	२४. विष्णो इह।
२५. जे अति।	२६. अग्ने ए।
२७. कस्मै अपि।	२८. रै अ:।
२९. ददौ अन्नम्।	३०. नौ औ।
३१. फले (dual) अत्र।	३२. गुरो ऋषी (Du.) इह।
३३. हे ऋषे।	३४. अहो बाल।

LESSON 2 : RECAPITULATION AND PARADIGMS OF CONJUGATION I, IV, VI AND IRREGULAR ROOTS IN EACH OF THEM

1. Conjugation One: Root takes guṇa of medial and final vowel. Remember two vowels are not permitted in a row, hence the substitution of the corresponding semi vowels of "ay" for "i" for "av" "u", and "ar" for "ṛi."

PARADIGMS TO HELP REMEMBER

खनामि	खनाव:	खनाम:	बोधामि	बोधाव:	बोधाम:
खनसि	खनथ:	खनथ	बोधसि	बोधथ:	बोधथ
खनति	खनत:	खनन्ति:	बोधति	बोधत:	बोधन्ति:
भवामि	भवाव:	भवाम:	गच्छामि	गच्छाव:	गच्छाम:
भवसि	भवथ:	भवथ	गच्छसि	गच्छथ:	गच्छथ
भवति	भवत:	भवन्ति:	गच्छति	गच्छत:	गच्छन्ति:

The following are irregular roots belonging to conjugation one :—

ऋ ऋच्छति	to rise upwards	पण् पणायति	to bargain
		पा पिबति	to drink
क्रम् क्रामति	to walk, go		
क्लम् क्लामति	to be weary	म्ना मनति	to think
गम् गच्छति	to go	यम् यच्छति	to restrain, err
गुप् गोपायति	to protect	रन्ज् रजति	to colour
गुह् गूहति	to hide	ष्ठिव् ष्ठीवति	to spit
घ्रा जिघ्रति	to smell	सन्ज् सजति	to adhere to
दंश् दशति	to bite	सद् सीदति	to sit
दा यच्छति	to give	सृ सरति	(dhāvati) to run*
दृश् पश्यति	to see	स्था तिष्ठति	to stand

* other verbal root form preferred.

ध्मा धमति to blow

2. Conjugation Four : No guṇa vowel change, semi vowel "y," is telescoped into the final consonant of the root.

A PARADIGM TO HELP REMEMBER

नृत्

नृत्यामि	नृत्याव:	नृत्याम:
नृत्यसि	नृत्यथ:	नृत्यथ
नृत्यति	नृत्यत:	नृत्यन्ति।

The following are irregular roots belonging to conjugation four :—

क्रम् क्राम्यति	to go, walk*
भ्रम् भ्रम्यति भ्राम्यति*	to roam (two forms)

क्लम् क्लाम्यति	to be weary *
मद् माद्यति	to be intoxicated
क्षम् क्षाम्यति	to forgive
छे छयति	to cut
व्यध् विध्यति	to pierce, strike
तम् ताम्यति	to be distressed
शम् शाम्यति	to grow calm
दम् दाम्यति	to tame, be tamed
शो श्यति	to sharpen
दिव् दीव्यति	to play, gamble
श्रम् श्राम्यति	to be tired
दो द्यति	to cut
सो स्यति	to kill, destroy
भ्रंश भ्रश्यति	to fall.

* Roots occuring in conj. I & IV.

3. Conjugation six : Resembles Conjugation One, *however, no vowel changes.*

A PARADIGM TO HELP REMEMBER

विश्

विशामि	विशाव:	विशाम:
विशसि	विशथ:	विशथ
विशति	विशत:	विशन्ति।

The following are irregular verbs of the VI conjugation:—

इष् इच्छति	to wish
कृत् कृन्तति	to cut
मुज् मुञ्जति	to leave
खिद् खिन्दति	to afflict

लिप् लिम्पति	to annoint, besmear
गृ गिरति	to swallow, devour
लुप् लुम्पति	to break
प्रच्छ् पृच्छति	to ask
विच्छ् विच्छायति	to go
भ्रस्ज् भृज्जति	to fry
विद् विन्दति	to get, gain
मस्ज् मज्जति	to sink
सिच् सिञ्जति	to sprinkle
व्यच् विचति	to defraud.

Review Exercise, conjugations I, IV, VI. Make the necessary Sandhi changes, then translate the following phrases. Refer to answer appendix.

Exercise *2*

१. नृपः जयति। २. ग्रामम् अभितः वृक्षाः रोहन्ति।
३. अश्वः अन्नम् खादति। ४. बालैः धावन्ति।
५. मित्रैः अटन्ति। ६. नरः च बालाः च ग्रामम् गच्छन्ति।
७. पुत्रः अर्हति। ८. पुत्रः इच्छति।
९. पुत्राः जयन्ति। १०. पतिः * जयति।
११. शतृः न अर्हति। १२. अग्निः दहति स्म।
१३. शत्रुः* चरति। १४. अद्य बालाः पश्यन्ति।
१५. अत्र अन्नम् पचतिं। १६. गृहम् त्यजनित स्म।
१७. अत्र मनस्। १८. पुनर् तरन्ति।
१९. अन्नम् यच्छति। २०. सुखम् इच्छामि।

पतिः = husband

शत्रुः = enemy

LESSON 3 : INTRODUCTION TO CONJUGATION X.

The endings are the same as in conjugations I, IV, and VI.

— Guṇa of the short medial vowel.

— Vṛiddhi of the final vowel.

— "aya" precedes the verbal endings. (Note! in Conjugation IV this semi-vowel is telescoped into final consonant, but in this conjugation it is separated.)

Paradigm: = चुर् to steal

चोरयामि	चोरयाव:	चोरयाम:
चोरयासि	चोरयथ:	चोरयथ
चोरयति	चोरयत:	चोरयन्ति

In this conjugation there are only two irregular verb stems :—

धू धूनयति to shake

प्री प्रीणयति to please

(N.B. In the appendices I have included many other verbs, so it is to your advantage to scan and investigate the Sanskrit — English appendix.)

Verb of the X Conjugation :—

कथ् कथयति to tell

क्षल् क्षालयति to wash

गण् गणयति to count

घुष् घोषयति to proclaim

चिन्त् चिन्तयति to think

चुर् चोरयति to steal

छद् छादयति to cover

दण्ड् दण्डयति to punish

धृ धारयति to owe

पाल्	पालयति	to protect
पीड्	पीडयति	to oppress
पूज	पूजयति	to worship
भूज्	भूजयति	to adore
भक्ष्	भक्षयति	to eat
भूष्	भूषयति	to adorn
रच्	रचयति	to arrange
सान्त्व्	सान्त्वयति	to counsel
स्पृह्	स्पृह्यति	to long for (+dative case)

Exercise 3

Translate the following sentences into English.

१. दासं सान्त्वयामः।

२. नरो बालं दण्डयति।

३. लोको धनं गणयति।

४. भक्तः पूजयति ईश्वरम्।

५. सनदर कूसुमात्ति रचयामः।

६. सत्यं घोषयति।

७. व्याघ्रोऽन्नं चोरयति।

८. ईश्वरो भक्तान् पालयति।

९. नराय उदार फलानि धारयसि।

१०. पत्रं छादयामि वचनैः।

Exercise 4

Set the following sentences into Sanskrit.

1. I protect the boys today.
2. They counted the flowers.
3. God adores the devotees.
4. Wash (your) two hands.
5. The clouds cover the moon and the rogues steal the jewels.

6. In this manner we shall eat the food.
7. I think and proclaim the Truth!
8. Why do you (sing.) cover the body?
9. The Jackal will steal the meet.
10. Why do you (pl.) punish the thief?

A preposition prefixed to a verbal root subtly changes the meaning of the original verb. Bear in mind the Sandhi rules when prefixing a preposition to a verbal root, but here is a brief introduction to them. [Consult the dictionary at the end of text to realize the impact of these prepositions.]

अति	over, beyond	अतिक्राम्यति	to go beyond, to cross
अधि	near, unto	अधिगच्छति	to go unto, to obtain
अनु	after, along	अनुसरति	to move after, to follow
अप	away from	अपचरति	to move away, to depart
अभि	towards	अभिधावति	to run towards, to attack
अव	downwards	अवदहति	to burn, to destroy
आ	unto, back	आनयति	to bring, to take unto
उद्	up, forth	उद्भवति	to arise, to be produced
उप	near	उपविशति	to sit near
नि	under	निक्षिपति	to throw under, to put down
निस्	away, out	निर्वहति	to carry out
परि	round, about	परिपतति	to fall around, to fly around
प्र	forward	प्रचलति	to move forward, to set out
प्रति	towards, against	प्रतिगच्छति	to go towards, to return
वि	apart, without	व्यस्यति	to throw apart, to scatter
सम्	together,	संक्षिपति	to put together, to summarize, summarize summarize fully

By means of the prepositional prefixing of verbs a whole

new perspective of grammatical construction ensues. The language of Sanskrit is very poetical, and ever consistent in mantric energy, intensified meanings, and filled with non-verbal meanings that are most difficult to transfer to other languages.

Prepositional prefixes. Exercises for Chapter 7.

Exercise 5

1. Death attacks (runs toward) the body.
2. The wind moves away from (departs) the lake.
3. The chariot goes unto the forest (acc.)
4. The two friends sit near the garden (acc).
5. God brings bliss unto the people (the world).
6. Strength follows (moves after) health.
7. The travellers go beyond the ocean.
8. We follow the moon.
9. The two men put down the two burdens and sit near the well (acc.)
10. The servants carry out the vessels.

Translate Sanskrit to English :

Exercise 6

१. शीष्यो ग्रामं प्रतिगच्छति।

२. भद्रो दु:खं अतिक्राम्यति अमृतं अधिगच्छति च।

३. मालिको बीजानि आरामं व्यस्यति।

४. पान्थ: पर्वतान् प्रचलति।

५. भक्तो दिव्यशास्त्रानि निर्वहति।

६. शास्त्रानि वचनानि संक्षिपत्ति।

७. बको ग्रामं परिपतति।

८. शृगालो मृगं अभिधावति।

९. सूखं योगं अनुसरति।

१०. बालो मस्तकं निक्षिपति सौन्दर्यं प्रतिगच्छति।

A complete list of the Masc. and Neuter Nouns ending in "a" ..... अ।

गुणः	quality	समुद्रः	ocean
रुपम्	body (spiritual)	इन्धनम्	fuel
बकः	crane	पुत्रः	son
ज्ञानम्	wisdom, knowledge	कनकम्	gold
शिष्यः	pupil	मूषिकः	mouse
अमृतम्	immortality	कमलम्	lotus
मृगः	deer	आरामः	garden
मृतम्	death	तृणम्	grass
भक्तः	devotee	चन्द्रः	moon
आसनम्	pose	पात्रम्	vessel, vase, jug
धर्मः	the way	पान्थः	traveller
वचनम्	sayings	शरीरम्	body (physical)
मनुष्यः	man	श्रृगालः	jackal
गृहम्	house	शीलम्	character
क्रोधः	anger	चौरः	thief
वनम्	woods, forest	स्थानम्	place
सर्पः	snake	मालिकः	gardener
पत्रम्	page, leaf	कुसुमम्	flower
अश्वः	horse	रथः	wheel, chariot
जलम्	water	जीवनम्	life
आचारः	conduct	लोकः	world, people
कुपम्	well	शीर्शम्	head
करः	hand	आनन्दः	bliss
मस्तकम्	head	भूषणम्	ornament
हस्तः	hand	गजः	elephant

पुष्पम्	flower	रत्नम्	jewel
काक:	crow	प्रसाद:	gift
पातकम्	sin	आरोग्यम्	health
ग्राम:	village	इद:	lake
सत्यम्	truth	काव्यम्	poem
जन:	person	अनिल:	wind
फलम्	reward, fruit	दैवम्	fate
दास:	servant	भार:	burden
शास्त्रम्	scripture	बलम्	strength
देश:	country	हंस:	swan
तीरम्	shore	मांसम्	meat
नर:	man	ईश्वर:	God
धनम्	wealth	मित्रम्	friend
नृप:	king	विनय:	modesty
अन्नम्	food	सौन्दर्यम्	beauty
पर्वत:	mountain	जनक:	father
चक्रम्	wheel	हलम्	plough
बाल:	boy	आकाश:	sky
हुतम्	family	उद्यनम्	garden
मेघ:	cloud	आगम:	arrival
दु:खम्	pain, misery	पापम्	sin
वृक्ष:	tree	शठ:	rogue
सुखम्	happiness	कारणम्	cause
राम:	Rāma	लोभ:	greed
भूतम्	a being	औषधम्	medicine

देवः	majesty, god	कामः	love
पुस्तकम्	book	क्षेत्रम्	field
रावणः	Rāvaṇa	योगः	union
ब्रीजम्	seed	दर्शनम्	sight, visionary.

CHAPTER VIII

Sandhi Rules continued, Readings from the Vedas. Introduction to the Imperfect Tense. Introduction to the Ablative, Genetive, Locative and Vocative Cases. Propositional Prefixes continued, Masculine Nouns in -i, -u, ri.

LESSON 1 : SANDIH RULES CONTINUED ....

More Sandhi Rules for memorization. To this point 11 rules have been introduced. (Refer to Chapters III and VII).

12. Find dental "n" (न्) before "j" (ज्)or "ś"(श्) converts to palatal "ñ" (ञ्).

    देवान् जयति = देवाञ्जयति।

    देवान् श्रयति = देवाञ्श्रयति or देवाञ्द्दयति *

*श more of ten becomes द (Note that the words coalesce!)

13. Final dental "n" (न्) before semi-vowel "l" (ल्) becomes anusvara (aṁ), and the words coalesce.

    एतान् लोकान् = एतां लोकान्।

14. Final dental "n" (न्), preceding "c, ch, ṭ, ṭh, t, or th (च्, छ्, ट्, ठ्, त्, or थ्

    Converts to anusvara (aṁ) + corresponding sibilant of same class, and coalesces.

शिष्यान् ताडयति = शिष्यांस्ताडयति

अश्वान् चोरयति = अश्वांश्चोरयति।।

15. Final dental "n" (न्), preceded by a short vowel and followed by any vowel becomes doubled (nna) न्न and coalesces.

स्मरन् इच्छाम् = स्मरन्निच्छाम्।

16. Within a word, "n" (न्) or "m" (म्), before a sibilant, become anusvara.

हंस वंश

17.* Internal dental "na" (न) when followed by a vowel or "na, ma, ya, or va," (न, म, य, व) cerebral "na" (ण) if preceded in same word at any distance by : "ri, rī, sa, or ra," ऋ , ॠ, ष, or र unless any palatal, cerebral or dental letters intervene, except "ya" (य). Note following examples carefully. Arrow shows why the change.

(out of anger) क्रोधेन = No change because न् and र् separated by dental ध

(with the arrow) शरेन =शरेण: न preceded by र्, no intervening palatal, cerebral, or dental)

(with the cakra) चक्रेन = चक्रेण: As above.

(with the eye) नेत्रेन =नेत्रेण: As above

(because of the jewel) रत्नेन = रत्नेन No change त् intervenes.

(with the ornament) भूषनेन = भूषणेन first न: no separation between ष् and न् but 2nd न्: intervening न or ण् (cerebral or dental)

(with/because of/the hero) वीरेन = वीरेण As above.

(with/because of health) आरोग्येन = आरोग्येण No intervening prohibited letters.

(w/because of desire) मनोरथेन = No change, dental separates र् and न्।

(out of/ because of human effort) पुरुषकारेन = पुरुषकारेण।

18. Sandhi of final consonants. If a hard consonant precedes a soft consonant or vowel, the final hard consonant changes to soft of its own class :—

क् = ग् वाक् वदति = वाग् वदति।

19. Final dental "t" (त्), becomes a "d" (द्) before "h" (ह) or a soft consonant, except before "j" (ज्) "l" (ल) and nasals, and the words coalesce.

(Frequently refers to the Ablative case.)

ग्रामात् अटति = ग्रामादटति।

पापात् रक्षात् = पापाद्रक्षात्।

20. Final "t" (त), preceding a "j" (ज्), "l" (ल्), or nasals, is changed to a doubled consonant.

मेघात् जलम् = मेघाज्जलम्

पापात् लोकात् = पापाल्लोकान्

गृहात् नयति = गृहान्नयति।

21. Final "t" (त्) preceding "c (च्) or ch (छ्)," becomes "c" (च्)

ग्रामात् च ग्रामाच्च)

22. Final "t" (त्), preceding "ś" (श्), becomes "c" (च्). [*Optioanl* : Initial "ś" (श्) = "ch" (छ्)।

शिष्यात् शिक्षति = शिष्याच्छिक्षति

23. Initial "ch" (छ), after a short vowel, a preposition, "ā" (आ), and prohibitive "mā" (मा), becomes "cch" (च्छ्), and the words coalesce.

अत्र छाया = अत्र च्छाया

अत्र छत्रम् = अत्र च्छत्रम्

अत्र छाग: = अत्र च्छाग:

अत्र छात्र: = अत्र च्छात्र:।

Correct the Sandhi in the following sentences and translate :

Exercise 1

1. आराम् पुष्पानि अधुना छादयन्ति।
2. अश्वान् शाम्यामि।
3. हुतात् चौरौ रत्नानि चोरयत:।
4. दास: बालान् लिम्पति।
5. ज्ञानात् शीलम् रोहति।
6. परशु: तरून् तुदति।
7. ग्रामात् जनक: गच्छति।

Change the following sentences to Sanskrit, incorporating all the Sandhi Rules learned thus far:

Exercise 2

1. The fruits fall from the tree.
2. The father praises the sons.
3. Do not cut the flowers.
4. The wind breaks the trees.
5. Water drops from the jug.
6. The baby notices the guests.
7. The body shines from asanas.

See Answer Appendix for this chapter.

LESSON 2 : READINGS FROM THE VEDAS : VISHNU

Samhita	Pada-Without Sandhi
१. विष्णोर्नु कं वीर्याणि प्रवोचं	विष्णो :। नु । कम् वीयोणि। प्र। वोचम्।
य: पार्थिवानि विममे रजांसि।	य:। पार्थिवानि। विऽममे। रजांसि।

यो अस्कभायदुत्तरं सधस्थं यः। अस्कभायत्। उत्ऽतरम्। सधऽस्थम्।

विचक्रमाणस्त्रेधोरुगाय:।। विऽचक्रमाणः। त्रेधा। उरुऽगायः।।

I will now proclaim the heroic powers of Viṣṇu, who has measured out the terrestial regions; who established the upper gathering place, having, wide-paced, strode out triply.

2. प्र तद्विष्णुः स्तवते वीर्येण प्र। तत्। विष्णुः। स्तवते। वीर्येण।

मृगो न भीमः कुचरो गिरिष्ठाः। मृगः। न। भीमः। कुचरः। गिरिऽस्थाः।

यस्योरुषु त्रिषु विक्रमणेष्व् यस्य। उरुषु। त्रिषु। विऽक्रमणेषु।

अधिक्षियन्ति भुवनानि विश्वा।। अधिऽक्षियन्ति। भुवनानि। विश्वा।।

By reason of his heroic power, like a dread beast that wanders at will, that haunts the mountains. Viṣṇu is praised aloud for that: he in whose three wide strides all beings.

3. प्र विष्णवे शूषमेतु मन्म प्र। विष्णवे। शूषमफ। एतु। मन्म।

गिरिक्षित उरुगायाय वृष्णे। गिरिऽक्षिते। उरुऽगायाय। वृष्णे।

य इदं दीर्घं प्रयतं सधस्थम् यः। इदम्। दीर्घम। प्रऽयतम्। सधऽस्थम्।

एको विममे त्रिभिरित्पदेभिः।। एकः। विऽममे। त्रिऽभिः। इत्। पदेभिः।

Let my inspiring hymn go forth for Viṣṇu, the mountain dwelling wide pacing bull, who alone with but three steps has measured out this long far-extended gathering place;

4. यस्य त्रीपूर्णा मधुना पदनन्य् यस्य। त्री । पूर्णा। मधुना। पदानि।

अक्षीयमाणा स्वधया मदन्ति। अक्षीयमाणा। स्वधया। मदन्ति।

य उ त्रिधातु पृथिवीमुत द्याम् यः। ऊं इति। त्रिऽधातु। पृथिवीम।

एको दाधार भुवनानि विश्वां।। एकः। दाधार। भुवनानि। विश्वा।।

Whose three steps filled with mead, unfailing, rejoice in bliss; and who in threefold wise alone has supported earth and heaven, and all beings.

Samhita	*Pada*
5. तदस्य प्रियमभि पाथो अश्यां	तत्। अस्य। प्रियम्। अभि। पाथः। अश्याम्।
नरो यत्र देवयवो मदन्ति।	नरः। यत्र। देवऽयवः। मदन्ति।
उरुक्रमस्य स हि बन्धुरित्था	उरुऽक्रमस्य। सः। हि। बन्धुः। इत्था।
विष्णोः पदे परमे मध्व उत्सः।।	विष्णोः। पदे। परमे। मध्वः। उत्सः।।

I would attain to that dear domain of his, where men devoted to the gods rejoice; for that, truly akin to the wide-strider, is a well of mead in the highest step of Viṣṇu.

६. ता वां वास्तून्युश्मसि गमध्यै	ता। वाम्। वास्तूनि। उश्मसि। गमध्यै।
यत्र गावो भूरिशृङ्गा अयासः।	यत्र। गावः। भूरिऽशृङ्गाः। अयासः।
अत्राह तदुरुगायस्य वृष्णः	अत्र। अह। तत्। उरुऽगायस्य। वृष्णः।
परमं पदमव भाति भूरि।।	परमम्। पदम्। अद। भाति। भूरि।।

We desire to go to those abodes of you two, where are the many horned nimble kine: there indeed that highest step of the wide-pacing bull shines brightly down.

Practice Readings from the Vedas: Surya

Sahitya : Including Sandhi	**Original Pada Before Sandhi**
१. उद्वेति सुभगो विश्वचक्षाः	उत्। ऊँ इति। एति। सुऽभगः। विश्वऽचक्षाः।
साधारणः सूर्यो मानुषाणाम्।	साधारणः। सूर्यः। मानुषाणाम्।
चक्षुर्मित्रस्य वरुणस्य देवश्	चक्षुः। मित्रस्य। वरुणस्य। देवः।
चर्मेव यः समविव्यक्तमांसि।।	सर्मऽइव। यः। समऽअविव्यक्। तमांसि।।

Up rises the genial all-seeing Sun, common to all men, the eye of Mitra and Varuṇa, the god who rolled up the darkness like a skin.

२. उदवे्ति प्रसवीता जनानां	उत्। ऊं इति। एति। प्रऽसविता। जनानाम
महान्केतुरर्णवः सूर्यस्य।	महान्। केतुः। अर्णवः। सूर्यस्य।
समानं चक्रं पर्याविवृत्सन्	समानं। चक्रम्। परिऽआविवृत्सन्।
यदेतशो वहति धूर्षु युक्तः।।	यत्। एतशः। वहति। धूःऽसु। युक्तः।।

Up rises the rouser of the people, the great waving banner of the Sun, desiring to revolve hither the uniform wheel, which Etaśa, yoked to the pole draws.

३. विभ्राजमान उषसामुपस्थाद्।	विऽभ्राजमानः। उषसाम्। उपऽस्थात्।
रेभैरुदेत्यनुमद्यमानः।	रेभैः। उत्। एति। अनुऽमद्यमानः।
एष मे देवः सविता चच्छन्द	एषः। मे। देवः। सविता। चच्छन्द।
यः समानं न प्रमिनाति धाम।	यः। समानम्। न। प्रऽमिनाति। धाम।

Shining forth he rises from the lap of the dawns, greeted with gladness by singers. He has seemed to me god Savitṛ who infringes not the uniform law.

Readings from the Vedas : Surya,

४. दिवो रुक्म उरुचक्षा उदेति	दिवः। रुक्मः। ऊरुऽचक्षाः। उत्। एति।
दूरेअर्थस्तरणिर्भ्राजमानः।	दूरेऽअर्थः। तरणिः। भ्राजमानः।
नूनं जनाः सूर्येण प्रसूता	नूनम्। जनाः। सूर्येण। प्रऽसूताः।
अयन्नर्थानि कृणवन्नपांसि।।	अयन्। अर्थानि। कृणवन। अपांसि।।

The golden gem of the sky, farseeing rises, whose goal is distant, speeding onward, shining. Now may men, aroused by the sun, attain their goals and perform their labours.

५. यत्रा चक्रुरमृता गातुमस्मै	यत्रा। चक्रुः। अमृताः। गातुम्। अस्मै।
श्येनो न दीयन्नन्वेति पाथः।	श्येनः। न। दीयन्। अनु। एति। पाथः।
प्रति वां सूर उदिते विधेम	प्रति। वाम्। सूरे। उतऽइते। विधेम।
नमोर्भिमित्रावरुणोत हव्यैः।।	नमः।ऽभिः। मित्रावरुणा। उत। हव्यैः।।

Where the immortals have made a way for him, like a flying eagle he follows his path. To you two, when the Sun has risen, we would pay worship with adorations. O Mitra-Varuṇa, and with offerings.

६. नू मित्रो वरुणो अर्यमा नम्	नु। मित्रः। वरुणः। अर्यमा। नः।
त्मने तोकाय वरिवो दधन्तु।	त्मने। तोकाय। वरिवः। दधन्तु।
सुगा नो विश्वा सुपथानि सन्तु	सुऽगा। नः। विश्वा। सुऽपथानि। सन्तु।
यूयं पात स्वस्तिभिः सदा नः।।	यूयम्। पात। स्वस्तिऽभिः। सदा। नः।।

Now may Mitra, Varuṇa, and Aryaman grant wide space to us ourselves and to our offsprings. Let all our paths be fair and easy to traverse. Do you protect us evermore with blessings?

LESSON 3 : THE IMPERFECT TENSE

In Sanskrit there are three past tenses :—

(a) Imperfect, past events where the speaker had been a witness.

(b) Perfect, past events of which the speaker had not been a witness.

(c) Aorist, used for immediate past. [not included in this text.]

In classical Sanskrit these three tenses are used indiscriminately, with the restriction that in the Perfect, the first person is rarely used.

To construct the imperfect tense the verbal root is prefixed with "a", and the same rules are used as in the First, Fourth, Sixth and Tenth Conjugations concerning the guṇa or vṛiddhi changes, and use of semi-vowels, etc.

Below is a comparison of the personal ending substitutes :—

Present & Future Tense Endings :—

	S.	Du.	Pl.
1.	āmi	āvaḥ	āmaḥ
2.	asi	athaḥ	atha
3.	ati	ataḥ	anti

Imperfect Personal Endings : prefix "a"

	S.	Du.	Pl.
1.	am*	āva	āma
2.	aḥ	atam	ata
3.	at	atām	an

* In the imperfect tense the first person singular uses a short "a", an exception to the rule.

Illustrative paradigms of present tense, and the Imperfect tense :—

पचामि	पचाव:	पचाम:	अपचम्	अपचाव	अपचाम
पचसि	पचथ:	पचथ	अपच:	अपचतम्	अपचत्
पचति	पचत:	पचन्ति	अपचत्	अपचताम्	अपचन्
नृत्यामि	नृत्याव:	नृत्याम:	अनृत्यम्	अनृत्याव	अनृत्याम
नृत्यसि	नृत्यथ:	नृत्यथ	अनृत्य:	अनृत्यतम्	अनृत्यत
नृत्यति	नृत्यत:	नृत्यन्ति	अनृत्यत्	अनृत्यताम्	अनृत्यन्
लिखामि	लिखाव:	लिखाम:	अलिखम्	अलिखाव	अलिखाम
लिखसि	लिखथ:	लिखथ	अलिख:	अलिखतम्	अपचत
लिखति	लिखत:	लिखन्ति	अलिखत्	अलिखताम्	अलिखन्
घोषयामि	घोषयाव:	घोषयाम:	अघोषयम्	अघोषयाव	अघोषयाम
घोषयसि	घोषयथ:	घोषयथ	अघोषय:	अघोषयतम्	अघोषयत
घोषयति	घोषयत:	घोषयन्ति	अघोषयत्	अघोषयताम्	अघोषयन्।

SPECIAL NOTE : In imperfect, verbal root prefixed with "a", and in the first person singular the personal ending is "am" NOT "ām".

Mnemonically refer back to previous verb lists and practice forming the imperfect tense.

If a verbal root has a prepositional prefix, the new augment of "a" is inserted between the preposition and the verbal root and will utilise the vowel Sandhi rules.

Examples :—

प्र + अ + विशत् = प्राविशत् = entered

अनु + अ + भवत् = अन्वभवत् = experienced

प्रति + अ + पतत् = प्रत्यपतत् = neglected

If the verbal root beings with a vowel, the augment "a" forms vṛiddhi with the initial vowel.

Examples :—

अस् = आस्यत् = threw

इष् = ऐच्छत् = wished

उष् = ओषत् = burned

ऋ = आर्त = went to

Again ! refer back to verb lists and mnemonically drill this construction.

Exercise 3

Translate Sanskrit to English.

१. गृहं नरोऽविशत्।

२. सत्ये देवोऽसृजत्।

३. वृक्षं गजोऽतुदत्।

४. इदं बाकान् प्रत्यपतन्।

५. भक्तागायन्।

६. गुरुं जनोऽलिम्पत्।

७. अन्नमक्षिपाम।

८. धर्ममन्वभवन्।

९. अपृच्छताम्।

१०. अलिखाव।

Exercise 4

English into Sanskrit : —

1. The horses ran to the forest.
2. Today the trees burned down.
3. The clouds moved in the sky.
4. The swans crossed the lake.
5. The two boys followed the teacher.
6. In this manner the people ate.
7. The tiger returned to the forest.
8. We read. (past tense)
9. You two played and ran.
10. They two worshipped.
11. Today she cooked the food.
12. She cried.*
13. All the people sang and danced.

LESSON 4 : INTRODUCTION TO ABLATIVE, GENETIVE, LOCATIVE AND VOCATIVE CASES.

Ablative case—used

1. Indicate the place from where action comes.
2. With the verbs which means, "to protect", to desert, to fear.
3. To express a derived "cause or motive from which action occurs.

The following prepositions are governed in this case :—

To the East of, before शक्

Before पूर्वम्

After अनन्तरम्

Until, since आ

Outside प्रभृति

* to cry = मुच्।

without बिना

except ऋते।

The endings attached to the nouns or substantives are as follows :—

Singular	Dual	Plural
āt	ābhyām*	ebhyaḥ*

**Special Note* :— In the Instr., Dat., and Abl. the endings are identical *DUAL NUMBER* in the Dat., and Abl. Plural, the endings are the same.

This applies to either Masculine or Neuter Nouns ending in "a".

From the forest, the deer goes. मृग: वनात् गच्छति = मृगो वनाद् गच्छति। *

He wanders from the village. ग्रामात् अटति = ग्रामादटति। *

She protects from evil. पापात् रक्षति = पापाद्रक्षति। *

Water from the cloud. मेघात् जलम् = मेघाज्जलम्। *

From an evil world. पापात् लोकात् = पापाल्लोकात्। *

She leads from the house गृहात् नयति = गृहान्नयति or गृहाद् नयति। *

He learns from the pupil. शिष्यात् शिक्षति = शिष्याच्छिक्षति। *

* Refer to information on external Sandhi related to a final "t" and a hard consonant meeting a soft one. (Lesson 1 of this chapter).

Exercise 5

Correct the following Sandhi exercises involving the Ablative case:

१. कुपात् पिबन्ति।

२. आरामात् धावन्ति।

३. ज्ञानात् स्मरिष्यति।

४. दुखात् शोचामः।

५. शास्त्रात् यजन्ति।

६. देवात् चिन्तावः।

७. ज्ञानात् रोहामः।

८. सत्यात् जयामि।

९. धर्मात् पठामि।

१०. आनन्दात् माद्यामः।

११. मृत्यात् गृंहतः।

१२. हुतात् अक्षाम्यन्।

१३. सुखात् माद्यामः।

१४. ज्ञानात् अस्मरन्।

१५. मेघात् जलम्।

Genetive case — Expresses relationship between the nouns showing possession and is like an apostrophy (') in English. The following prepositions are used in this case.

उपरि above, अधः below, पुरतः in front of, पश्चात् behind,

अग्रे-समक्षम् in presence of, कृते for the sake of, परतः beyond

The declension endings for Masculine and Neuter Nouns are :—

Singular	*Dual*	*Plural*
asya	ayoḥ	ānām

Exercise 6

For practice copy the following Sanskrit to English Sentences and especially note the karmadhāraya compounds, Sandhi rules, and tenses involved.

१. पर्वतानां वृक्षानवदहन्।

२. अन्धनृपस्य पुत्रोऽपचरति।

३. वृद्धदासस्य इन्धनमधो गृहम् निक्षिपर्तिस्म।

४. दिव्याचार्यस्य वचनानि धर्मम् संक्षिपन्ति।

५. नीलकमलस्य पुष्पानि उदभ्वन्ति।

६. शीघ्राभयोऽ न्नं व्यास्यत्।

७. शास्त्रानाम् विश्वपुस्तकानपठन्।

८. शुक्लकमलस्य पत्रानि क्षेष्यन्ति।

९. वनस्य नवग्रामोऽवादहत्।

१०. मनुष्यस्य पुस्तकमपतत्।

Exercise 7

English to Sanskrit exercises:

1. Man's conduct
2. Servant's two hands
3. King's misery
4. Tree's fruits
5. Horses's food (pl.)
6. Rāma's wealth
7. Life's misery
8. Deer's grass
9. For the sake of the blind man the people sing.
10. Behind the little tree swift water flows.
11. The devotees have a teacher.
12. In the presence of the king the people are quiet.
13. I have endless wealth.

Special notes :

1. Remember the new Sandhi rules.
2. Remember there is no word in Sanskrit for "have."
3. Practice karmadharaya compounds.
4. Practice present, future and imperfect tenses.
5. Review all nouns and adjectives for future reference.

[Three mantras to dwell on]

१. शीलम् नरस्य भूषणम्।

२. सत्यम् लोकस्य दीपः।

३. मुर्खस्य नास्ति औषधम्।

The Locative Case is used :

(a) to indicate the *place where the action takes place* -- prepositions "in", 'at", "on", "upon", "among", etc.

वने भक्तश्चिन्नति। (The devotee ponders in the forest.)

(b) to indicate the *time when the action takes place.*

शरदे (In the Autumn. f. noun)

(c) *after verbs indicating movement* such as "to fall", "to place", "to throw", "to send", "to enter", etc.

विशति गृहे। (He enters the house.)

(d) to translate expressions like "*concerning*", " *in the matter of* ", etc.

बालः पुस्तकानि शास्त्रेषु पठति। (The boy studies books concerning the Sastras.)

(e) to indicate the *object of emotions and feelings:*

नरो नृपे इर्ष्यिति। (The man is jealous of the king.)

The last case to be introduced is the Vocative Case.

Masculine Nouns ending in "a" :—			*Neuter Nouns ending in "a" :—*		
Sing.	*Dual*	*Plural*	*Sing.*	*Dual*	*Plural*
a	au*	āḥ*	a	e*	āni*

*Note same endings as in the Nominative.

The Vocative case is used for addressing, calling or evoking!

There are many particles used, but here are the most common:—

हे = Oh! अये = Ho! Joy! अहो = Surprise, anger, joy, praise, blame, surprise.

हे बाल Oh child!

अहो नृप Oh joy, king

Review of all the cases :— A brief summary, but go back and re-read each case again!

Nominative = the subject

Accusative = the direct object, or to where the action is carried.

Instrumental = By, with, for because of, on account of, are the inferred prepositions.

Dative = The indirect object

Ablative = From where the action started.

Genetive = Shows onwership, or belonging to, possession like English (').

Locative = Where the action is taking place.

Vocative = To evoke or to call.

In learning these first declensional endings, look for similarities rather than for differences. In all the future declensions you will find a great many similar endings which can only be understood in context.

Masculine Nouns : "a"				*Neuter Nouns : "a"*			
N.	ah.	au*	āh*	N.	am*	e*	āni*
A.	am	au*	ān	A.	am*	e*	āni*
I.	ena	ābhyām*	aiḥ				
D.	āya	ābhyām*	ebhyaḥ*				
A.	āt	ābhyām*	ebhyaḥ*				

ALL OTHER ENDINGS SAME AS MASCULINE

G.	asya	ayoḥ*	ānām				
L.	e	ayoḥ*	eṣu				
V.	a	au*	āḥ*	v.	a	e*	āni*

* Note same endings which will occur in future declensions!

LESSON 5 : CONTINUATION OF VERBAL PREPOSITIONAL PREFIXES THE VERB.

कृ = to do spiritually, to make. Although it is highly irregular and belongs to the non-conjugational, VIII conjugation it is a most important verb with many nouns, adjectives and substantives.

Present Tense			*Imperfect Tense*		
करोमि	कुर्वः	कुर्मः	अकरवम्	अकुर्व	अकुर्म
करोषि	कुरुथः	कुरुथ	अकरोः	अकुरुतम्	अकुरुत
करोति	कुरुतः	कुर्वन्ति	अकुरोत्	अकुरुताम्	अकुर्वन्।

कुरु is the imperative form.

In the previous chapter sixteen prepositional prefixes were introduced and now attention is drawn to particular prepositional-prefixed roots which are very important because of their refined inflection, alteration of meaning and for future construction of nouns, adjectives and substantives too. Here are a few, but please courageously skim through the Sanskrit-English dictionary in the appendix for others. Remember when a prefix precedes a verb the Sandhi rules must be observed, and when the imperfect tense is constructed the "a" is inserted between the prefix and the root and of course Sandhi is to be observed.

अर्थ् x, to request	कृ VIII, to do, to make spiritually
अभि = to beg	अधि = to refer to
प्र = to ask, to wish	अनु = to imitate
प्रति = to challenge	अप = to harm
	अलभ = to adorn
ऊह् = I, to guess	आविस् = to reveal
अप = to remove	उप = to help
प्रति = to impede	उपस्कृ = to decorate
वि = to arange troops.	तिरस् = to abuse

कृ VIII, to do, make spiritually

परिष्कृ = to polish

प्रति = to surround

वि = to change

विप्र = to tease

व्या = to explain

संस्कृ = to refine

कृष् = I, to pull

आ = to attract

उद् = to enhance

नि = to lessen

क्षिप् = VI, to throw

अधि = to offend, to abuse

आ = to allude

नि = to put down, to intrust

सम् = to abridge

खन् I, to dig

उद् = to uproot

नि = to bury

गण् X to count

अधि = to praise

नमस् = to salute, to revere

परि = to surround

गम् I, to go

अधि = to acquire

अनु = to follow

अभि = to approach

अव = to know, to understand

आ = to come

उद् = to rise

उप = to approach

नसि् = to go out

प्रति = to return

वि = to pass away

गै I, to sing

अव = to censure

चर् I, to move, walk, go

अप = to depart

अनु = to follow

अभि = to offend

आ = to practise, to perform

उप = to serve

प्र = to set forth

जि् I, to conquer

अव = to deprive of

अव = to disregard

परि = to consider

जीव् = I, to live, to be alive

अति = to survive + acc.

अनु = to live upon +acc.

उद् = to live again

उप = to maintain oneself

तड् = X to beat

परि = to strike

वि = to wound

तुष् = IV, to be pleased

परि = to be satisfied

सम् = to rejoice in

तॄ = I & VI, to cross over, transcend

अति = to overcome

अव = to descend

उद् = to escape

निस् = to overcome

वि = to bestow

त्यज् = I, to abandon

परि = to forsake

सम् = to give up

निस् = to overcome

त्रस् = I, to tremble

अप = to flee

परि = to be afraid

सम् = to dread

दिश् =VI, to show

अनु = to refer to

अप = to feign

आ = to prescribe, to command

उद् = to point out

उप = to instruct, to advise

निस् = to specify

सम् = to assign

दृश् = I, see visionary, insight

अनु = to behold

उप = to observe

प्र = to foresee

सम् = to perceive

द्रु = I, to melt, flow, run, ooze

अनु = to pursue

अप = to flee

अभि = to assail

उप = to hasten

प्र = rush upon

वि = to flee, to burst

धृ = X, to hold, to support, to owe

अव = to determine

उप = to support

निस् = to pick out

नन्द् = I, to rejoice

अभि = to congratulate

प्रति = to receive joyfull

नी = I, to lead

अनु = to request

अप = to carry away

अभि = to act (on the stage)

आ = to bring

उद् = to raise

उप = to offer

निस् = to decide

परिणी = to marry

वि = to dispel

सम् = to unite

बुध् = I, to know, to understand

अनु = to think of

अव = to perceive

उद् = to awaken

प्रति = to observe

वि = to learn

सम् = to recognize

मू = I, to be, to become

अनु = to experience

अभि = to overcome

उद् = to arise

परा = to vanquish

परि = to surpass

प्र = to be produced, to rule

सम् = to be possible

भ्रम् = I & IV, to roam, to err

परि = to turn around

वि = to be perplexed

सम् = to fall into error

पत् = I, to fall

अति = to neglect

अभि = to rush at

उद् = to fly up

नि = to fall down

प्रणि = to prostrate oneself

मद् = IV, to rejoice

उद् = to be mad

प्र = to neglect

मन्त्र् = X, to consult
अभि = to address
आ = to take leave of
नि = to invite
सम् = to consult

मुच् = VI, to release (liberate)
अति = to avoid
अभि = to discharge
आ = to put on
उद् = to free
निस् = to loosen
परि = to abandon

मुह्=IV, to faint, to lose sense
अति = to be at a loss
परि = to be confused
वि = to faint

रक्ष् I, to protect
अभि = to observe
परि = to guard
प्र = to save
सम् = to preserve

रुह् = I, to grow, to ascend
अधि = to mount
अव = to descend
आ = to ascend
प्र = to grow
वि = to shoot up
सम् = to grow

रुप् = X, to represent (a form, shape)
नि = to observe
प्र = to explain
वि = to disfigure

लिख् = I, to write, to scratch
अभि = to write
अव = to erase
आ = to sketch
उद् = to polish
परि = to copy
प्र = to draw
सम् = to summarize

वद् = I, to speak
अप = to abuse
अभि = to address
परि = to blame

वस् I, to dwell

अधि = to occupy

आ = to abide

उप = to stay, to fast

नि = to dwell

प्र = to live abroad

वि = to depart

विश् = VI, to enter

अभि+नि = to resort to+acc.

आ = to overpower

उप = to sit down

प्र = to enter

स्मृ = I, to remember

वि = to forget

स्था I, to stand, to halt

अधि = to dwell

अनु = to perform

हस् = I, to laugh

परि = to ridicule

हृ = I, to take

अभि = to offer

व्यव = to behave

आ = to obtain, to eat

व्या = to utter

समा = to collect

उद् = to lift, to rescue

उप = to offer

परि = to avoid

प्र = to strike

वि = to enjoy oneself

सम् = to check

In conjugating these inflected verbs remember :

1. Rules governing each conjugation [I, VI, IV, & X].
2. Remember the particular verb roots which are irregular.
3. For the imperfect tense, the "a" is inserted between prep. and root, and if prep starts with "a", remember the Sandhi change.
4. Consult appendix for future stems.
5. Practice in writing and in speaking for drill work!
6. Go very slow!!!

LESSON 6 : INTRODUCTION TO MASCULINE NOUNS ENDING IN "I" AND "U"

To this point we have been concerned with only masculine and neuter nouns which ended in "a." Learning the first set of declensional endings is perhaps the firmest groundwork for all nouns to come. Now we commence to expand our vocabulary, but bear in mind the following : —

a. Accusative singular in all declensions ends with "m."
b. Accusative plural in most declensions ends with "n."
c. Ablative and Genetive singular are always the same.
d. Nominative, Accusative and Vocative Dual are always the same.
e. Instrumental, Dative and Ablative Dual are always the same.
f. Nominative and Vocative Plural are always the same.
g. Dative and Ablative Plural are always the same.
h. The Genetive Plural will always end in a "-nām," formation.
i. The Locative Plural will always end in a "-ṣu," formation.
j. Look for similarities, rather than completely new endings.
k. The "i," and "u," nouns employ samprasarana (the guna or semivowel interchange). Refer to earlier chapter showing this.
l. Go very slowly and perhaps write your own alphabetical diary of all the Nouns, adjectives, verbs that we have covered so far. DO NOT BE AFRAID TO CONSULT THE DICTIONARIES IN THE APPENDIXES

A paradigm of the new declensional presentation.

	Sin.	*Dual*	*Plural*
Nom.	रविः	रवी	रवयः
Acc.	रविम्	रवी	रवीन्

Inster	रविना	रविभ्याम्	रविभि:
Dative	रवये	रविभ्याम्	रविभ्य:
Ablative	रवे:	रविभ्याम्	रविभ्य:
Genitive	रवे:	रव्यो:	रवीनाम्
Locative	रवी	रव्यो:	रविषु
Vocative	रवे	रवी	रवय:

रवि: = The Sun

Master list of Declensional Paradigms : Note similarities that occur as opposed to a maze of different varied endings. Remember in the cases where i, u, ṛi. occur either the guṇa or vṛiddhi or corresponding semivowel may be used. I corresponds to either e or ya, u corresponds to o or va, ṛi corresponds to ar, ār, or ra, etc. The most important part of learning the declension endings is in the *similarities* as opposed to the variances!

	Masculine Nouns: "a"				*Neuter Nouns : "a"*		
N.	ah.	au	āḥ	N.	am	e	āni
A.	am	au	ān	A.	am	e	āni
I.	ena	ābhyām	aiḥ				
D.	āya	ābhyām	ebhyaḥ				
A.	āt	ābhyām	ebhyaḥ				

ALL OTHERS SAME AS MASCULINE ENDINGS

G.	asya	ayoḥ	ānām				
L.	e	ayoḥ	eṣu				
V.	a	au	āḥ	v.	a	e	āni

	*Masculine Nouns: "i"**				*Masculine Nouns : "u"**		
N.	iḥ	ī	ayaḥ	N.	uḥ	ū	avaḥ
A.	im	ī	īn	A.	um	ū	ūn
I.	inā	ibhyām	ibhiḥ	I.	unā	ubhyām	ubhiḥ

D.	aye	ibhyām	ibhyaḥ	D.	ave	ubhyām	ubhyaḥ
A.	eḥ	ibhyām	ibhyaḥ	A.	oḥ	ubhyām	ubhyaḥ
G.	eḥ	-yoḥ	īnām	G.	oḥ	-voḥ	ūnām
L.	au	-yoḥ	iṣu	L.	au	-voḥ	uṣu
V.	e	ī	ayaḥ	V.	o	ū	avaḥ

Feminine Nouns: "ā"				*Feminine Nouns : "ī"*			
N.	ā	e	āḥ	N.	ī	-yau	-yaḥ
A.	ām	e	āḥ	A.	īm	-yau	īḥ
I.	ayā	ābhyām	ābhiḥ	I.	-yā	ībhyām	ībhiḥ
D.	āyai	ābhyām	ābhyaḥ	D.	-yai	ībhyām	ībhyaḥ
A.	āyāh	ābhyām	ābhyaḥ	A.	-yāḥ	ībhyām	ībhyaḥ
G.	āyāḥ	ayoḥ	ānām	G.	-yāḥ	-yoḥ	īnām
L.	āyām	ayoḥ	āsu	L.	-yām	-yoḥ	īṣu
V.	e	e	āḥ	V.	ī	-yau	-yaḥ

* refers to substitution of guṇa, vṛiddhi, or semivowel and / or telescoping into the consonant.

Additional Nouns to be learned and added into your personal diary :—

Masculine :— "a"	*Neuter : — "a"*
ईश्वर: God	आरोग्यम् Health
गुण: Quality, Personality trail	काव्यम् Poem
विनय: Modesty	दैवम् Fate
जनक: Father	बलम् Strength
आकाश: Sky	मांसम् Meet
प्रसाद: Offering	मित्रम् Friend
भार: Burden	वचनम् Sayings, Quotation
अनिल: Wind	सौन्दर्यम् Beauty
वीर: Hero	हलम् Plough
घट: Jar, Vessel	तीरम् Shore, Bank of river

आदेशः Order
क्रोधः Anger
लोभः Greed
कामः Lust, Desire
मोहः Illusion
नाशः Destruction
आश्रमः Place of learning
शरः Arrow
सूतः Charioteer
स्तेनः Thief
वधः Killing
पुरुषकारः Human effort
उद्यमः Effort
मनोरथः Desire

भूषणम् Ornament
रत्नम् Jewel
कार्यम् Work
उद्यानम् Garden
औषधम् Medicine
क्षेत्रम् Field
नेत्रम् Eye
भयम् Fear
दर्शनम् Visionary sight, Seeing
हस्यम् Ridicule
चक्रम् Wheel, Energy center
सख्यम् Friendship
गानम् Song

N.B. In the Genetive and Locative Dual endings the telescoping here as opposed to the "ayoḥ" which occurs in the Masculine and Neuter Nouns in "a."

New Vocabulary list of Masculine Nouns ending in "i" and "u". [Add to your own personal diary!]

अग्निः Fire
अतिथिः Guest
अरिः Enemy
कविः Poet
गिरिः Mountain
मुनिः Sage
रविः Sun
राशिः Heap

इन्दुः Moon
इषुः Arrow
गुरुः Dispeller of Darkness; Teacher
तरुः Tree
परशुः Axe
पशुः Beast
बन्धुः Relative
बाहुः Arm

उदधिः Ocean
कलिः Quarrel
अलिः Bee
कपिः Monkey
नृपतिः King (Benevolent)
ऋषिः Seer
ध्वनिः Sound
निधिः Treasure
पाणिः Hand
विधिः Fate
रश्मिः Ray

बिन्दुः Drop, Point
शिशुः Baby
वायुः Wind
मृत्युः Death
प्रभुः Lord, Master
शत्रुः Enemy
हेतुः Cause
साधुः Honest man

Exercise 8

Sanskrit to English Exercises :

१. अग्निर्गिरिषु तरूनवादहत्।

२. रवैरश्मयः प्रकाशन्ति आकाशे।

३. न्याघ्रागजाकपयश्च पशून्भवीन्त।

४. लोभः प्रभुं न तुष्यति।

५. हे शिशो खाद।

६. कविः सत्येन संलिखति।

७. प्रभोगृहम् साधून् चिन्तयति।

८. मृत्युः शत्रुर्न भवति।

९. मुनिर्वने माद्यति।

१०. इषवस्तृणस्य गिरौ रोहन्ति।

११. कलिना बन्धूनपाचरत्।

१२. मुनयः रविम् यजन्ति।

Exercise 9

English to Sanskrit Exercises :

1. He punishes the enemies in the presence of the king.
2. Why do the wild elephants attack (rush at) people?
3. When will you go to the mountains?
4. From the ocean Rama brings food to the devotees.
5. The mean arrows fell into the lake.
6. The scriptures are a Divine treasure.
7. The guru sat near the mountain and chanted (sang).
8. Desire is misery's cause; enough with desire!
9. In the forest people obtain truth, happiness and great treasures.
10. Because of the poet's beautiful words, many devotees read (his) books.

Recapitulation and Grand Review.

1. Describe each of the eight declensional cases.
2. What is the purpose of the past passive participle construction?
3. Both write and read aloud complete paradigms of the following nouns :—
   1. Mountain both masc. in "a" and in "i".
   2. Ocean both the masc. in "a" and in "i".
   3. King both in the masc. in "a" and in "i".
4. Both write and read aloud the conjugations in present, future and imperfect tenses of the following verbs :—
   1. भू I
   2. व्यध् IV
   3. मुच् VI
   4. मन्त्र् X.
5. Review and write the prepositions which govern Acc., Instr., Dat., Gen, and Abl. cases.

6. Draw the samprasaraṇa triangles including AUM.
7. Consult the Sanskrit English dictionary in the appendix and list some of the nouns or adjectives formed directly from verbal roots of any conjugation!
8. From this chapter choose any four prepositional-prefixed verbs and both write and recite them in the present, future and imperfect tenses.

CHAPTER IX

Feminine Nouns in -ā and -i. Introduction of Middle Voice. Feminine Nouns in -i and -u. Introduction to Passive Voice. Personal Pronouns.

LESSON 1 : FEMINE NOUNS ENDING IN "ā" AND "I"

In the previous chapter a preview was given of the new declensional endings, but here they are again. Please make careful note in the case of the "ī" nouns where the "y" (य्) is telescoped into the previous consonant, as is the case in the fourth conjugation. If you look for similarities rather than differences, the task at hand can be more pleasant.

	Feminine Nouns: "ā"				*Feminine Nouns : "ī"*		
N.	ā	e	āḥ	N.	ī	-yau*	-yaḥ
A.	ām	e	āḥ	A.	īm	-yau*	īḥ
I.	ayā	ābhyām	ābhiḥ	I.	-yā*	ībhyām	ībhiḥ
D.	āyai	ābhyām	ābhyaḥ	D.	-yai*	ībhyām	ībhyaḥ
A.	āyāḥ	ābhyām	ābhyaḥ	A.	-yāḥ*	ībhyām	ībhyaḥ
G.	āyāḥ	ayoḥ	ānām	G.	-yāḥ*	-yoḥ*	īnām
L.	āyām	ayoḥ	āsu	L.	-yām*	-yoḥ*	īṣu
V.	e	e	aḥ	V.	i	-yau*	-yaḥ*

* represents the endings which are telescoped into the previous consonant.

New Vocabulary list (added to your own) of :

Feminine Nouns ending in "ā"	*Feminine Nouns ending in "ī"*
गंगा The Ganges	नगरी Town, City
रम्भा A plantain tree	नदी river
मुद्रा Seal, Coin, Gesture	धात्री Nurse
शोभा Splendour	पृथ्वी The Earth
भार्या Wife	वाणी Voice, speech
छाया Shade, Shadow, Splendour	राज्ञी Queen
संध्या Twilight	सिंही Lioness
भाषा Speech, Language	जननी Mother
सभा Assembly	नारी Woman
माला Garland	पत्नी Wife
लता Creeper	भगिनी Sister
बालिका Girl	गृहिणी Housewife
कन्या Girl, daughter	शर्वरी Night
चिन्ता Reflection, Thought, Anxiety	
इच्छा A wish	
वीणा A lute (musical instrument)	
सेवा Service (spiritual)	
पूजा Worship, Honour	
हिंसा Injury, Harm	
करिया Action	
विद्या Knowledge	
तारा Star, Pupil of the eye	
श्रद्धा Faith	

Exercise 1

Copy and translate Sanskrit-to-English Exercises. (Refer to Answer pages in the appendix). All Sandhi rules are now cumulative!!

१. प्रगमिष्यामि गङ्गम्।

२. कन्या दीणाम् नृपम् अनुष्ठात्।

३. नृपेन राज्या च नगर्या जना माद्यन्ति।

४. जनन्या शोचति भगिनी बालिकाया मृत्युना।

५. राज्ञी गृहिणी न भवति।

६. रामः कुसुमानि तीरात् नद्या व्यास्यत्।

७. बालस्य श्रद्धा विद्याम् संक्षिपति।

८. संध्या नगर्यै छायमानयति।

९. कविरस्मतं् राज्ञीम् सुन्दरवचनैः।

१०. सिम्या वाणी सुन्दरभवति वा शृगालस्य न भवति

Exercise 2

English to Sanskrit exercises.

1. The people are glad because of the Queen's voice.
2. The Master will return to the Ganges.
3. The enemies throw arrows at the heros.
4. Today I shall give beautiful garlands to the seer.
5. How does faith bring happiness?
6. At night the animals roam in the forest.
7. Beautiful flowers grow around the mountain (giri).
8. Truth is a treasure remembered by the devotees.
9. The honest man creates good health, happiness and union with God!
10. A creeper, garland, grows under the trees near the shore of the river.

LESSON 2 : INTRODUCTION TO THE MIDDLE VOICE : ĀTMANPADĪ.

Parasmaipada – (active voice) – Voice infering an action done for another which we have studied in privious lesson.

Atmanepada – (middel voice) —Where action is done for oneself.

Note :— P for parasmaipada and A for Atmanepada will be used.

Some verbs especially neuter as in which the result of the action occures to the agent are conjugated in the A only. The following is an abbreviated list, by conjugation, of some verbal roots only used A.

Paradigm of atmanepada endings :—

	S.	*Du.*	*Pl.*	व्यथ्	A. to be afraid	
1.	e	āvahe	āmahe	व्यथे	व्यथावहे	व्यथामहे
2.	ase	ethe	adhve	व्यथसे	व्यथेथे	व्यथध्वे
3.	ate	ete	ante	व्यथते	व्यथेते	व्यथन्ते

[Conj.I]

अय् to go

कल्प् to be able

गर्ह् to blame, censure

त्रप् to be ashamed

त्रै (त्राय) to defend from, protect

त्वर् to make haste, hurry

दय् to sympathize with, pity

बाध् to trouble, oppress

भाष् to speak, say

भिक्ष् to beg for

लभ् to obtain, get

लोक् to look at, examine

वन्द् to revere inwardly, salute

वृत् (वर्त्) to exsist

वृध् (वर्ध्) to grow

व्यथ् to be afraid, suffer

शिक्ष् to learn

श्लाघ् to praise

सह् to endure, bear

सूद् to hurt, strike

यत् to try	स्पर्ध् to challenge
रम् to rejoice, sport	स्वञ्ज् to embrace
	क्षम् to forgive, to suffer, to bear

All middle reflexive verbs!

[Conjugation IV, Ātmanepada verb roots.]

क्लिश् to suffer, be afflicted	मन् to think
खिद् to be distressed	युज् to meditate, concentrate
जन् (जा) to be born, to be produced	युध् to fight
दू to suffer pain	ली to adhere to
प्री to be satisfied, feel affection	सू to bring forth
बुध् to know	

[Conjugation VI, Ātmanepada verb roots..]

जुष् to be pleased, like

दृ + आ = आद्रिय to respect, honour

मृ (म्रिय) to die

विज् to fear, to shake

[Conjugation X, Ātmanepadae verb roots ..]

चित् (चेत्) to perceive	विद् to tell, etc.
भू to obtain	स्पश् to embrace
मन्त्र् to consult	लल् to fondle
मृग् to seek, to hunt	

[Most of the X conjugation verbs can be both P. & A.]

The following verb roots use the A. endings, but have P. translations.*

यतते strives, रमते sports, लोछते sees, वर्तते is, शोभते shines, सहते endures, सेवते serves and स्मयते smiles. All belong to Conj. I.

मृयते belongs to Conj. VI.

जयते to be produced, पद्यते go, उध्यते fight, and विद्यते exists, All belong to Conj. IV.

* These are classed as deponent verbs, using A. endings with P. meaning!

[It is essential that you check the verb appendix and note when verbs are P. or A. or both P. & A. called Ubhayapada or those used both ways . I do hope that for your organic-growth process you are making your own personal list of all Nouns, Adjectives, and verbs as you progress!]

Both the present tense and future tense use the same A. endings : —

	S.	*D.*	*Pl.*
1.	e	āvahe	āmahe
2.	se	ethe	adhve
3.	te	ete	ante

IN THE IMPERFECT TENSE ĀTMANEPADE CONSTRUCTIONS, IN ADDITION TO THE "a" PREFIX

TO THE ROOT, A NEW SET OF ĀMANEPADE ENDINGS IS USED!

	S.	*D.*	*Pl.*
1.	e	āvahe	āmahi
2.	athaḥ	ethām	adhvam
3.	ata	etām	ante

Here are paradigms of both constructions in conj. I, IV, VI, X. both P. & A.

Pres. Tense. P. "to dig"			*Imperfect Tense P.* "dug"		
खनामि	खनावः	खनामः	अखनम्	अखनाव	अखनाम
खनसि	खनथः	खनथ	अखनः	अखनतम्	अखनत
खनति	खनतः	खनन्ति	अखनत्	अखनताम्	अखनन्

Future Tense P. "will dig"

खनिष्यामि	खनिष्याव:	खनिष्याम:
खनिष्यसि	खनिष्यथ:	खनिष्यथ
खनिष्यति	खनिष्यत:	खनिष्यन्ति

N.B. All actions done for oneself!

Pres. Tense A/.			*Imperfect Tense A*		
खने	खनावहे	खनामहे	अखने	अखनावहि	अखनामहि
खनसे	खनेये	खनध्वे	अखनथा:	अखनेथाम्	अखनध्वम्
खनते	खनेते	खनन्ते	अखनत	अखनेताम्	अखनन्त

Future Tense A.

खनिष्ये	खनिष्यावहे	खनिष्यामहे
खनिष्यसे	खनिष्येथे	खनिष्यध्वे
खनिष्यते	खनिष्येते	खनिष्यन्ते

Paradigm of Conj. IV. लष् to wish.

Pres. Tense P.			*Imperfect Tense P.*		
लष्यामि	लष्याव:	लष्याम:	अलष्यम्	अलष्याव	अलष्याम
लष्यसि	लश्यथ:	लष्यथ	अलष्य:	अलष्यतम्	अलष्यत
लष्यति	लष्यत:	लष्यन्ति	अलष्यत्	अलष्यताम्	अलष्यन्

Future Tense P.

लषिष्यामि	लषिष्याव:	लषिष्याम:
लषिष्यसि	लषिष्यथ:	लषिष्यथ
लषिष्यति	लषिष्यत:	लषिष्यन्ति

Present Tense A			*Imperfect Tense A*		
लष्ये	लष्यावहे	लष्यामहे	अलष्ये	अलष्यावहि	अलष्यामहि
लष्यसे	लष्येथे	लष्यध्वे	अलष्यथा:	अलष्येथाम्	अलष्यध्वम्
लष्यते	लष्येते	लष्यन्ते	अलष्यत	अलष्येताम्	अलष्यन्त

Future Tense A

लषिष्ये	लषिष्यावहे	लषिष्यामहे
लषिष्यसे	लषिष्येथे	लषिष्यध्वे
लाषष्यते	लषिष्येते	लषिष्यन्ते

Paradigm Conj. VI विश् to enter

Present Tense P.			*Imperfect Tense P.*		
विशामि	विशाव:	विशाम:	अविशम्	अविशाव	अविशाम
विशसि	विशथ:	विशथ	अविश:	अविशतम्	अविशत
विशति	विशत:	विशन्ति	अविशत्	अविशताम्	अविशन्

Future Tense P.

वेक्ष्यामि	वेक्ष्याव:	वेक्ष्याम:
वेक्ष्यसि	वेक्ष्यथ:	वेक्ष्यथ
वेक्ष्यति	वेक्ष्यत:	वेक्ष्यन्ति

Present Tense A.			*Imperfect Tense A.*		
विशे	विशावहे	विशामहे	अविशे	अविशावहि	अविशामहि
विशसे	विशेथे	विशध्वे	अविशथा:	अविशेथाम्	अविशध्वम्
विशते	विशेते	विशन्ते	अविशत	अविशेताम्	अविशन्त

Future Tense A.

विक्ष्ये	वेक्ष्यावहे	वेक्ष्यामहे
वेक्ष्यसे	वेक्ष्येथे	वेक्ष्यध्वे
वेक्ष्यते	वेक्ष्येते	वेक्ष्यन्ते

Paradigm Conj. X चिन्त् to think

Present Tense P.			*Imperfect Tense p.*		
चिन्तयामि	चिन्तयाव:	चिन्तयाम:	अचिन्तयम्	अचिन्तयाव	अचिन्तयाम
चिन्तयसि	चिन्तयथ:	चिन्तयथ	अचिन्तय:	अचिन्तयतम्	अचिन्तयत
चिन्तयति	चिन्तयत:	चिन्तयन्ति	अचिन्तयत्	अचिन्तयताम्	अचिन्तयन्

Future Tense P.

चिन्तयिष्यामि	चिन्तयिष्याव:	चिन्तयिष्याम:
चिन्तयिष्यसि	चिन्तयिष्यथ:	चिन्तयिष्यथ
चिन्तयिष्यति	चिन्तयिष्यत:	चिन्तयिष्यन्ति

Present Tense A.			*Imperfect Tense A.*		
चिन्तये	चिन्तयावहे	चिन्तयामहे	अचिन्तये	अचिन्तयनावहि	अचिन्तयामहि
चिन्तयसे	चिन्तयेथे	चिन्तयधवे	अचिन्तयथा:	अचिन्तयेथाम्	अचिन्तयध्वम्
चिन्तयते	चिन्तयेते	चिन्तयन्ते	अचिन्तयत	अचिन्तयेताम्	अचिन्तयन्त

Future Temse A.

चिन्तयिष्ये	चिन्तयिष्यावहे	चिन्तयिष्यामहे
चिन्तयिष्यसे	चिन्तयिष्येथे	चिन्तयिष्यध्वे
चिन्तयिष्यते	चिन्तयिष्येते	चिन्तयिष्यन्ते

SPECIAL NOTES TO REMEMBER THE P. & A. ENDINGS ....

1. In the P. both present tense and future tense have same endings :

	S.	D.	Pl.	
1.	āmi	avah	āmah	
2.	asi	athah	atha	verb
3.	ati	atah	anti	[Check the index for future each time.]

2. In the P. the imperfect tense endings are : Prefix root with "a".

	S.	D.	Pl.	
1.	am*	āvā	āma	[Ist. per. sing. short "a".]
2.	aḥ	atam	ata	
3.	at	atām	an	

3. In the A. both present tense and future tense have same endings :

	S.	D.	Pl.	
1.	e	āvahe	āmahe	verb
2.	se	ethe	adhve	[Check the index
3.	te	ete	ante	future each time!]

4. In the A. the imperfect tense endings are : Prefix root with "a".

1.	e	āvahi	āmahi
2.	athāḥ	ethām	adhvam
3.	te	ete	ante

LESSON 3 : FEMININE NOUNS ENDING IN "I" AND "U"

The feminine nouns ending in "i" and "u", borrow most of their declensional endings from the masculine nouns which end in "i" and "u".

SPECIAL NOTE :Where a dash [—] Orecedes the ending it means the ending is telescoped into the preceding consonant! Aslo note the alternate endings in the D. Ab1., Gen and Loc. singular endings.

Feminine Nouns in "i". *Feminine Nouns in "u".*

	S.	Du.	Pl.		S.	Du.	P.
N.	iḥ	ī	ayaḥ	N.	uḥ	ū	avaḥ
A.	im	ī	īḥ	A.	um	ū	ūḥ
I.	-yā	ibhyām	ibhiḥ	I.	-vā	ubhyām	ubhiḥ
D.	-yai/aye	ibhyām	ibhyaḥ	D.	-vai/ave	ubhyām	ubhyaḥ
A.	-yāḥ/eḥ	ibhyām	ibhyaḥ	A.	-vāḥ/oḥ	ubhyām	ubhyaḥ
G.	-yāḥ/eḥ	-yoḥ	īnām	G.	-vāḥ/oḥ	-voḥ	ūnām
L.	-yām/au	-yoḥ	iṣu	L.	-vām/au	-voḥ	uṣu
V.	e	ī	ayaḥ	V.	o	ū	avaḥ

New Vocabulary list of Feminine Nouns ending in "i" and "u".

मतिः mind	धेनुः cow
शक्तिः energy, power	चञ्चुः beak

भक्तिः devotion

तृप्तिः satisfaction

नीतिः conduct

केलिः jest

भूमिः earth

धूलिः dust

रात्रिः night

मुक्तिः liberation, salvation, release

प्रतिपत्तिः fame, acquirement, confidence

तनुः the body

रज्जुः rope

रेणुः dust, pollen

हनुः jaw

A FEW IDIOMATIC EXPRESSIONS :

मतिं करोमि I turn my mind + Loc.

करे करोमि I take in my hand.

पदम् करोमि I set foot + Loc.

क्षणम् करोमि I wait one moment.

शीर्षं करोमि I place on my head.

Sample paradigms of Femine nouns in "i" and "u."

	S.	Du.	Pl.	"the night"
N.	रात्रिः	रात्री	रात्रयः	
A.	रात्रिम्	रात्री	रात्रीः	
I.	रात्र्या	रात्रिभ्याम्	रात्रिभिः	
D.	रात्र्ये/रात्रये	रात्रिभ्याम्	रात्रिभ्यः	
A.	रात्र्याः/रात्रेः	रात्रिभ्याम्	रात्रिभ्यः	
G.	रात्र्याः/रात्रेः	रात्र्योः	रात्रीनाम्	
L.	रात्र्याम्/रात्रौ	रात्र्योः	रात्रिषु	
V.	रात्रे	रात्री	रात्रयः	

	S.	Du.	Pl.	"the cow"
N.	धेनुः	धेनू	धेनवः	
A.	धेनुम्	धेनू	धेनू	
I.	धेन्वा	धेनुभ्याम्	धेनुभिः	
D.	धेन्वै/धेनवे	धेनुभ्याम्	धेनुभ्यः	

A.	धेन्वा/धेनोः	धेनुभ्याम्	धेनुभ्यः
G.	धेन्वा/धेनोः	धेन्वोः	धेनूनाम्
L.	धेन्वाम्/धेनौ	धेन्वो.	धेनेषु
V.	धेनो	धेनूः	धेनवः

Note alternative endings in D., A., G., and Loc. singular.

Exercise 3

Sanskrit — English exercise. (Remember the A. construction!)

१. मतिर्वर्तते च अविद्याविवर्तते।

२. मतिं करोमि विद्यायाम्।

३. साधुनीतिः शक्तिमानयति।

४. चञ्चवा काको मांसहरते।

५. रज्जुं करे करोमि।

६. तन्वा योगमभिनिविशते।

७. भूम्यास्तृणम् धेनुः खादति।

८. बालौ तनुम् रात्रौ अयच्छताम्

९. आदेशेन गुरौ रमावहे कायाभ्याम्।

१०. भक्तिः तृप्तिर्भवति।

Exercise 4

English to Sanskrit exercise.

1. I wait one moment for Kṛṣṇa. (Use idiomatic constr.)
2. I place on my head a beautiful white garland of flowers. (Idiomatic)
3. I turn my mind to the scriptures. (Idiomatic)
4. The cow and the horse does not have a beak!
5. For myself I obtain truth and Divine knowledge.*

---

* Remember "for myself" signals usage of Atmanepade

6. I consult the teacher in the forest near the village.
7. The crow attacks the mean snake.
8. I place on my head a jar filled with water.
9. I respect the power of the Guru.
10. We all desist from anger, untruth and ignorance.**

A review list of speical *Ātmanepade verbs* by conjugation.

Conjugation I :—

ईक्ष् ईक्षते to see

कम्प् कम्पते to tremble, to shake

गाह् गाहते to dive within

डी =डयते Conj. I डी = डीयते Conj. IV, to fly

रुच् रोचते to be pleased + dative case.

वि + जि = विजयते to conquer

परा + जि = पराजयते to defeat

वि + वद् = विवदते to disagree

वृत् वर्तते to exist

प्र + वृत् = प्रवर्तते to proceed

नि + वृत् = निवर्तते to desist from

भाष् भाषते (for oneself) to speak

लभ् लभते to obtain

Conjugation IV ......

जन् जायते to be born, to be produced

मन् मन्यते to think

आ + दृ = आद्रियते Conjugation VI : to respect

---

* Remember "for myself" signals usage of Atmanepade

** desist = निवृत् (A) + Abl.

Conjugation X :—

मन्त्र् मन्त्रयते to consult

मृग् मृगयते to search for.

(Have you put all of the Ātmanepade and deponent verbs in your diary?)

LESSON 4 : INTRODUCTION TO PASSIVE VOICE

The passive voice is used when the subject is acted on by someone or something else. It is constructed on the root and not the base or irregular form. "Y," is added, and in the X conjugation it loses the additional "a". The construction will be presented in steps.

Step One :— "Y" is telescoped into the root form, and ātmane endings are used :

Active	*Passive*
पचति	पच्यते
चरति	चर्यते
गम् गच्छति	गम्यते
पतति	पत्यते
बुध् बोधति	बुध्यते

Step Two : A final short "i" or "u" is lengthened.

जि जयति	जीयते
श्रु श्रवति	श्रूयते
क्षि क्षयति	क्षीयते
द्रु द्रवति	द्रूयते

Step Three :— The following rts change their final vowel to "ī".

दा दीयते। गै गीयते। पा पीयते। स्था स्थीयते।

Step Four : Final "ṛi" after a single consonant becomes "ri."

हृ ह्रियते। धृ ध्रियते। भृ भ्रियते। सृ स्रियते। मृ म्रियते।

Step Five : Final "ṛi" after a double consonant uses guṇa form of "ar".

स्मृ समर्यते

Step Six :— Irregular forms. Incomplete list consult verb glossary at end of text.

खन् खायते

वद् उद्यते

वह् उह्यते

वप् उप्यते

वस् उष्यते N.B. REFER TO VERB GLOSSARY!!!

वे ऊयते

सृप् सृप्यते

ह्वे हूयते

जृ जीर्यते

ग्रह् गृहयते।

Step Seven : In changing from active voice to passive voice note following changes of declensional case. [All Sandhi rules are applied!]

	Active Voice	*Passive Voice*
ex. :	Nom : The man	Instr : By the man
	Verb : cooks	Verb : is cooked
	Acc : the fruit	Nom : the fruit

Active Voice : The man cooks the fruit. नरः फलम्पचति।

Passive Voice : The fruit is cooked by the man. नरेण फलम्पच्यते।

Exercise 5 — Constructing active, and then passive voice.

Fire :	अग्निः	अनलः	
Moon :	इन्दुः	विधुः	चन्द्रः
Man :	नरः	जनः	मनुष्यः

Tree :	तरु:	वृक्ष:	द्रुम:
Mountain :	गिरि:	पर्वत:	शैल:
King	नृप:	नृपति:	
God :	देव:	सुर:	ईश्वर:
Wind :	अनिल:	वायु:	

Using the above vocabulary, write two forms for each of the following sentences :

1. ACTIVE VOICE : The fire burns the trees.
2. PASSIVE VOICE : The trees are burned by the fire.
3. ACTIVE VOICE : The moon lights the sky.
4. PASSIVE VOICE : The sky is lit by the moon. (प्रकाश् 10 PA)
5. ACTIVE VOICE : The man adorns the woman.
6. PASSIVE VOICE : The woman is adorned by the man.
7. ACTIVE VOICE : The trees protect the village from the wind.
8. PASSIVE VOICE : The village is protected from the wind by the trees.
9. ACTIVE VOICE : The clouds cover the mountains.
10. PASSIVE VOICE : The mountains are covered by the clouds.
11. ACTIVE VOICE : The king blames the servants.
12. PASSIVE VOICE : The servants are blamed by the king.
13. ACTIVE VOICE : The man sees the truth. (ईक्ष 1A)
14. PASSIVE VOICE : Truth is seen by the man.

Note : (a) Remember declension of the noun.

(b) Remember necessary Sandhi.

(c) Each word will have two sentences.

(d) After completing the exercises consult the answer glossary.

LESSON 5 : THE PERSONAL PRONOUNS.

In the Ist and 2nd person no difference in gender is shown. The optional short forms may not be used at the beginning of a sentence, or in connection with : च and, वा or, एव just, indeed. Remember the dual endings are not subject to vowel Sandhi, and very slowly memorize the declensional endings.

1st. Person : अस्मद्

	S.	Du.	Pl.
N.	अहम्	आवाम्	वयम्
A.	माम्	आवाम्	अस्मान्
	मा	नौ	नः
I.	भया	आवाभ्याम्	अस्माभिः
D.	महयम्	आवाभ्याम्	अस्मभ्यम्
	मे	नौ	नः [Short forms occur in Acc. Dat. & Gen.]
A.	मत्	आवाभ्याम्	अस्मत्
G.	मम	आवयोः	अस्माकम्
	मे	नौ	नः
L.	मयि	आवयोः	अस्मासु

2nd, person : युष्मत्

	S.	Du.	Pl.
N.	त्वम्	युवाम्	यूयम्
A.	त्वाम्	युवाम्	युष्मान्
	त्वा	वाम्	वः
I.	त्वया	युवाभ्याम्	युष्माभिः

D.	तुभ्यम् / ते	युवाभ्याम् / वाम्	युष्मभ्यम् / वः
A.	त्वत्	युवाभ्याम्	युष्मत्
G.	तव / ते	युवयोः / वाम्	युष्मकाम् / वः
L.	त्वयि	युवयोः	युष्मासु

Personal Pronouns in the 3rd person are Masc., Fem., and Neuter Genders तद्

Masuline form of "he"

N.	सः	तौ	ते
A.	तम्	तौ	तान्
I.	तेन	ताभ्याम्	तैः
D.	तस्मै	ताभ्याम्	तेभ्यः
A.	तस्मात्	ताभ्याम्	तेभ्यः
G.	तस्य	तयोः	तेषाम्
L.	तस्मिन्	तयोः	तेषु

Feminine form of "She"

N.	सा	ते	ताः
A.	ताम्	ते	ताः
I.	तया	ताभ्याम्	ताभिः
D.	तस्यै	ताभ्याम्	ताभ्यः
A.	तस्याः	ताभ्याम्	ताभ्यः
G.	तस्याः	तयोः	तासाम्
L.	तस्याम्	तयोः	तासु

Neuter form of "it"

N.	तत्	ते	तानि
A.	तत्	ते	तानि

ALL OTHERS ARE THE SAME AS THE MASCULINE FORM !!

एतत् "This" follows all the above patterns in Masc. Fem., and Neuter.

saḥ and eṣaḥ drop their visarga before any consonant and before any vowel except "a. Before "a" the visarga becomes "o" the "a" is substituted with an avagraha.

सः पतति = स पतति। एषः वदति = एष वदति।

सः अहम् = सोऽहम्। एषः अवदत् = एषोऽवदत्।

Exercise 6

Sanskrit to English Exercise : —

१. स चिन्तयति।

२. तदटति।

३. शिष्यश्चलति।

४. वयंगूहिष्यामहे।

५. ताः तृप्यन्ते।

६. स दूयते।

७. तानि नश्यन्ति।

८. अन्नं तस्मै दिशमि।

९. सा भुञ्जते।

१०. यूवाम् संलिखामः।

११. अहमनयम्।

१२. आवाम् भक्षयावः।

१३. सा मण्डयते।

१४. अस्मान् मन्त्रयामहे।

१५. तदवादहत

Exercise 7

English to Sanskrit Exercise :—

1. She entered.
2. Thou singest.
3. Rāma gives it to her.
4. Because of sorrows, I wish happiness for her.
5. It multiplied.
6. We two cook for ourselves.
7. The two girls will understand. (अवगम्)
8. We two (f.) learn.
9. The two girl's books.
10. I shall proclaim!
11. We two desist.
12. She is protected.
13. They two (f.) are nourished.
14. It is pursued.
15. All the flowers are scattered.

Review

1. What is the difference between Parasmaipada and Atmanepada?
2. What is meant by deponent verbs?
3. What is the purpose of prepositional prefixing of verbs?
4. Write out the declension for : mother / mind / energy / treasure.
5. What is the difference between active voice and passive voice?
6. Write out conjugation in Pres., Imperfect and Future Tense of : Both P. & A.

   To think/ To be/ To understand.
7. Orally practice the Masc., Fem, and Neuter pronouns.

CHAPTER X

Masculine and Feminine Nouns in ṛi, Usage of Adjectives continued (Agreement), Comparison Superlative Forms. The Imperative Mood Continued. Introduction to Potential (Optative) Mood. Neuter Nouns in-i, -u, -ṛi.

LESSON 1 : MASCULINE AND FEMININE NOUNS IN - ṚI. —

There are two types of masculine nouns in "ṛi', agent-nouns and nouns of relations. Their declension differs only in the nominative and vocative dual and plural and in the accusative singular and dual; in which case the final "ṛi", of the agent-nouns takes vṛiddhi (ār) while that of nouns of relations takes guṇa (ar).

Paradigm of endings : Masculine agent-nouns :

	Masculine agent-nouns :			*Masculine nouns of relation:*		
	S.	Du.	Pl.	S.	Du.	Pl.
N.	ā	arau*	āraḥ*		arau	araḥ
A.	āram	ārau*	ṛīn	aram	arau	
I.	rā	ṛbhyām	ṛibhiḥ			
D.	re	ṛibhyām	ṛibhyaḥ			
A.	—uḥ	ṛbhyām	ṛibhyaḥ	(all others the same as masculine agent-nouns)		
G.	—uḥ	—roḥ	ṛīṇam			
L.	ari	—roḥ	ṛiṣu			
V.	ar	ārau*	āraḥ		arau	araḥ

Paradigm of endings : Feminine relations—nouns :

	S.	Du.	Pl.
N.	ā	arau*	araḥ*
A.	aram*	arau*	rīḥ
I.	rā	ṛibhyāṃ	ṛibhiḥ
D.	re	ribhyām	ṛibhyaḥ
A.	—uḥ	ribhyām	ṛibhyaḥ
G.	—uḥ	—roh	ṛīṇam
L.	ari	—roḥ	ṛiṣu
V.	ar	arau*	arah*

* Indicates the difference where guṇa and vṛiddhi occur!

Paradigm Declensions of दातृ

दाता	दातारौ	दातार:
दातारम्	दातारौ	दातृन्
दात्रा	दातृभ्याम्	दातृभि:
दात्रे	दातृभ्याम्	दातृभ्य:
दातु:	दातृभ्याम्	दातृभ्य:
दातु:	दात्रो:	दातृणाम्
दात्री	दात्रो:	दातृषु
दातर्	दातारौ	दातार:

The following masculine nouns although names of relations are declined like दातृ.

भर्त = husband

नप्तृ = grandson

Feminine nouns in "ṛi" are all nouns of relations. They are declined like pitṛi except in the accusative plural which ends with "ṛiḥ"; svasṛi (sister), however is delcined like netṛi except in the accusative plural.

Nominative and Accusative of मातृ mother, and स्वसृ sister.

	S.	Du.	Pl.	S.	Du.	Pl.
N.	माता	मातरौ	मातः	स्वसा	स्वसारौ	स्वसारः
A.	मातरम्	मातरौ	मातृः	स्वसारम्	स्वसारौ	स्वसृः

New Vocabulary list :—

Masc. Relation Nouns : "ṛi"

दातृ donor	मुक्तिःf. salvation, release
कार्तृ doer	गोपालः Gopāla
नेतृ leader	सुमतिः Sumati
श्रोतृ hearer	
जेतृ conqueror	वधः killing
सवितृ Sun	दर्शनम् Visionary sight
नप्तृ grandson	सीता f. Sītā
पितृ father	आशा f. hope
भ्रातृ brother	कन्या daughter
जामातृ son-in-law	लज्जा shame.

Fem. nouns : 'ṛi".

दुहितृ daughter

मातृ mother

ननांदृ sister-in-law

स्वसृ sister.

Prepositional prefixed verbs both P. & A.

प्र + वृत् = प्रवर्तते	to proceed
प्र + भू = प्रभवति	to arise, to be produced
क्लृप् = कल्पते	A. to be fit for + dat.
अव + गम् = अवगच्छति	to know

उद् + स्था = उत्तिष्ठति to rise
आ + दिश् = आदिशति to order, command
प्र + बुध् = प्रबोधति to wake up
अधि + क्षिप् = अधिक्षिपति to abuse
आ + गम् = आगच्छति to come
पद् = पद्यते A. to go, obtain for self
वि + पद् = विपद्यते A. to fall into misfortune
सम् + पद् = सम्पद्यते A. to prosper for self
वि + स्मृ = विस्मरति to forget
प्र + दा = प्रयच्छति to bestow
सह् = सहते A. to endure for self
शिक्ष् = शिक्षते A. to learn for self
भृ = भरति to feed, to support

Sanskṛit to English Exercise 1.

१. दाता प्रवर्तते।

२. सविता प्रकाशति।

३. जेता त्यजति।

४. दुहिता च माता प्रबोधन्ति।

५. पिता च भ्राता गच्छन्ति।

६. स्वसा गुरौ सागच्छति।

७. जामाता मुक्तिम् शिक्षते।

८. दाता जनान् भरति।

९. ननांदा स्वसरि सुखं प्रयच्छति।

१०. नेता निधिना विपद्यते।

English to Sanskṛit Exercise 2

1. The father will learn the truth.

2. Rāma and Sītā feed the people.
3. Why are the brother and sister-in-law enemies?
4. The conquerors abuse the devotees in the village.
5. When will the sun shine above the clouds near the mountains?
6. The doer does āsanas for himself.
7. All the daughters fall into misfortune.
8. Gopala and Sumati will not forget the people.
9. Enough with killing!
10. Oh Gopāla! the disciples are abused by the ignorance of the conqueror.

LESSON 2 : THE USAGE OF ADJECTIVES.

In chapter V the karmadhāraya compounds were introduced. This was an easy way to use adjectives without the complications of sandhi rules and declensions at that point of our learning. Now will be presented the full usage of the adjectives as we are prepared more adequately. The adjective, whether it be used as an epithet or as a predicate, agrees with the noun it qualifies in gender, number and case. [Refer to paradigms of various masc., fem, and neuter nouns.]

Step One : Adjectives ending in अ form their feminine in आ and neuter in अम्

ex: Masculine like: कूप: प्रिय:

Feminine like: कन्या प्रिया

*Neuter like: वनम् प्रियम् [Using प्रिय = dear.]

Step Two : Adjectives ending in इ. Using the adjective शुचि pure.

Masculine like: मुनि: शुचि:

Feminine like: मति: शुचि:

*Neuter like: वारि शुचि

Step Three : Adjective endings in उ. Using the adjective मृदु soft/sweet

Masculine like: शिशुः मृदुः

Feminine like: धेनुः मृदुः

*Neuter like: मेधु मृदु

Step Four : Adjective endings in. ऋ. Using दातृ generous.

Masculine like: नेता दाता

Feminine like: they have the forms inई नदी! दनत्री

*Neuter like: धातृ दातृ

* Note : In the neuter declension, the endings are the same as the masculine endings, except in the Nominative, Accusative and Vocative cases.

List of Adjectives that end in अ

अन्ध = blind नव = new

उदार = generous नित्य = regular, obligatory

कुशल = skillfull वृद्ध = old

कृत्रिम = artificial व्याधित = sick

कृपण = wretched हत = killed

क्षुद्र = small, mean प्रसन्न = favourable, clear

खञ्ज = lame पीन = fat

तीव्र = sharp, acute मृत = dead

दुर्लभ = difficult to get to

Adjectives ending in इ Adjectives ending in उ

सुगन्धि = sweet smelling बहु = much, many

सुरभि = fragrant साधु = virtuous

शुचि = pure आशु = swift

चारु = lovely

मृदु = soft, sweet

स्वादु = sweet

Adjectives ending in ऋ

दातृ = generous

जेतृ = victorious

वक्तृ = eloquent

Refer back to earlier chapter and to glossary at end of text.

Exercise 3 : Combining adjectives with a noun or substantive :

Using the model adjective, make them agree with the nouns in Number/Gender/Case.

Blind [अन्ध] जनैः - नारीषु - कविना - शत्रवे

Pure [शुचि] बालौ - जले - मती - दुहितरः

Lovely [चारु] कुसुममं - वारिणा - बालिकया - नद्याम्

Eloquent [वक्तृ] नृपेण - मित्राभ्याम् - गृहिणी - श्वश्रूणाम्

LESSON 3 : DEGREES OF COMPARISON IN THE ADJECTIVE AND ADVERBIAL FORMS

The comparative or superlative of adjectives is generally formed by the suffixes तर or तम to the stem.

ex :			
	मन्द	मन्दतर	मन्दतम
	slow	slower	slowest
	शुचि	शुचितर	शुचितम
	pure	purer	purest
	धीमत्	धीमत्तर	धीमत्तम
	wise	wiser	wisest
	धनिन्	धनितर	धनितम
	rich	richer	richest

When तराम् or तमाम् is used attached to a verbal construe it is translated adverbally.

ex: पचतितराम् He, she or it cooks better.

पचतितमाम् He, she or it cooks best.

In the construction of the comparative and superlative there are many irregular construes, especially for adjectives denoting qualities. Some of the construes use तर or तम, or have a substitute base, and others use ईयस् or इष्ठ so carefully read aloud the following tabulations with their English equivalents.

Adjective	Substitute —	Comparative —	Superlative
अन्तिक 'near'	नेद	नेदयिस्	नेदिष्ठ
अल्प 'little'	कन	कनीयस्	कनिष्ठ
उरु 'large'	वर	वरीयस्	वरिष्ठ
ऋजु 'straight'	ऋज	ऋजीयस्	ऋजिष्ठ
कृश 'thin—lean'	क्रश	क्रशीयस्	क्रशिष्ठ
क्षिप्र 'quick'	क्षेप	क्षेपीयस्	क्षेपिष्ठ
क्षुद्र 'small—mean'	क्षोद	क्षोदीयस्	क्षोदिष्ठ
गुरु 'heavy'	गर	गरीयस्	गरिष्ठ
तृप्र 'satisfied'	त्रप	त्रपीयस्	त्रपिष्ठ
दीर्घ 'long'	दघ	द्राघीयस्	द्राघिष्ठ

दूर	दव	दवीयस्	दविष्ठ
'distant'			
दृढ	द्रढ	द्रढीयस्	द्रढिष्ठ
'firm'			
परिवृढ	परिव्रढ	परिव्रढीयस्	परिव्रढिष्ठ
'eminent'			
पृथु	प्रथ	प्रथीयस्	प्रथिष्ठ
'broad'			
प्रशस्य	श्र	श्रेयस्	श्रेष्ठ
'good'			
(वृद्ध) जरठ	ज्या	ज्यायस्	ज्येष्ठ
'old'			
प्रिय	प्रे	प्रेयस्	प्रेष्ठ
'dear'			
Adjective	Substitute	Comparative	Superlative
बहु	भू	भूयस्	भूयिष्ठ
'much, frequent'			
बहुल	बंह	बंहीयस्	बंहिष्ठ
'much'			
भृश	भ्रश	भ्रशीयस्	भ्रशिष्ठ
'excessive'			
मृदु	म्रद	म्रदीयस्	म्रदिष्ठ
'soft'			
युवन्	यव	यवीयस्	यविष्ठ
'young'			
वाढ	साध	साधीयस्	साधिष्ठ
'firm—thick'			
वृद्ध	वर्ष	वर्षीयस्	वर्षिष्ठ
वृन्दरक	वृन्द	वृन्दीयस्	वृन्दिष्ठ
'excellent'			

स्थिर	स्थ	स्थेयस्	स्थेष्ठ
'firm—stable'			
स्थूल	स्थव	स्थवीयस्	स्थविष्ठ
'gross—bulky'			
स्फिर	स्फ	स्फेयस्	स्फेष्ठ
'turgid'			
ह्रस्व	ह्रस	ह्रसीयस्	ह्रसिष्ठ
'short'			

LESSON 4 : THE IMPERATIVE MOOD

In Sanskrit the imperative mood, with its own set of personal endings, is used in four principle ways:

1. to express a command or advice (Do, should)
2. to express a wish or prayer (May)
3. to express possibility or doubt (Might)
4. with the negative मा to expression prohibition (Shouldn't)

You, eat! त्वं खाद। You, don't eat! त्वं मा खाद।

You, dance! त्वं नृत्य। You, don't dance! त्वं मा नृत्य।

You, speak! त्वं वद। You, don't speak! त्वं मा वद।

The formation of the base follows the rules set down for the present tense in conjugations I, IV, VI and X.

To the base the following endings are added:

	परस्मैपद			आत्मनेपद		
	S.	D.	P.	S.	D.	P.
1st p.	āni	āva	āma	ai	āvahai	āmahai
2nd p.	a	atam	ata	asva (e)	āthām	dhvam
3rd p.	atu	atām	antu	atām (e)	ātām	antām

Study the following paradigms of the verbs बुध् (Par.) and मन् (Atm.) conjugated in the imperative mood :

	S.	D.	P.	S.	D.	P.
1st p.	बोधानि	बोधाव	बोधाम	मन्यै	मन्यावहै	मन्यामहै
2nd p.	बोध	बोधतम्	बोधत	मन्यस्व	मन्येथाम्	मन्यध्वम्
3rd p.	बोधतु	बोधताम्	बोधन्तु	मन्यताम्	मन्येताम्	मन्यन्ताम्

Note the various meanings of the form : बोधानि

1. I should know.
2. May I know.
3. I might know.
4. I may not know (with the particle मा).

In the passive imperative mood the stem ending is "atām".

श्रूयताम्	Let it be heard!
क्रियताम्	Let it be done!
दृश्यताम्	Let it be seen!
उच्यताम्	Let it be told!

Exercise 4 : Conjugate fully in the Imperative Mood the following verbs.

Next to each form write the various possible translations :

a. वस् (वसति)

b. तृप् (तृप्यति)

c. मुंच् (मुञ्चति)

d. कथ् (कथयति)

Exercise 5 Sanskrit/English Sentences to translate :

1. आसनेषु रमामहै।
2. मातर्शिशु ललयस्व।
3. नेतारो मुक्तिं मृगयध्वम्। प्रतिपत्तिं या मृगयध्वम्।
4. आशां प्रभवताम्।
5. दर्शनं मतिं प्रबोधतु।

6. भूमि: सहताम्।

7. केलिं मोहस्य मा विस्मराम।

8. ईश्वरो भक्तिमस्मभ्यं प्रयच्छतु।

9. सत्यं चेतयामहै।

10. मा क्लिश्येयाम्।

Exercise 6 English/Sanskrit Sentences to translate :

1. May the donors give wealth to the people of the village.
2. Let it be grown!
3. May the conqueror not punish the people of the country.
4. May the father not carry the stick in anger.
5. May the brothers and sisters live in peace.
6. May sin, the cause of misery, perish!
7. Boys, do not leave the house!
8. May we two know truth through union.
9. May we learn for ourselves.
10. Becuase of the illusion, they might not see.

LESSON 5 : THE POTENTIAL (OPTATIVE) MOOD

Neuter Nouns in i, u, ṛi

A. The Potential Mood :

also called the Optative Mood, is used:

1. To express a wish or request.
2. To express advice.
3. To express possibility or doubt.
4. To express probability or doubt.
5. In conditional clauses, see examples.

Note the similarity to the Imperative Mood for #1—4

	Parasmaipada			*Atmanepada*		
	S.	D.	P.	S.	D.	P.
1.	eyam	eva	ema	eya	evahi	emahi
2.	eḥ	etam	eta	ethāḥ	eyāthām	edhvam
3.	et	etām	eyuḥ	eta	eyātām	eran

These endings are added to the verbal base, following the rules for the Ist, 4th, 6th and 10th conjugations.

(*Note* : the actual endings all begin with ī, but as the base ends in —a, these vowels combine to form —e, which has been used in the above paradigms)

Examples :

भू = to become, 1p. मृग् =to search, 10A.

	S.	D.	P.	S.	D.	P.
1.	भवेयम्	भवेव	भवेम	मृगयेय	मृगयेवहि	मृगयेमहि
2.	भवेः	भवेतम्	भवेत	मृगयेथाः	मृगयेयाथाम्	मृगयेध्वम्
3.	भवेत्	भवेताम्	भवेयुः	मृगयेत	मृगयेयाताम्	मृगयेरन्

Imperative and Potential Moods of the verb कृ (to do, 8p)

	Imperative			*Potential*		
	S.	D.	P.	S.	D.	P.
1.	करवणि	करवाव	करवाम	कुर्याम्	कुर्याव	कुर्याम
2.	कुरु	कुरुतम्	कुरुत	कुर्याः	कुर्यातम्	कुर्यात
3.	करोतु	कुरुताम्	कुर्वन्तु	कुर्यात्	कुर्याताम्	कुर्युः

Examples of the Imperative Mood and the potential Mood :—

[Imperative Mood]

जलमानय Bring water!

शिशुं मा पीडय Do not annoy the baby!

[Potential Mood]

नरः सदा सत्यं वदेत्! Man should always tell the truth!

मातरं पश्येयुर्बाला। May the boys see their mother!

Conditional clause : यदि माता नागच्छेत् शिशुम्रियेत If the mother does not come, the baby will die!

SPECIAL NOTE : All visargas met with in previous lessons stand in the place of a final स्.

जनः = जनस् नमथः = नमथस् (The visarga was used because स् is not permitted as a final. Also final र् bcame a visarga.)

नेतर् = नेत:, मातार् = माता:, पुनर् = पुन:, प्रातर् = प्रात:

The visarga standing for र follows the general rules of sandhi with the exception.

The visarga standing for र् when preceded by अ or आ and followed by a vowel or soft consonant is changed to र्.

ex: पुन: अपि = पुनरपि

पित: वदसि = पितर्वदसि

मात: इन्दुं पश्यसि = मातरिन्दुं पश्यसि।

When a visarga is changed to र् and followed by र्, the first र् is dropped and the preceding vowel, if short, is lengthened.

ex : इन्दु: राजते = इन्दू राजते।

भ्रात: रचयसि = भ्राता रचयसि।

[Two "r's" sare not permitted in a row!]

To illustrate the usage of the Potential Mood, here follows "An Invocation for Peace, "memorize it as a beautiful mantra for meditation. It is from the Kathopaniṣad!

सह नाववतु।

May he protect us (The Preceptor and the Disciple)

सह नौ भुक्तु

May he nourish us both.

सह वीर्य करवावहै

May we both work together with great energy.

तेजस्वि नावधीतमस्तु।

May our study be thorough and fruitful

मा विद्विषावहै।

May we never hate each other.

शान्ति: शान्ति: शान्ति:

PEACE PEACE PEACE

Exercise 7. Sanskrit English — Identify if it is Imperative or Potential Mood, then translate.

१. त्वं खाद।

२. तत् माम् अवतु = तम्मामवतु।

३. विषादं भवतु।

४. श्वश्रूर्वध्वै न कुप्येत्।

५. प्रभुर्नन्त्रयेत्।

६. शिष्यः कवेः पुस्तकानि गृहिण्या लभेत्।

Exercise 8. English Sanskrit—Identify if it is imperative or Potential Mood, then translate.

1. Thou reflect for thyself.
2. May the guru be pleased.
3. If the sanke bites you, you will die.
4. Let the Truth be known!
5. Oh girl, learn.
6. Adorations to the Divine.
7. If you speak good words, you will obtain liberation.
8. May you (pl.) do āsanas.
9. May wisdom be worshipped everywhere.
10. May that protect me!

Neuter Nouns [See previous lesson on adjectives of same endings] that end in "i", "u", and "ṛi". They are all declined on the same pattern!

वारि (water)			मधु (honey)		
वारि	वारिणी	वारीणि	मधु	मधुनी	मधूनि
वारि	वारिणी	वारीणि	मधु	मधुनी	मधूनि
वारिणा	वारिभ्याम्	वारिभिः	मधुना	मधुभ्याम्	मधुभिः
वारिणे	वारिभ्याम्	वारिभ्यः	मधुने	मधुभ्याम्	मधुभ्यः
वारिणः	वारिभ्याम्	वारिभ्यः	मधुनः	मधुभ्याम्	मधुभ्यः

वारिण:	वारिणो:	वारीणाम्	मधुन:	मधुनो:	मधूनाम्
वारिणि	वारिणो:	वारिषु	मधुनि	मधुनो:	मधुषु
वारि वारे	वारिणी	वारीणि	मधु मधो	मधुनी	मधूनि

धातृ (dispenser)

धातृ	धातृणी	धातृणि
धातृ	धातृणी	धातृणि
धातृणा	धातृभ्याम्	धातृभि:
धातृणे	धातृभ्याम्	धातृभ्य:
धातृण:	धातृभ्याम्	धातृभ्य:
धातृण:	धातृनो:	धातृणाम्
धातृणि	धातृनो:	धातृषु
धातृ धातर	धातृणी	धातृणि

NEW VOCABULARY-NEUTER NOUNS

वारि = water

मधु = honey

अश्रु = tear

अम्बु = water

जानु = knee

वस्तु = thing

दारु = wood

धातृ = dispenser.

Note carefully the alternate forms in the Voc. Sing. Case, and the usage of the internal "ṇ" Sandhi rule change.

CHAPTER XI

Introduction to the Perfect Tense. The Conjuctive Participles, The Infinitive, Nominal and Adverbial Clause Constructions. Interrogative and Relative Pronouns. Essential Sanskrit Philosphical Terms.

LESSON 1: INTRODUCTION TO THE PERFECT TENSE.

In Classical Sanskrit the three past tenses are used indicriminately, with the restriction that in the Perfect Tense, the first person singular is rarely used. The three Past Tenses are :

1. Imperfect where the speaker had been a witness.
2. Perfect where the speaker had not been a witness.
3. Aorist used for immediate past. [Not included in this text!]

The construction of the Perfect Tense requires reduplication of the root which is followed by the same rules of construction as of Conjugation I, IV, VI, X.

Rules of Reduplication of the root:—

1. An initial aspirate loses its aspiration.

   भिद् = बिभिद्

   भ्रम् = बभ्रम्

2. An initial gutteral is changed to the corresponding palatal, and an initial "h" is changed to "j".

क्रम् = चकम्

गम् = जगम्

हस् = जहास्

3. When a root begins with a conjunct consonant, its first consonant alone appears in the reduplication form.

क्षिप् = किक्षिप् = चिक्षिप्

4. When a root begins with a sibilant followed by a hard consonant, it is the *latter* which appears in the reduplicated form.

स्तु – तुष्टु (sandhi) स्मृ = सस्मृ

5. A long vowel becomes short in reduplication.

नी = निनी

6. Medial (e) becomes (i) in reduplication, and medial (o) and (au) becomes (u).

7. Final (e) (ai) and (o) becomes (a) in reduplication.

गै = जगै

8. "rī" or "ṛī" becomes (i) in reduplication.

भृ = बिभृ

The termination for the third person singular is "a" but if the root ends in "ā" the termination becomes "au". Most of the stems are to be found in the verb glossary at the end of the text, but here are a few examples for immediate usage.

भू = बभूव he went	पत् = पपात he fell
गम् = जगाम he became	बुध् = बुबोध he knew
चर् = चचार he went	वद् = उवाद he spoke
जि = जिगाय he conquered	वस् = उवास he dwelt
तृ = ततार he crossed over	वह् = उवाह he carried

त्यज् = तत्याज he abandoned	भ्रम् = बभ्राम he wandered/erred
दा = ददौ he gave	शुच् = शुशोच he sorrowed for
दह् = ददाह he burned	श्रि = शिश्राय he served
दृश् = ददर्श he saw	श्रु = शुश्राव he heard
द्रु = दुद्राव it flowed	सृ = ससार he went
पा = पपौ he drank	सृप् = ससर्प it crept
पच् = पपाच he cooked	स्मृ = सस्मार he remembered
	हस् = जहास he laughed
	हृ = जहार he took.

Exercise 1

Sanskrit English Exercise using the Perfect Tense.

(Can you change the construction to simple past with particle "sma" too?)

१. रावणं जिगाय रामः।

२. गिरिं ततार कविः।

३. पुत्रस्तत्यज पितरम्।

४. अन्नं किमर्थं न पपाच माता।

५. भक्तः शास्त्रं बुबोध।

६. पिता पुत्रयोवाद।

७. अश्वो नरमुवाह।

८. व्याघ्रो वनं ससर्प।

Exercise 2

English to Sanskrit exercise using the Perfect Tense.

(Can you change the construction to the simple past with particle "sma" too?

1. The devotee became a disciple.
2. The father gave knowledge to his son.

3. Sītā spoke to her sisters.
4. The woman sorrowed for the child's death.
5. The horse fell into the lake.
6. The daughter served her mother.
7. I remembered the scriptures.*
8. The son took the jewels.
9. He laughed!
10. Why did the person burn the trees near the house?

Note : The 3rd person singular form is also used for Ist person singular.

LESSON 2 : INTRODUCTION TO THE CONJUCTIVE PARTICIPLE.

The Past Passive Participle dealt with in chapter VI was treated like an adjective, and was subject to the rules of agreement with the noun or substantive which it qualified. The Conjunctive participle, also called past participle active gerundive is *never declined!* In the sentence 'Rāma conquered Rāvaṇa and went to his house,' the former action may be expressed by a Participle; "Having conquered Rāvaṇa, Rāma went to his house." This is an example of the conjunctive participle and it ends with the suffix "tvā," except in participles which are compounded with a prefix, in which case the ending is "ya." The Gerund is indeclinable in both its forms, but all sandhi rules must be observed in the sentence construction.

ex: Rāma having conquered Rāvaṇa went to his house.

रामो रावणं जित्वा गृहं जगाम।

The following is a list of the two constructions, but do consult the verb index at end of text for a more complete listing.

कृ = कृत्वा having done/made

पच् = पक्त्वा having cooked

क्रम् = क्रान्त्वा having walked

पा = पीत्वा having drunk

क्षि = क्षित्वा having decayed

बुध् = बुधित्वा having known

खन् = खात्व having dug

मन्त्र = मन्त्रयित्वा having consuled

गम् = गत्वा having gone

वच् = उक्त्वा having said

घ्रा = जिघ्रित्वा having smelled

वद् = उदित्वा having spoken

चिन्त् = चिन्तयित्वा having thought

वस् = उषित्वा having dwelt

जि = जित्वा having conquered

वह् = ऊढ्वा having carried

ज्ञा = ज्ञात्वा having known

शुच् = शोचित्वा having grieved/ sorrowed for

तॄ = तीर्त्वा having crossed over, transcended

स्था = स्थित्वा having stood

त्यज् = त्यक्त्वा having abandoned

स्मि् = स्मित्वा having smiled

दह् = दग्ध्वा having burned

हस् = हसित्वा having laughed

दा = दत्त्वा having given

हृ = हृत्वा having taken away

दृश् = दृष्ट्वा having seen.

Exercise 3 : Sanskrit — English

Carefully note difference between the Perfect Tense construction, and the Conjunctive Participle!

१. मातान्नं पक्त्वा बालेभ्य उवाद।

२. कविं श्रुत्वा शिष्यः पापं तत्याज।

३. पुत्रः स्मृत्वा पितॄनुवाद।

४. मधु खादित्वा वारि बालः पपौ।

५. नेता चिन्तयित्वा ईश्वरं शिश्राय।

६. नप्ता भ्रातरं मन्त्रयित्वा बुबोध।

Exercise *4:* Englsih —Sanskrit

1. The water, having oozed towards the ocean, was gone.
2. The daughter, having remembered the shame, endured for herself.
3. The blind man, having grieved, heard the guru's words.
4. The girl, having gone to the city, spoke to virtuous people.
5. The fragrant wood, having stood near the house, burned down.
6. The elephant, having drunk the water, went back to the forest.

Feminine Nouns ending in "ū" ऊ

They are declined with the same pattern as नदी where नदी has इ ई and य् feminine nouns in "ū' have उ ऊ and व् respectively. Besides, their Nominative singular takes visarga.

वधू = bride, young woman

वधूः	वध्वौ	वध्वः
वधूम्	वध्वौ	वधूः
वध्वा	वधूभ्याम्	वधूभिः
वध्वै	वधूभ्याम्	वधूभ्यः
वध्वाः	वधूभ्याम्	वधूभ्यः
वध्वाः	वध्वोः	वधूनाम्

वध्वाम्	वध्वोः	वधूषु
वधू	वध्वौ	वध्वः

NEW VOCABULARY FEM. NOUNS Ū

वधूः bride, young woman

चमूः army

A review of all the declensions presented in this text :

1. Nouns ending in अ & आ	2. Nouns ending in इ	3. Nouns ending in उ
Masculine कूपः	Masc मुनिः	Masc. शिशुः
Feminine लता	Fem. मतिः	Fem. धेनुः
Neuter वनम्	Neu. वारि	Neu. मधु
4. Nouns ending in ऋ	5. Nouns ending in ई	6. Nouns ending in ऊ
Masculine नेतृ पितृ	Fem. नदी	Fem वधूः
Feminine मातृ		
Neuter धातृ		

A review of all the rules for the I, IV, VI, and X Conju—gations :

Conjugation I : guṇa of short medial vowel and final vowel, "a" before termination.

Conjugation IV: "ya" is telescoped into last consonant, "a" before termination.

Conjugation VI: No guṇa changes, "a" before final termination.

Conjugation X: guṇa short medial vowel, vṛiddhi offinal vowel, "ay" preceeding termination.

Review of Case meanings :—

Nominative : The subject, subjective compliment or a noun standing in opposition to the subject.

Accusative : The direct object of a transitive verb and its complement.

Instrumental : To indicate the instrument which is used to do the action; "by, with, for, because of, on account of, etc. To indicate the agent of a passive verb.

Dative : The indirect object, after verbs meaning "to give, to send, to promise, to show," etc. After verbs meaning "to be angry with, to long for, and to desire". To express the purpose of the action. To indicate the person or thing for whose advantage the action is done. After verbs indicating movement.

Ablative : To indicate the place from which the action begins. After verbs meaning "to desist from, to protect, to fear." To express the cause or motive.

Genetive : No relation with the action of the verb. It indicates a relation between the nouns, usually translated in English by preposition "of." showing ownership.

Locative : To indicate place where action occurs. In English like prepositions "in, at, on, upon, among, etc." To indicate the time when the action takes place. To translate expressions like "concerning, in the matter of, etc." To indicate the object of emotions and feelings.

Vocative: To evoke, call or address a subject.

Review the difference between Parasmaipada, Ātmanepada, and Ubhayapada.

कृ belongs to the VIII conjugation, but is very important. The present and future constructions have been given, and now here is the Imperative and Potential Mood of this crucial verb.

IMPERATIVE MOOD :			*POTENTIAL MOOD :*		
करवाणि	करवाव	करवाम	कुर्याम्	कुर्याव	कुर्याम
कुरु	कुरुतम्	कुरुत	कुर्याः	कुर्यातम्	कुर्यात
करोतु	कुरुताम्	कुर्वन्तु	कुर्यात्	कुर्याताम्	कुर्युः

LESSON 3 : THE INFINITIVE, THE NOUN CLAUSE, NOMINAL SENTENCE CONSTRUCTION, THE ADVERBIAL CLAUSE, PARADIGMS OF INTERROGATIVE DECLENSIONS, REVIEW.

(a) The infinitive is formed by adding तुम् to the root of the verb after gunating a short medial and final vowel. Here are a few examples, but because many are irregular, consult the appendix of "verbal-roots and their forms!

जि = जेतुम् to conquer, to win

कृ = कर्तुम् to do spiritually

दृश् = द्रष्टुम् to see

ध्यै = ध्यातुम् to meditate

भू = भवितुम् to be, to exist

खन् = खनितुम् to dig

चुर् = चोरयितुम् to steal

चिन्त् = चिन्तयितुम् to think, to reflect

दण्ड् = दण्डयितुम् to punish

Example showing infinitive used to express an action.

पातुम्	to drink		
अस्मि	I am	पातुमसमर्थोऽस्मि	= I am unable to drink.
असर्थः	unable		
इच्छति	He wishes		
श्रोतुम्	to hear	गीतं श्रोतुमिच्छति	= He wishes to hear the song.
गीतम्	the song		
आरम्भ	He began		
धावितुम्	to run	धावितुमारभत	= He began to run.

The infinitive can also be used with अर्ह् in the sense of polite request.

रक्षितुम् to protect

माम् me   मां रक्षितुमर्हसि = You should reverently protect me.

अर्हसि you should (reverently)

भक्ता: the devotees

इच्छन्ति wish

गान्तुम् to go भक्ता: पर्वतं गन्तुमिच्छन्ति = The devotees wish to go to the mountain.

पर्वतम् to the mountain

The infinitive has no passive form. When passive is to be expressed, the verb accompanying the infinitive is put in the passive :—

(Active Voice) I begin to see the trees.

वृक्षान् द्रष्टुमारभे।

(Passive Voice) The trees begin to be seen by me.

मया वृक्षान्द्रष्टुमारभन्ते।

(b) The Noun clause is introduced by the conjunction "that" and is constructed with a double accusative.

ex : He thinks that Rama is a hero.

रामं वीरं चिन्तयति।

A Noun clause introduced by a conjunctive pronoun connects to an adjective clause.

ex : What he says is true = That which he says is true.

यद् वदति तत्सत्यम्।

Indirect speech does not exist in sanskṛit and must be turned into direct speech and the end of the direct speech is marked with इति. इति espresses an attitude of mind, the ground upon which something is done : 'because,' in order that,' etc.

ex : They stop to hear him speak further. (He is speaking again, so-thinking they stop.

पुनर्वदतीति तिष्ठन्ति।

ex : He told me that he had conquered the enemies. = I have conquered the enemies, so he told me.

अहं शत्रूनजयमिति सोऽवदत्।

(c) Nominal sentence construction contains no verb. Adjectives used predicatively must agree in number, gender and case with their substantive. (All sandhi rules are cumulative and must be observed.)

शीघ्रौ अश्वौ = शीघ्रावश्वौ The two horses are swift.

रमणीयः बालः = रमणीयो बालः The boy is pleasant.

स्वल्पम् सुखम् क्रोधः स्वल्पं सुखं क्रोधः Anger is a small pleasure.

When the subject is a pronoun and predicate a substantive, the pronoun agrees in number, and gender of the predicate.

सुर्यः सः = That is the sun.

(d) The adverb clause expresses a particular circumastance of the action of the main clause. In sanskrit the adverb clause generally precedes the main clause and is introduced by a conjunctive adverb to which a simple adverb corresponds in the main clause. [The tree lies where it fell = "Where the tree fell, there it lies.]

NOTE IN THE FOLLOWING TABULATION OF ADVERBS THE FOLLOWING :—

a. All the interrogatives start with क्।

b. All of the conjunctives start with य्।

c. All of the simple conjunctives start with त्।

d. Adverbs are tabulated according to 'time, "place," "manner," "cause," "condition," and "concession."

CHART OF CONJUNCTIVE ADVERBS :–

	Interrogatives	conjunctive	simple	indefinite
TIME	कदा When?	यदा When	तदा then	कदाचित् at times
		यावत् while	तावत्(–)	सर्वदा always
PLACE	कुत्र क्व Where?	यत्र where	तत्र there	सर्वत्र every-where
MANNER	कथम् How? Why?	यथा as	तथा so	कथञ्चित् some-how
CAUSE	किम् Why?	यत: because	तत: then	------------
CONDITION	-----------	यदि if	तर्हि then	------------
CONCESSION	---------	यद्यपि although	तथापि yet	------------

ex : You came when the guests had gone.

यदातिथयो गतास्तदा त्वमागच्छ:।

यदा अतिथय: गता: तदा त्वम आगच्छ:।

ex : He does not speak because his friends have left him.

यतो मित्राणि तमत्यजन् स न भाषते।

यत: मित्राणि तम् अत्यजन् स: न भाषते।

ex : If your mother comes, you should serve her.

यदि मातागच्छेत् तां सेवेथा:।

यदि माता अगच्छेत् ताम् सेवेथा:।

ex : Although I live in the forest, I still remember my friends.

यद्यपि वने वसानि तथापि मित्राणि स्मरामि।

ex : Sit down while I bring water.

यावदहं जलमानयामि तावदुपविश।

यावत् अहम् जलम् अनयामि तवात् उपविश।

ex : They stood where the hero fell.

यत्र वीरोऽपतत् तत्र ते तिष्ठन्।

यत्र वीरः अपतत् तत्र ते अतिष्ठन्।

ex : Virtues adorn the heart as flowers adorn the tree.

यथा पुष्पानि वृक्षं तथा गुणा हृदयं भूषयन्ति।

यथा पुष्पानि वृक्षम् तथा गुणाः हृदयम् भूषयन्ति।

e. Interrogative and Relative Pronouns :

किम् Which? What? (Interrogative Pronouns)

	Masculine				*Neuter*		
N.	कः	कौ	के	N.	किम्	के	कानि
A.	कम्	कौ	कान्	A.	किम्	के	कानि
I.	केन	काभ्याम्	कैः				
D.	कस्मै	काभ्याम्	केभ्यः	ALL OTHERS SAME AS			
A.	कस्मात्	काभ्याम्	केभ्यः	MASCULINE			
G.	कस्य	कयोः	केषाम्				
L.	कस्मिन्	कयोः	केषु				

	Feminine		
N.	का	के	काः
A.	काम्	के	काः
I.	कया	काभ्याम्	काभिः
D.	कस्यै	काभ्याम्	काभ्यः
A.	कस्याः	काभ्याम्	काभ्यः
G.	कस्याः	कयोः	कासाम्
L.	कस्याम्	कयोः	कासु

Relative Pronoun :— Which ? Who ?

MASCULINE				*NEUTER*		
N.	यः	यो	ये	N. यत्	ये	यानि
A.	यम्	यौ	यान्	A. यत्	ये	यानि
I.	येन	याभ्याम्	यैः			
D.	यस्मै	याभ्याम्	येभ्यः	ALL OTHERS SAME AS		
A.	यस्मात्	याभ्याम्	येभ्यः	MASCULINE		
G.	यस्य	ययोः	येषाम्			
L.	यस्मिम्	ययोः	येषु			

FEMININE : RELATIVE PRONOUN Which, Who

N.	या	ये	याः
A.	याम्	ये	याः
I.	यथा	याभ्याम्	याभिः
D.	यस्यै	याभ्याम्	याभ्यः
A.	यस्याः	याभ्याम्	याभ्यः
G.	यस्याः	ययोः	यास्मान्
L.	यस्मान	ययोः	यासु

In this last set of Sanskrit to English exercises, break down all the individual words and put analysis of their construction, then write them correctly remembering all of the cumulative Sanskṛit sandhi rules.

Exercise 5

१. जेतुमिच्छामि क्रोधम्।

२. ध्यातुम् सा शिक्षते।

३. दण्डयितुम्पुत्रं माता चेष्टते।

४. पठितुं तुष्यामि शास्त्रानि।

५ कन्यानन्तुं गुरुं सा गच्छति।

६. मां रक्षितुमर्हसि।

७. सुन्दराकन्या।

८. रक्तम्फलम्।

९. तुङ्गावृक्षाः।

१०. आविलंनगरम्।

११. शुचिर्कृष्णः।

१२. शुक्लम्कमलंप्रियम्।

१३. यदा माता त्यजेत् आगच्छेः।

१४. यावतहंशिक्षे त्वण्खाद।

१५. यत्र वीरो म्रियन्ते तत्र तान्यशोचन्।

१६. यथालंकारान्मन् तथा गुणा हृदयं भूषयन्ति।

१७. यतो मित्रणि तमन्यजन् स न हसते।

१८. यदि मातागच्छतु तां नमथाः।

Exeracise 6

In the following English to Sanskrit exercisess follow same pattern as previously done.

1. The deer wishes to eat the food.
2. My brother enters the house to show us girfts.
3. We wish to hear the Gītā.
4. The tiger began to run.
5. You should protect me from sin.
6. The women wish to go to the large city.
7. I know that Sītā is beautiful.
8. What she says is true. (That which she says is true.)
9. He told me that he had conquered the enemies. (I have conquered the enemies, so he told me.)
10. The women are strong. (Nominal construction)

(11. The Divine mountain shines.) " "

12. Friends are blissful. (Nominal construction)
13. Āsanas are healthy. " "
14. You understood when the guru spoke.
15. Wait here while I bring fuel.
16. We cried where the men died.
17. Love adorns the Soul as Peace fills the world.
18. She does not speak because her friends have left her.
19. If the king comes, you should honour him.
20. Although I live in a cave, I still remember the village.

"Grand Review : Sanskrit to English." Explain each construction.

Exercise 7

१. सा पचति।

२. सा पचते।

३. सा पचतीति।

४. यदा सा गायति तदा सा पक्ष्यति।

५. धने ममत्वं कर्तव्य्ं प्रश्नं।

६. अश्रुभिर्माता शोचनीया शमेत्।

७. सत्यमं लोकस्य दीप:।

८. संभवामि युगे।

९. सा शान्तिं अधिगच्छति।

१०. अत्र स्थातुमुचितम्।

११. सत्यमेव जयते मृतम्।

१२. तव पुस्तकं कुत्र वर्तते।

English to Sanskrit exercises, follow above pattern.

Exercise 8

1. A pure mind is like a fragrant flower.
2. The teacher has summarized many new things.

3. You tremble out of fear of God; You should worship God out of devotion.
4. If the mother does not come, the children will mourn.
5. You desire happiness: desist from greed.
6. Because of the clouds and dust, the cows do not eat the grass.
7. I sit in the shade of the tree and meditate.
8. I wish to learn the āsanas.
9. The men are fond of fruits.
10. In both villages there is neither water nor food.
11. I shall swim in the lake in the summer.
12. I study yoga to know truth, peace and love.

LESSON 4 : THE PHILOSPHICAL TERMS OF SANāTANA DHARMA

In this last lesson of this humble opus of a new approach to learning Sanskrit, let me reiterate that this is not an exhaustive treatise on this Divine Language, but an introduction and an aid to why knowing the grammatical construction is so important. Our purpose in studying this highly inflective ancient language of non-verbal communion is to feel the meanings of the terms and not to rely solely on translations or sectarian points of view. The basic terms are intensified inwardly when you can recognize the verbal root energy forms springing forth from the construes. Keep in mind the importance of the vowel changes, the prefixes, suffixes and infixes for the terms, and above all be sure to review the prepositional prefixes in the terms.

In the Judaic-Christian-Muslim faiths life is like a straight line; we are born, we live and then die. In the Sanātana Dharma life is a continuum resembling a circle. We appear as a point somewhere in this circle bringing a great deal with us and continue with the hopes of eventual "Liberation or Self-Realization." It is a very optimistic and lovely concept to dwell with!

In the following sections the terms will be given showing the verb roots from whence they were derived. Try to feel the meanings as opposed to resorting to academic or sectarian interpretations. First the scriptures, then the terms of the upaniṣads, the systems and finally terms of yoga. By no means will this section be exhaustive, but a good start for why you are learning Sanskrit. Be patient and in the Bibliography is a very selected listing of reference materials highly recommended for further study.

The term is listed first, followed by the affixes which influence them.

4a. The Scriptures :

1. Vedas, "vyadh"
2. Ṛig-Veda, "ṛik"
3. Sāma-Veda, "sāman"
4. Yajur-Veda, "yaj"
5. Atharva-veda "athar"
6. Sukta or Mantra, "su+ukta/man+tṛi"
7. Brāhmaṇas, "bṛih+man"
8. Āraṇyakas, "āraṇya"
9. Upaniṣads, "upa+ni+ṣad"
10. Saṁhita, "sam+hita"
11. Sutra, "su+tṛī"
12. Vedāṅga, "vyadh+aṅga"
13. Bhaṣyas, "bhaṣ"
14. Upa-vedas, "upa+vid"
15. Āyur-vedas, "ayus, medecine"
16. Dhanur-vedas, "dhanus, bow"
17. Śāstra-Śāstra, "śās +tṛī"
18. Gandharva-veda, "gandhar"
19. Stapatya-Veda, "stā+pat,architecture"
20. Śilpa-Śāstra, "śilpa+śas+tra,fine arts"
21. Śikṣā-vedaṅga, "sikṣ=vid=aṅga, phonetics"
22. Chandas, "chand, prosody"
23. Vyākaraṇa, "vyak+kṛi, grammar.

24. Nirukta, "nir+ukta, etymology"
25. Jyotiṣa, "jyut, astronomy"
26. Kalpa, "kḷrip, ceremonial"
27. Purāṇas, "purāṇa, history"
28. Trimurit, "tri+mārga, trinity"
29. Brāhma, "brih+mā" Creater
30. Viṣṇu, "viś, Preserver
31. Śiva, "śiv/Rudra—rud"
32. Rāma, "ram"
33. Īsvāra, "Ī+īś+vṛit"
34. Mānavadharmaśāstra, "man+ava-dhṛi+mā+śās+ tṛī"
35. Āgamas, "ā+gam"
36. Itihāsa, "iti+ha+āsa, so it was!"
37. Mahābhārata, "maha"bhṛi"
38. Bhagavadgītā, "bhagavan+gai"
39. Sāvṛitī, "sa+vṛit"
40. Mahākāvyas, "mahā+kavi"
41. Nātakas, "nṛit"
42. Kāma-sutra, "kām+mā+su+tra"
43. Artha-śāstra, "artha+śās+tra"
44. Bṛhatsaṁhitā, "bṛih+saṁ+hitā"
45. Nīti-śastra, "nī+śās+tra"
46. Pañchatantra, "pañch+tān+tra"
47. Hitopadeśa, "hito+upa+deśa"

4b. The Classical Systems :

1. āstika, "a+tika"
2. svāstika, "sva+tika"
3. śad-darśana, "śaḍ+dṛiś"
4. nyāya, "nī"
5. vaiśeṣiha, "vi+śis"

6. saṅkhyā, "saṅ+khyā"
7. yoga, "yuj"
8. purva-mimāṁsa—vedānta, "pur+va+man+sa+vid+ anta"
9. uttara-mimāṁsa-vedānta, "uttāra+man+sa+vid+anta"
10. Cārvaka/lokāyata, "car+vac/loka+yā"
11. Jain, "jina"
12. Sautrāntīka-Hinayāna Buddhism, "sau+trā+tīka+hiṇa+yāna+budh"
13. Vaibhāsika-Hiṇayāna Buddhism, "vai+bhaṣ"
14. Mādhyamika-Mahāyāna Buddhism, "madhya+mahā+Budh"
15. Yogācāra-Mahāyana Buddhism, "yuj+car+mahā+Budh"

4c. Upanisad Terms :

1. tat, "pronoun that"
2. Idam, "pronoun this"
3. Haṁsa, "aham+saḥ"
4. Puruṣa, "pū+ūṣ"
5. Ekatva, "eka+tvā"
6. amṛita, "a+mṛita"
7. prabhu, "pra+bhū"
8. dhātṛi-dhātā, "dhā+tri"
9. anuṣṭāna, "anu+stā"
10. āvṛitti, "ā+vṛit"
11. jnāna, "jna"
12. ajnāna, "a+jnā"
13. antaryāmin, "antar+yāmin"
14. jīvātman, "jīv+āt+man"
15. prāna, "pra+an"
16. vyāna, "vi+ātan"
17. apāṇa, "apa+an"

18. udāṇa, "ud+a+an"
19. kośa, "kuś"
20. annamayakośa, "annam_maya_kuś"
21. prāṇamayakośa, "prāṇa+maya+kuś"
22. manomayakośa, "manas+maya+kuś"
23. vijnānamayakośa, "vijnāna+maya+kuś"
24. ānandamayakosā, "ānanda+maya+kuś"
25. ānandamayapuruṣa, "ānanda+maya+pū+ūṣa"
26. ātman, "āt+man"
27. cit/cidmayakośa-caitanya puruṣa, "(See foregoing breakdowns!)
28. sacchidānanda, "āt+cit =ānanda"
29. avasthās, "ava+stā"
30. jāgrat, "jāgṛi"
31. svapna, "svap"
32. suṣupti, "su+ṣup"
33. samādhi, "saṁ+ādhi"
34. turīya, "catur"
35. jīvātman
36. bhūtātman
37. prāṇātman
38. sthūlātman, "sthūla+āt+man"
39. Cakras, "kṛi"
40. Sahasrāra or padma cakra, "sahasra-padma-kṛi"
41. ājnā cakra, "ā+jnā+kṛi"
42. anāhata cakra/hṛitpadma cakra"
43. viśuddhi cakra, "vi+śuddha+kṛi"
44. Manipūra/nābhipadma cakra "maṇi+puri+kṛi"
45. Svādhiṣṭhāna cakra, "svā+ādhi+sthā+kṛi"
46. Mūlādhāra cakra, "mūlā+dhṛi+kṛi"
47. tattva, "tat+tva"
48. avyakta, "a+vi-anj"
49. avyakta, "aham+kṛi"

50. tanmātra, "tan+ma+tṛi"
51. Mahābhūtas'Pāncabhautikas, "mahā+bhū/panca+bhū+tika" (5 Tanmatras)

śabda—sound	ākāśa—ether
sparśa—touch	vāyu—air
rūpa—sight	tejas—fire
rasa—taste	apas—water
gandha—smell	pṛithivī—earth

52. niyantri, "ni+yam" (5 Sense Organs)

śrota—ear	diśah—Quarters of Space
Tvak—skin	vayu—the Wind—God
Cakṣu—eye	Āditya—Sun—God
akṣu	
jihvā—tongue	Varuṇa—God of the Expanse
ghrāṇa—nose	Aśvins—Horsemen of the Sun

53. karmendriya, "karma+indriya" Organs of Action

vāc—voice, larynx	agni—God of Fire, Divine Will
pāni—hand	indra—God of the Firmament, Mind
pādas—foot	viṣṇu—the All—Pervader
pāyus—anus	mitra—God of Harmony
upastha—Organ of generation	prajāpati—Lord of Creation

54. Yuga, "yuj, Age or Cycle"
55. Satyayuga, "satya+yuj" (Truth-prevails!)
56. krityayuga, "kṛi+yuj" (Age of Innocence)
57. Tretāyuga, "¾ of truth"
59. Kaliyuga, "dark ages"
60. Yugasandhyā, "Age of the 'evening or morning or twilight"
61. Yugadharma, The True law of the age.
62. Catur Āśrama, "catur+āś+rāma"
63. Brahmacarya, "bhram+acar+ya"
64. Gṛihastha, "gṛiham-+sthā"

65. Vanaprastha, "vanam+pra+sthā"
66. Saṁnyāsa, "saṁ+yā+sa"
67. Puruṣartha, "pū+ūṣ+artha"
68. Kāma
69. Dharma. "dṛiś+mā" or "dhṛi+mā"
70. Mokṣa, "Muc"
71. śarīra, "sṛī"
72. sṛiṣṭi, "sṛij"
73. sambhāva, "saṁ+bhū"
74. saṁbhūti, "saṁ+bhū"
75. asambhāva, "a+saṁ+bhū"
76. gāyatrī, "gai+tṛī"
77. udgita, "ud+gai"
78. jyoti, "jyut"
79. prakāśa, "pra+kaś"
80. akṣara, (Syllable for AUM!).
81. praṇava, "pra+ṇu"
82. nādabrahman, "nad+brahm+man"
83. siddhi, "sidh"
84. tarka, "tark"
85. upāsana, "upa+sad"
86. satsanga, "sat+sanga"
87. viveka, "vi+vic"
88. āśā, "ā+śaṇs"
89. śānta, "śam"
90. sāṁskāra, "saṁ+kṛi"

4d. Yoga Philosophical Terms :

1. haṭhayoga, "ha + ṭha + yuj"
2. karmayoga, "kṛi +mā+yuj"
3. Bhaktiyoga, "bhaj + yuj"
4. Jnānayoga, "jnā+yuj"

5. Rājayoga, "raj + yuj"
6. aṣṭaṇgyoga, "aṣṭa+aṅga+yuj"
7. japayoga/mantrayoga, "jap+yuj/man+tṛi+yuj"
8. Kuṇḍalinī or Tantra yoga, "kuṇḍ+laya/tan+tṛī +yuj"
9. ātmavicārayoga, "at+mā+vi+car+yuj" [Ramāṇa Maharṣhi Vendānta Yoga]
10. Pūrṇayoga, "pūrṇa+yuj" {Sri Aurobindo's Integral Yoga]
11. kṛiyayoga, "kṛi+yuj"

[Interesting comparison of Patanjali's aṣṭaṇgayoga and aṣṭaṇgamārga of Buddhism.]

Patañjali	*Buddha's Eightfold Path*
1. Yama, Self control	1. Right view, samyak, right; dṛiṣṭi-view.
2. Niyama, Religious observances.	2. Right speech, samyagvāk
3. Āsana, Postures	3. Right resolve, saṁkḷrip.
4. Prāṇayāma, Breath Control.	4. Right conduct, samyakkarmānta.
5. Pratyāhāra, Withdrawal of Seṇseconsciousness.	5. Right livelihood, saṁyagājīva.
6. Dhāraṇā, Concentration	6. Right Effort, Saṁyagvyāyāma.
7. Dhyāna, Meditation	7. Right recollection, Saṁyaksmṛiti.
8. Saṁadhi, Realization of Self.	8. Right contemplation, Saṁyaksaṁādhi.

CHAPTER XII

Summary, Deity Name Clarifications, Short Mantra, The Haṭhayoga Postures (84), Longer Mantras from the Vedas, Gītā and Sutras.

LESSON 1 : CONCLUDING SUMMARY.

As stated earlier in the text, although an English-Sanskrit dictionary is included and also a Sanskrit-English dictionary, I suggest your own continuous listing of the nouns, substantives, adjectives and verbs by conjugations I, IV, VI, and X will prove to be most consequential to you. Please do consult the dictionaries for further words to expand you grammatical composing.

Your determination at learning this Divine Language will be rewarded by your ability to feel the philosophical intent of the non-verbal terms. As witnessed in the previous chapter, whenever translations occur, the translator cannot help but include his own convictions, and whenever you utilize translations of a sectarian nature, the terms again will be redefined, hence, you are the best source of understanding. I can refer you to a magnificent text by the late Dr. Judith Tyberg called "The Language of The Gods,:as a tremendous font of further investigation into the inner-meaningfulness of the terms. It is recommended that you obtain this text to augment your broader understanding.

Again, a book carried is not a fulfillment of your work. In India this text would fulfill at least two levels of accomplishment and represent quite a large step in your venturesome learning. Mnemonic practicing of the paradigms, and constures will serve you well. (These too constitute mantric-meditations!) Again, restating dedication, detachment and discipline as your way of learning is appropriate. Congratu-lations to your perseverance and fortitude! It is encouraged that you try to write short paragraphs, stories, and perhaps even your own mantras with the facility that you have acquired at this point. This author would welcome questions, corrections and reactions to this text. When there is enough demand, volume two will become available, and/or cassettes when requested.

LESSON 2 : A CLARIFICATION OF VARIOUS NAMES OF DEITIES FOR MEDITATION.

Symbology and various names that you will encounter in learning the mantras is very important. Here is set forth a miniscule articulation of the various names, and a brief explanation.

THE TRINITY : BRĀHMA, VIṢṆU, ŚIVA.

Brahma represents the inner personality of man; mind, ego, intellect and conditional consciousness. He is the Creator of the Universe in a total abstract conceptualization. His consort is *Sarasvati*. She is the female aspect of illumined knowledge, Goddess of the Arts, Sciences, Speech and the embodiment of love, beauty, cheerfulness, who brings harmony. She increases intuition, good-will and all forms of learning.

Viṣṇu represents the aspect of preservation and God Absolute. He is the deity of preservation and unlike Brahma, does have concrete symbols and becomes incarnate in ten forms.

1. Matsya, the fish symbolic of the beginning of man and saving of the fine seeds of man-to-be.
2. Kūrma, the tortoise, representing the vital physical man to be churned out of the ocean of Infinity. [The Flood]
3. Vahāra, the boar, symbolizes animal man struggling to master the earth.
4. Narasimha, the Man-Lion, bridging man and the animal who turns towards conscious power.

5. Vāmana, the dwarf, undeveloped Godman taking possession of existence.
6. Parasurāma, Rāma with the axe, the vital rajasic man who brings ethics into social life by destroying the physical forces of the ksatriyas.
7. Rāma, Hero of the Rāmāyana, the sattvic mental man, the ideal human.
8. Kṛṣṇa, the overmental spiritual man, bringer of ānanda into life.
9. Buddha, A negative supreme liberation which reveals the oneness of all beings and hence led to his compassionate abnadonment of nirvaṇa to raise mankind.
10. Kalki, a White-Horse, the Divine Man, strength of power of all colours. Conquers death, Yama, of all duality, all opposition and all darkness. Divine Man on Earth, One with the Infinite Divine.

Hence Viṣṇu is also noted by all these names of Rāma, Kṛṣṇa, Buddha, and sometimes as Gopala and Govinda.

His consort is *Lakṣmi*, the Goddess of fortune, prosperity and the dynamic force behind Viṣṇu. She grants the devotees unlimited material wealth as well as prosperity and spiritual attainments. Rāma, the seventh incarnation of Viṣṇu has as his consort Sītā. Hanuman represents Rāma's perfect nature of human perfection.

Śiva is the deity of regeneration who destroys personality attributes which keep us from realizing our True Nature. His consort is *Durga* also known as Parvati, Uma, Kālī : the Divine Mother Aspect! Kālī is the destructful force of change, to control the senses and the awareness of the Absolute and Oneness with the Original State.

Gaṇeśa rules the ganas or spirits who preside over the five elements: fire, earth, air, water, either common to all religions.

Subramanya is the second son of Śiva who destroys ignorance and is in control of all spiritual qualities.

Dattatreya represents the totality of the Trinity : Brāhma, Viṣṇu and Śiva as ONE SPIRIT.

In the various mantras alternate or descriptive names will be invoked to align one with the various aspects of the Trinity. Brahmanism is totally abstract and scholastic, Viṣṇu does have some symbolism, and Śiva has total symbolism and is most popular.

Mantras are the vehicles through which man can reach beyond the limits of his perceptions, they are the links between different order of things. A way of remembering from the depths of the mind. They are basic thought forms or seeds. The power of the mantra brings down the Deity and makes it enter the image. The first perception of a mantra is always attributed to a direct contact between a human being and a divinity.

LESSON 3 : SHORT MANTRAS FOR MEDITATION AND 84 MAIN POSTURES.

It must be stated that the āsanas are indeed the finest form of becoming the vehicle of the transcendental inflow. Āsanas themselves are valuable aids for better health, but are intensive postures for receiving the Divine Inflow. Here is recommended one of the finest books that perhaps you might obtain for good reference : "Light of Yoga," Iyengar. Now follows a list of the eighty-four most important Āsanas.

१. सिद्धासन, The posture of attainment : purifies the seventy-two thousand arteries and veins of the body and infuses them with new blood. It greatly increases the power of the mind to grasp ideas, delusions decrease, and the mind inclines towards Divinity and Liberation.

२. प्रसिद्धसिद्धासन, The posture of Celebrated-attainment which destroys physical ailments and makes a man humble.

३. पद्मासन, The Lotus posture which brings all desired

results and inclines the mind towards spiritual experiences.

४. बद्धपद्मासन, The Bound Lotus Posture which brings pesce.

५. उत्थित पद्मासन, The raised—Lotus posture; gives super—human sight (divyadṛiṣti), opens the heart's center and cures respiratory disorders.

६. उर्ध्वपद्मासन, The high—lotus posture; strengthens the spinal chord and stimulates blood circulation.

७. सुप्तपद्मासन, The sleeping—lotus posture; cures digestive ailments.

८. भद्रासन, The posture of prosperity' makes the mind alert and interested in all works.

९. स्वस्तिकासन, The auspicious posture; has the vitures of its name!

१०. योगासन, The posture of communion; stabilizes the mind's substance (citta) leads to the eight attainments and cures disorders of sleep.

११. प्राणासन, The Life-Breath Posture or Breath Control Posture (prāṇāyāma), purifies the mind's substance as well as the blood and all the nervous and circulatory systems.

१२. मुक्तासन, The Liberated Posture; leads to all the attainments (siddhis).

१३. पवनमुक्तासन, The Free-From-Wind Posture; facilitates the inner functions.

१४. सूर्यासन, The Sun (Solar) Posture, increases the firey element!

१५. सूर्यभनासन, Piercing-of-the Sun Posture, cures eye diseases.

१६. भास्त्रिकासन, The Pouch-Posture; regulates the temperature of the body, eliminates all kinds of fevers, regulates digestion and cleanse the blood.

१७. सावित्री समाधि, Posture of Identification with Solar-Rhythm; gives brilliance, strength and memory.

१८. अचिन्तनियासन, Posture of the Inconceivable; develops powers of consciousness.

१९. ब्रह्मज्वरान्कुषासन, The Posture of the Driving-Hook-Of-The-Elephant, Principial-Fever; masters all diseases.

२०. उद्धारकासन, The Drawing-Out Posture; strengthens lower part of digestive tracts.

२१. मृत्युभञ्जकासन, The Posture of Splitting-Death; masters the air elements in body.

२२. आत्मारमासान, The Posture of Self-Delight; gets rid of worries. It is said to have been the first (ādi) of all the postures.

२३. भैरवासन, The Posture of the Fearful-Śiva; makes restless the basic coiled energy (kuṇḍalini); the subtle centers, or lotuses, open of themselves; all troubles of the heart and spleen are cured.

२४. गुरुदासन, The Posture of Wings-Of-Speech; makes people enterprising and swift.

२५. सिंहासन, The Lion Posture; strengthens intellectual faculties.

२६. गोमुखासन, The Cow-Muzzle-Posture; cures diseases of the face.

२७. वातायनासन, The Horse-Posture; brings speedy progress.

२८. सिद्धमुक्तावलि आसन, The Pearl-String-of-Attainment-Posture, makes one feel happy.

२९. नेत्यासन, The-Water-Inhaling-Posture; makes one feel clean.

३०. पुर्वासन, The Past or East Posture; makes one remember past events.

३१. पश्चिमोत्तनासन, The-Drawing-In-Or-Westward-Posture; destroys internal parasites, cures weak digestion.

३२. बज्रासन, The Thunderbolt Posture; lengthens life and does away with minor ailments.

३३. चक्रासन, The Wheel-Posture; soothes the basic coiled energy.

३४. गर्भासन, The Foetus Posture; gives energy to bear pain.

३५. शीर्षासन, The Head-Stand-Posture; of ten kinds, they increase health, beauty, strength, sexual powers, swiftness, activity and archenergy (mahā śakti).

३६. सर्वाङ्गोत्तानासन, The-All-Limbs-Raised-Posture; brings independence and Self-control.

३७. हस्तदाङ्गुष्टासन, The-Hand-And-Toe-Posture; strengthens the neck, waist, nose and stomach.

३८. पदाङ्गुष्टासन, The Toe Posture; strengthens sight.

३९. उत्रानपदासन, The Raised-Feet Posture; purifies the life-breath.

४०. जनुलग्नासन, The Touching-Of-The-Knee Posture; purifies the life-breath.

४१. एकपद शीर्षासन, The One-Foot_To-The-Head Posture; gives a perfect figure.

४२. द्विपद शीर्षासन, The Two-Feet-To-The-Head Posture; gives pleasure.

४३. एकहस्तासन, The One-Hand-Posture; prevents inter-costal pain.

४४. पदहस्तासन, The Hand-To-Feet Posture; increases strength.

४५. कर्नपिदमुलासन, The Root-Posture-Covering-The Ears; increases digestive powers.

४६. कर्नासन, The -Angle-Posture; purifies the digestive organs.

४७. त्रिकोनासन, The-Triangular-Posture; cures lumbago.

४८. चतुष्कोनासन, The-Quadrangular-Postures; increases mental powers.

४९. कन्दपिदासन, Pressing-the-bulb-below navel posture; opens the knot of the marrow.

५०. तुलितासन, The-balance-posture; gives balance and stability.

५१. वृक्षासन, The-tree-posture; strengthens the nerves.

५२. धनुषासन, The-bow-posture; develops heroism, courage and endurance; cures laziness and helps in the practice of visual concentration.

५३. वियोगासन, The-posture-of-separation; cures enlarged spleen.

५४. विलोमासन, The-inverted-posture; cures prolonged illnesses.

५५. योन्यासन, The-yoni-posture; strengthens the lower orifices of the body.

५६. गुप्ताङ्गासन, The-posture-of-the-secret-parts; cures secret diseases.

५७. उत्कासन, The-raised-posture; increases strength of the feet.

५८. षोकासन, The-sorrow-posture; cures epilepsy.

५९. सन्कतासन, The posture-of-suffering; cures lumbago.

६०. अन्धासन, The-blind-posture; removes night-blindness & other visual defects.

६१. रुन्दासन, The-headless-posture; makes a man fearless.

६२. शवासन, The-corpse-posture; makes the inner organs function freely.

६३. वृषासन, The-Bull-Posture; prevents the flow of semen.

६४. गो पुच्हासन, The-cow-tail-posture; purifies from sin.

६५. उष्ट्रासन, The-camel-posture; helps a man bear heat and cold.

६६. मर्कतासन, The-monkey-posture; improves the nerves and blood vessels of the navel region

६७. मत्स्यासन, The-fish-posture; gives firmness.

६८. मत्स्येन्द्रासन, Posture-of-the-Great-Teacher-Matsendra; (Lord of the Fishes) increases virility.

६९. मकरासन, The-sea-monster-posture; increases strength.

७०. कुर्मासन, The-tortoise-posture; renders the mind unswerving.

७१. मदुकासन, The-frog-posture; renders the body invisible.

७२. उत्तनासन, The-raised-frog-posture; gives power to cross into the world beyond (tāraṇa Śakti).

७३. हंसासन, The-swan-posture; gives peace.

७४. बकासन, The-crane-posture; helps a man to bear the shock of water.

७५. मयूरासन, The-peacock-posture; helps a man to hear a long way and cures diseases of the liver, spleen and intestines.

७६. कुक्कुतासन, The-cock-posture; calms erotic impulses.

७७. फोद्यासन, *The-phodia-posture; cures nose and gum bleeding.

७८. षलभासन, The-locust-posture; increases physical strength.

७९. वृष्छिकासन, The-scorpion-posture; makes a man feared.

८०. सर्पासन, The-serpent-posture; cures weak digestion.

८१. हलासन, The-plough-posture; makes a man powerful.

८२. वीरासन, The-hero-posture; gives courage.

८३. शान्ति प्रियासन, The-peace-loving-posture; brings all kinds of happiness.

* The meaning of this term is historically unknown.

As we approach the end of this opus, a few random abstract reflections!

— The purpose of our study was to *feel* the non-verbal construes of the Sanskrit philosophicla terms.

— Translations into English bear the inner thoughts of a translator, with the exception of such polyglots as Radhakrishnan, Ramana-Maharshi, Bhandarkar, Monier-Williams, etc.

— In the previous chapter it is hoped that you could *feel* the meanings of the terms in relationship to your work in the grammar.

— The purpose of 'yoga,' is not to convert, but to help one fully realize one's highest potential spiritual unfoldment. It helps you to become more intense in your spiritual heritage!

— In the suggested bibliography there are texts which are quite valuable for further understanding in English.

— Without a question of a doubt, the āsanas are intrinsically the finest medium of meditation. Re-read the potential aspects of the 84 āsanas and carefully note their value to your spiritual and physical body.

— Next to the āsanas the saṁprasaraṇa fulfills your meditational needs when time is limited!

— If you have more time available, you can utilize the full inner and outer chanting of the cakra letters and the interpolation of the bijam mantra.

— Next will follow short mantras for daily meditation.

Do include familiar religious mantras of your own faith too!

— The longer mantras require more time, but do consideretting aside a special time each day, according to your busy schedule and needs.

— When using mantras, unlike prayers of supplication, neither ask for something, nor expect anything. Just let the Divine inflow fill your vṛitti with 'true-knowledge!'

— Always remember to be patient, and dedicated, disciplined, and detached when doing any form of meditation. Disallow the time-space relationship, and gradually work towards Self-Realization and Liberation

— In chanting mantras remember to sound each syllable as opposed to a complete word. The syllables have a direct mathematical relationship to releasing energy!

Lesson 4 : Short traditional mantras followed by longer mantras drawn from Gītā. The Upanisadas, the Vedas and other Sacred exts.

ॐ हरि ॐ।

ॐ नमो भगवते वासुदेवाय्।

ॐ नमो नारायणाय।

ॐ नमः शिवाय।

ॐ योग उच्चते।

ॐ दत्तात्रेयाया नमः।

ॐ ब्रह्मवेदं सर्वम्।

ॐ अयं आत्म शन्त।

ॐ असङ्ग अयं पुरुष।

ॐ सर्वम् खल्विदं ब्रह्म।

ॐ अहं ब्रह्मास्मि।

ॐ नमो ब्रह्मणे।

शीलं नरस्य भूषनम्।

यथा कर्म तथा फलम्।

आशा दुखस्य कारणम्।

कथं बन्धः कथं मोक्षः।

का विद्या कोऽविद्येति।

जग्रत् स्वप्न सुषुप्ति तुरीयं कथम्।

ॐ अहं युक्तः।

एकं एवद्वित्यं।

सत्यं ज्ञानम् अनन्तं ब्रह्म।

ॐ इति मया श्रुतम्।

असतो मा सद्गमय।

तमसो मा ज्योथिर्गमय।

सत्यान् नास्ति परो धर्मः।

सत्यमेव जयते नानृतम्।

ॐ विद्या सर्वत्र पुज्यते।

ॐ सनातन धर्म।

ॐ समन्य धर्म।

ॐ विशेष धर्म।

ॐ वर्णाश्रम धर्म।

ॐ स्वधर्म।

ॐ युगधर्म।

ॐ मानवधर्म।

ॐ स्थरीधर्म।

ॐ प्रवृत्तिधर्म।

ॐ निर्वृत्तिधर्म।

ॐ सच्छिदेकं ब्रह्म।
ज्योति शक्ति शान्तिः।
ॐ तत् त्वम् असि।
ॐ तत् सत्।

The Traditional "Gāyatrī Mantra" Rig Veda III, 62, 10

भूर् भुवः स्वः
तत् सवितुर् वरेण्यम्
भर्गो देवस्य धीमहि
धियो यो नः प्रचोदयात्।

अश्वत्तः सर्ववृक्षाणाम् B.G. X—26
देवर्षीणाम् च नारदः
गन्धर्वाणाम् चित्ररथः
सिधानां कपिलो मुनिः।

सत्वानुरूपा सर्वस्य B.G. XVII—3
श्रद्धा भवति भारत
श्रद्धामयोऽयं पुरुषो
यो यच्छ्रद्धः स एव सः।

ऋलिभिर् बहुधा गीतम् B.G. XIII—4
चन्धोभिर् विविधैः पृथक्
ब्रह्मसूत्रपदैश्चैऽव
हेतुमद्भिर् विनिश्चितैः।

ध्यानेनाऽत्मनि पश्यन्ति B.G. XIII—24
केचिद् आत्मानम् आत्मना
अन्ये संख्येन योगेन
कर्मयोगेण चऽपरे।

समं सर्वेषु भूतेषु B.G. XIII—27
तिष्ठन्तम् परमेश्वरम्

विनस्यत्स्व विनस्यन्तं
य: पश्यति स पश्यति।

समं पश्यन् हि सर्वत्र B.G. XIII—28
समवस्थितं ईश्वरम्
न हिनस्त्यात्मनाऽत्मानं
ततो याति परां गतिम्।

अशोच्यान् अन्वशोचस्त्वं B.G. II—11
प्रज्ञावादांश्च भाषसे
गतासून् अगतासूंश्च
नानुशोचन्ति पण्डिता:।

न जायते म्रियते वा कदाचित् B.G. II—20
नायं भूत्वा भविता वा न भूय:
अजो नित्य: शाश्वतोऽयं पुराणो
न हन्यते हन्यमाने शरीरे।

वासांसि जीर्णानि यथा विहाय B.G. II—22
नवानि गृह्णाति नरोऽपराणि
तथा शरीराणि विहाय जीर्णाणि
अन्यानि संयाति नवानि देही।

जातस्य हि ध्रुवो मृत्युर् B.G. II—27
ध्रुवं जन्म मृतस्य च
तस्माद् अपरिहार्येऽमे
तं त्वं शोचितुम् अर्हसि।

न तु मां शक्यसे द्रष्टुम् B.G. XI—8
अनेनैऽव स्वचक्षुषा
दिव्यं ददामि ते चक्षु:
पश्य मे योगम् ऐश्वरम्।

यो माम् अजं अनादिं च B.G. X—3
वेत्ति लोकमहेश्वरम्

असंमूढः स मर्त्येषु
सर्वपापैः प्रमुच्यते।

अहं सर्वस्य प्रभवो B.G. X—8
मत्तः सर्वं प्रवर्तते
इति मत्वा भजन्ते मां
बुद्धा भावसमन्विताः।

तेषां सततयुक्तानां B.G. X—10
भजतां प्रीतिपूर्वकम्
ददामि बुद्धियोगं तं
येन मां उपयान्ति ते।

सुखदुःखे समे कृत्वा B.G. II—38
लाभालाभौ जयाजयौ
ततो युद्धाय युज्यस्व
नैवं पापम् अवप्स्यसि।

त्रैगुण्यावषया वेदा B.G. II—45
निस्त्रैगुण्यो भवाऽर्जन
निर्द्वन्द्वो नित्यसत्त्वस्थो
निर्योगक्षेम आत्मवान्

योगस्यः कुरु कर्माणि B.G. II—48
सङ्ग त्यक्ता धनंजय
सिद्ध्यसिद्ध्योः समो भूत्वा
समत्वं योग उच्चते।

क्रोधाद् भवति संमोहः B.G. II—63
संमोहात् स्मृतिविभ्रमः
स्मृतिभ्रंशाद् बुद्धिनाशो
बुद्धिनाशात् प्रणश्यति।

एषा ब्राह्मी स्थितिः पार्थ B.G. II—72
नैनां प्राप्य विमुह्यति

स्थित्वा स्यां अन्तकालेऽपि
ब्रह्मनिर्वाणाम् ऋच्छति।

अक्षराणम् अकारोऽस्मि B.G. X-33
द्वन्द्वः सामासकस्य च
अहम् एवाऽक्षयः कालो
धाताऽहं विश्वतोमुखः।

पितामहस्य जगतो B.G. IX-17
माता धाता पितामहः
वेद्यं पावनं ऊँकार
ऋक् साम यजुर् एव च।

पतञ्जलि

अथ योगानुशासनम्। I-१

योगश्चित्तवृत्तिनिरोधः। I-२

वृात्तसारूप्यमितरत्र। I-४

ईश्वरप्रणिधानाद्वा। I-२३

तपःस्वाध्यायेश्वरप्रणिधानानि।
क्रियायोगः। II-१

यमनियमासेनप्राणायाम। II-२९
प्रत्याहारधारणाध्यान।
समाध्योऽष्टावङ्गानि।

अहिंसासत्यास्तेय। II-३०
ब्रह्मचर्यापरिग्रहा यमाः।

शौचसंतोषतपःस्वाध्यायेश्वर। II-३२
प्राणधानानि नियमाः।

स्वाध्यायाद् इष्टदेवता संप्रयागः। II-४४

समाधिसिद्धिरीश्वरप्रणिधानात्। II-४५

APPENDIX - A

Sanskrit	*English*
sam	with
pari	round
upari	above (upper)
prati	towards
pra	before
antar	within
na	no (negative)
ca	and
dvi	two
trī	three
chatvara	four
panchan	five
shaṭ	six
saptan	seven
ashṭan	eight
nayan	nine
daśan	ten
dānạ	gift
bhū	to be, I was
tan, tanomi	stretch
janus	birth, kind
jña	to know
ajñāta	unknown
nāman	name, surname

ad	to eat
sarp	to creep
sarpa	serpent
vas	to clothe
vāta	wind
anj	to annoint
man, manye	I think, remember
manas	mind, intellect
kar, karomi	to do, fulfill, create
vam	vomit
sveda	sweat
mar	to die
mṛityu	death
martya	mortal
amṛita	immortal
āloka	light
vach	speak, call
matra	measure, meter
yuj, yunajmi	to yoke, join
yuktos	joined
yuga	yoke
much	remove, free, wipe
suryas	sun
agni	fire
ap	water
dant	tooth
pitar	father
mater	mother
nānā	mother, aunt
bhrater	brother
svasar	sister,
duhitar	daughter
naptar, napet	grandson, cousin.

jamatar	son-in-law
pitṛiviya	father's brother
vīra	man, hero, virile
jaras	old age
jaran	old man
ātman	breath, soul, vapour
an (to breathe)	wind, mind
kṛip (to make)	body
kṛidaya	heart
kapala	head
akshi	eye
nasika	nose
bhrū	eyebrow
asthi	bone
pāda	foot
janu	knee
udara	belly
āyus	life
vi	bird
kokila	cuckoo
ulūka	owl
Dyaus	sky, Zeus
divya	celestial, divine
naktā	night
tāra	star
madhu	honey, wine
apas	work
pur, purī	city
dama	house
scapna (sleep)	sleep
ṅau	ship
vanas (to love)	beauty, Venus
pathin	road, path

dhūma	smoke, spirit
chakra	wheel, circle
marmara	murmur
manḍa	ornament, world
kūpa	hole, well
phulla	flower, leaf
guru	heavy
manhishtha	greatest, venerable
barbara	barbarous
sama	like
mala (dirt)	dirty, bad, black.

APPENDIX - B

Counting Cognates

	Sanskrit	*Hindi*	*English*
1.	eke = १	ek	one
2.	dvī = २	do	two
3.	tri = ३	tīn	three
4.	catur = ४	cār	four
5.	pañca = ५	pañc	five
6.	ṣas = ६	chha	six
7.	saptā = ७	sāt	seven
8.	aṣṭā = ८	āṭh	eight
9.	nava = ९	nuv	nine
10.	dasa = १०	dus	ten.

APPENDIX - C

Summarizing Exercises

Sanskrit to English		*English to Sanskr*	
धावति	He runs.	I eat	खादामि
यजति	He worships.	We become	भवामः
वदावः	We two speak.	You two protect.	रक्षथः
त्यजसि	You (sing.) abandon.	They abandon.	त्यजन्ति
पततः	They (two) fall.	He speaks.	वदति
स्मरामः	We remember.	We know.	बोधामः
पचथः	You (two) cook.	They two dwell.	वसतः
बोधामि	I understand.	We rove.	अटामः
द्रवति	It melts.	She grieves.	शोचति
जयथ	You (plural) conquer.	He is worthy.	अर्हति
नमन्ति	They revere.	We two play.	क्रीडावः

The mouse digs.	अश्वौ धावतः।
The boy grow.	बालाः स्मरन्ति।
Both Rāmas remember.	रावणो जयति।
The servant cooks.	शिष्यौ पटावः।
The horses run.	श्रृगालाः क्रीडन्ति।
The king, the hero, is speaking.	मेघश्चरति

Sanskrit to English	*English to Sanskrit*
The two travellers +	
Murmur* जल्प् Root.	पुत्र वीरा भवन्ति।
The moon grows.	जनौ वदत:।
Rāma leads.	दास: क्रोधति + क्रुध Root.
The village burns.	सर्पौ सर्पाव:।
The two devotees worship.	वृक्षा दहन्ति।

Illustration of Sandhi Rule # 3*

नर इच्छति।	The man wishes.
दास ईर्ष्यति।	The servant envies.
रथ ईरयति।	The chariot moves.
पान्थ इष्यति।	The traveller goes.
वृक्ष ओष्यति।	The tree burns.
नृप ऋष्यति।	The king prospers.
मालिक उष्छति।	The gardener gleans.
हस्त ईरयति।	The hand moves.
चौर ऋष्यति।	The thief prospers.
राम इच्छति।	Rāma wishes.

* Note -These are only example sentences.

Illustrations of Sandhi Rule # 4

ब्राह्मणोऽटति।	The Brahmin wanders.
पान्थोऽटति।	The Traveller wanders.
शिष्योऽर्हति।	The disciple is worthy.
दासोऽर्हति।	The servant is deserving.
भक्तोऽर्च्चति।	The devotee worships.
मनुष्योऽर्चति।	The man worships.

बालोऽर्जति।	The boy earns.
मालिकोऽर्जति।	The gardener earns.
नृपोऽवति।	The king protects.
रामोऽवति।	Rāma protects.

Illustration of Sandhi Rule #5

ब्राह्मणा बोधन्ति।	The brahmins understand.
कपोता रोहन्ति।	The pigeons grow.
रथा द्योतन्ति।	The chariots shine.
मृगा जलं पिबन्ति।	The deer drink the water.
मूषिका अन्नम् हरन्ति।	The mice take the food.
दासा वयन्ति।	The servant weave.
देवा भवन्ति।	The Gods exist.
जना नयन्ति।	The people lead.
चौरा धनं गूहन्ति।	The thieves hide the wealth.
बका इयन्ति।	The cranes fly.

Illustration of Sandhi Rule #6

मुनिर्सत्यं बाधति।	The sage knows the truth.
कविर्दुःखं स्मरति।	The poet remembers sorrow.
अरिर्शोचति।	The enemy grieves.
गुरूर्नयति।	The guru leads.
अग्नी रथं दहति।	The fire burns the chariot.
शिशुर्फलं श्रयति।	The baby reaches the fruit.
उदधिश्रयति।	The ocean swells.
इषू रावणं श्रयति।	The arrow reaches (pierces) Rāvana.
मुनी रूपं जयति।	The sage conquers the body.
गुरुर्शास्त्रं स्मरति।	The guru remembers the sacred precepts.

Illustration of Sandhi Rule #7

पुष्पं नरश्चेचतति।	The man notices the flower.
चौरश्चलति।	The thief goes astray.
भक्तश्चन्द्रं यजति।	The devotee worships the moon.
करश्चरति।	The hand moves.
शिष्यश्चिन्तति।	The disciple reflects.
अन्नं बकश्चयोतति।	The crane drops the food.
मृतमानन्दस्तरति।	Bliss transcends death.
पान्थस्तीरं श्रयति।	The traveller reaches the shore.
दासश्चक्रं चरति।	The servant moves the wheel.
मेघस्तरतिं।	The cloud crosses over.

Illustration of Sandhi Rule #8

सत्यं दुःखं च सुखं च तरति।	Truth transcends both pain and happiness.
कुलं गायति।	The family sings.
मृतं रूपं जयति।	Death conquers the body.
पुष्पं रोहति।	The flower grows.
वनं तृणं रक्षति।	The forest protects the grass.
पातकं दुःखं वपति।	Sin sows pain.
मुतं कमलं चिन्तति।	A being ponders a lotus.
पत्रं शास्त्रं धरति।	The page holds the sacred precepts.
ज्ञानं धनं तरति।	Knowledge transcends wealth.
भुतंम् अमृतं नमति।	A being reveres immortality.

Illustration of Sandhi Rule #9

पुनः क्रोडति।	Again he plays.
पुनश्चन्द्रः शोभति।	The moon shines again.
or	or
पुनश्चन्द्रच्छेभति।	The moon shines again.

मृगौ क्रीडतः पुनः।	The two deer are playing again.
पुनर्नमामः।	Again, we revere.
देवः (from देवस्)।	God.
पुनश्चौरश्चलति।	Again, the thief goes astray.
पुनर्वपावः।	We both plant again.
आनन्दस् = आनन्दः पुनर्	Bliss!
पुनस्तृणम्रोहति।	Again the grass grows.

Illustration of Sandhi Rule #10

भुतमटति।	A being wanders.
कुलमटति।	The family wanders.
पुस्तकमर्हति।	The book is worthy.
खादति फलम्।	He eats the fruit.
पठति शास्त्रम्।	He studies the sacred precepts.
भुतमीर्ष्यति।	The being is jealous.
बालः खादति अन्नम्।	The boy eats food.
दुःखम्म्लायति।	Pain fades.
दहति इन्धनम्।	Fuel burns.
अमृत जयति मृतम्।	Immortality conquers death.

Illustration of Sandhi Rule #11

शास्त्रन्नमति।	He reveres the sacred precepts.
पत्रन्दहति।	The page burns.
रूपङ्क्षयति।	The body decays.
सत्यं तरति।	Truth transcends.
पात्रं जलन्धरति।	The jug holds water.
कमलम्प्लवति।	The lotus floats.
सुखं दुःखञ्जयति।	Happiness conquers sorrow.
कुलं गायति।	The family sings.

कनकन्द्योतति।	Gold shines.
बीजञ्च्योतति।	The seed drops.

Illustration of the use of the Conjugation च

नरश्च बालश्च धावन्ति।	Both the man and the boy are running.
दासश्च नृपश्च यजन्ति।	Both the servant and the king worship.
सुखं च दुःखं म्लायन्ति।	Happiness and sorrow fade.
पान्थश्चाश्चश्च ग्लायन्ति।	Both the traveller and the horse are weary.
कपोते बकश्च डयन्ति।	The pigeon and the crane are flying.
नृपो जनाश्च जयन्ति।	The king and the people conquer.
भक्तश्च ब्राह्मणश्च गायन्ति।	Both the devotee and the Brahmin are singing.
मालिकश्च शिष्यश्च पुष्पं धरन्ति।	Both the gardner and the disciple hold a flower.
फलंच पुष्पानि क्षयन्ति।	Fruit and flowers decay.
रामश्च रावणश्च ग्लायन्ति।	Both Rāma and Rāvaṇa are weary.

Illustration of the use of न

चन्द्रो न शोभति।	The moon does not shine.
चौरो न धनं अर्हति।	The thief does not merit wealth.
मृगो न व्याघ्रं चेतति।	The deer does not notice the tiger.
नरो न यजति।	The man does not worship.
अश्वो न कर्षति।	The horse does not pull.
बाह्मणो न शोचति।	The brahmin does not grieve.
वृक्षो न रोहति।	The tree is not growing.
पान्थो न ग्लायति।	The traveller is not weary.
क्रोधो न जयति।	Anger does not conquer.
जना न नन्दन्ति।	The people are not satisfied.

CHAPTER IV

Exercise 1 Sanskrit English

1. They protect the men.
2. In that manner, they (dual) go to the mountain.
3. The disciple remembers the devotees.
4. The men reflect upon happiness.
5. The horses run near the trees.
6. The devotee thinks the truth.
7. The tiger smells the food.
8. The boys drink water and eat fruit.
9. The traveller sits near the village.
10. Rāma, the hero, restrains the boy.

Exercise 3 Sanskrit to English

1. The king goes to the village with the servants.
2. He eats the fruits with (his) two hands.
3. He is delighted with happiness.
4. Because of truth and character the trees decay.
5. Without water the trees decay.
6. The boys are weary with sorrow.
7. The snake goes to the country with the deer.
8. The chariot does not move without wheels.
9. The men remember Rāma, the immortal.
10. You (dual) go with the traveller.

Exercise 2 English to Sanskrit

१. अश्वः समया वनं धावति।

२. कपोतौ जलं पिबतः।

३. ग्रामं उभयतो मूषिकः सर्पति।

४. बाला शिष्यान् यजन्ति।

५. अत्र धर्मो द्योतति।

६. रामो दुःखं निन्दति।
७. क्रोधं यच्छति च नन्दति।
८. अद्य भक्तो न खादति।
९. अभि आरामं जलं मर्षति।
१०. स्तयं न वदथः।
११. अधुना नृपो दासान् रक्षति।
१२. सर्वत्र जना गायन्ति च नन्दन्तिच।
१३. सर्पो बालं दशति।
१४. चन्द्रः (चन्द्रोऽति) अति मेधान् शोभति।
१५. तथा समया ग्रामं खनामंः।
१६. भक्तो न शोचति।
१७. तत्र वृक्षो क्षयति।
१८. ब्राह्मणो दुःखं यच्छति।
१९. उप आरां तिष्ठावः।
२०. स्तयं च सुखं च भवन्ति।

Exercise 4 English / Sanskrit

१. पापेन नरश्चिन्तति।
२. जलेन बीजानि वपामः।
३. कमलाभ्यां शिष्यं नमामः।
४. अलं हुतेन।
५. जलेन पुष्पानि मर्षसि।
६. ईश्वरेन योगश्चेतति।
७. सुखेन तरथः।
८. रामो वीरो रावणं क्रोधेन यच्छति।
९, मृतेन रूप क्षयति।
१०. नरोऽनेन नन्दति स्म।

CHAPTER V

Exercise 1 : Sanskrit English

1. The man is pleased.
2. The boys dance near the village.
3. The person feeds the elephant.
4. The king forgives the servant.
5. The boy is thirsty and drinks water.
6. Rama is hungry and eats fruits.
7. The men destroy the trees and are wrong.
8. Tigers and elephants roam on all sides of the village.
9. The traveller is pleased.
10. The world is afflicted with misery and praises wisdom.

Exercise 2 : English / Sanskrit Contd.

१. बालो दुःखेन सह किल्स्यति।

२. जना सर्पान् च न्याग्रान् द्रुहयन्ति।

३. ब्राह्मणो भक्तान् क्षाम्यति।

४. सत्यं अज्ञानं स्यति।

५. पत्रानि नश्यन्ति च भ्रश्यन्ति।

६. भक्तो दुष्यति च क्रोधेन वदति।

७. जलं विना गजो महयति च क्षुभ्यति।

८. जना नृपंमभितो नृत्यन्ति च तुष्यन्ति।

९. आज्ञानेन सत्येन च जन ऋध्यति।

१०. ब्राह्मणो बोधति शास्त्रैर्हप्यामि च

Exercise 3 : Sanskrit / English

1. The elephant will dwell.
2. The thief will leave.
3. The deer will ramble.

4. The student will be worthy.
5. The god will remember.
6. The food will burn.
7. The snake will creep.
8. The sage will roam.
9. The fruit will decay.

Exercise 4 : English / Sanskrit

१. बाला वनं गमिष्यन्ति।

२. रामो जलं पास्यति मदिष्यति।

३. जना मोक्ष्यन्ति।

४. नरो दासान् क्षंस्यति।

५. ब्राह्मणो ग्रामं समया सत्स्यति।

६. दुःखं यंस्यामि।

७. मृगः स्थास्यति च वनं वत्स्यति।

८. बकः कुसुमानि घ्रास्यति।

९. कमले जलं विना रोक्ष्यतः।

१०. ज्ञानं अज्ञानं व्यत्स्यति।

११. वृक्षान् धक्ष्यामि।

१२. हस्ताभ्यां अन्नं खादिष्यामि।

१३. नरो ब्राह्मणो भविष्यति।

१४. मित्रानि स्मरिष्यावः।

१५. शंसिष्यन्ति वदिष्यन्ति च।

Exercise 5 For Practicing the Karmadāraya Compounds.

१. विश्वधर्मान् बोधामः।

२. वने कृष्णशुक्लव्याघ्रोऽतत।

३. नीलपात्रं।

४. जनैर्महातमुनिर्वदति।

५. सुन्दरकन्या खादति।

६. दिव्यहुतं।

७. योग्यपुस्तकं पठति।

८. साधुअन्नं शिष्यान् पोक्ष्यति*।

९. मन्दवचनं।

१०. अनुचितवचनं।

११. विस्मितमुनिः।

१२. पुराणशास्त्रं।

१३. साधुमनेन।

१४. सुन्दरगृहे।

१५. दूरतीरात्।

१६. स्थिरगाच्छति।

१७. दिव्यवदति।

१८. अनन्तधुःखेन।

१९. बालिकेन।

२०. दक्षिणवने।

*irregular future construction.

CHAPTER VI

Exercise 1 Sanskrit/English

1. A person ploughs near the garden.
2. The form (body) releases a seed.
3. The sons write the family.
4. Oh, you two boys, anoint the two disciples.
5. The beings ask (search for) the truth.
6. Truth will release ignorance.
7. The man strikes the serpent with his two hands.
8. Misery and sacrifice find happiness.
9. With happiness, the mother (*see glossary) will write the sons.
10. The dharma cuts (destroys) anger.

Exercise 2 English/Sanskrit Contd.

१. पठान् बाला लेखिष्यन्ति पठिष्यन्ति च।

२. महतानिलो वृक्षान् लोपस्यति।

३. आसनानि दुःखं मोक्ष्यन्ति।

४. हे नरे यज।

५. अन्नं सर्पा न विन्दन्ति।

६. हस्ताभ्यां लिम्पामि सुन्दरकन्या।

७. भक्ता गृहं वेक्ष्यन्ति।

८. क्षुद्रनरः पुनर् नृत्यति च मुह्यति।

९. ज्ञानं सत्यं देक्ष्यति।

१०. ईश्वरो नरं सृजति।

११. धनेन कनकेन च जना हसन्ति।

१२. हुतं आसनानि च योगं सृजन्ति।

१३. पान्थाः पुष्पानि स्पृशन्ति च फलानि खादन्ति।

१४. शृगाले बालं दशति च ग्रामं विशति।

१५. मा लिख।

१६. कुशलशिष्यो धर्मं बोधिष्यति।

Exercise 3 Sanskrit / English

1. Truth is remembered by the man.
2. Rama is conquered by the enemy.
3. The tigers seen by the man will move.
4. The man went to the village.
5. The Śastras are remembered by the brahmin.
6. Food is taken by the hand.
7. Restrained anger (Anger is restrained).
8. Anger is conquered by the devotee.

Exercise 4 English / Sanskrit

१. धनं चौरेण हतम्।

२. कपोतो नरेण दृष्टो जलं पिबति।

३. शास्त्रं श्रुतं भक्तैः।

४. ज्ञानं बोधितं बालैः।

५. अन्नं दृष्टं जनैः।

६. पाठः पठितः शिष्यैः।

७. इन्धनं दग्धम्।

८. जलं पीनम्।

९. सत्यं त्यक्तम्।

१०. खलं खातम्।

Exercise 5 Sanskrit/English

1. Where is the boy?
2. When shall I go to the forest?
3. What is she/he saying?
4. Where does she/he live?

5. Why doesn't the girl remember the boy?
6. How will they cook the food?
7. Why is the mother grieving?
8. When will the son feed the people?
9. Where are the clouds going?
10. What does the poet know?

Exercise 6 English / Sanskrit

१. किमर्थं पाठान् पठामि।

२. कुत्र कुलं वसति।

३. किमर्थं न आगच्छति।

४. कदा वृक्षा रात्स्यन्ति।

५. किं वचनं भवति।

६. कथं नरं स्मरिष्यति।

७. कथं वृद्धीगजो भवति।

८. किं नरा पक्ष्यन्ति।

९. कथं सुन्दरकन्या भवति।

१०. किमर्थं नरो न प्रतिगच्छति।

* 4th conj. verb राध्

Exercise 7 Sanskrit/English

1. The boys give the flowers to the disciple.
2. Salutations to Kṛṣna.
3. The man carries the book to the devotee.
4. She/he digs the garden for (the) son.
5. I am angry with (my) son.
6. The fruits grow for the person.
7. Today I go to the village because of the holy precepts for the devotees.

8. Hail truth!
9. Rama chants wisdom for the sage.
10. Sin leads to fighting.

Exercise 8 English/ Sanskrit

१. शिवाय नमः।

२. कन्या बालेभ्योऽन्नं यच्छति।

३. बालेभ्यः क्रोपिष्यामि।

४. नृपः पुष्पानि वीराय यच्छति।

५. चन्द्रं बालाभ्यं दिशतः।

६. पापेन कृतम्।

७. नृपाय स्वस्ति।

८. अत्र सुखेन बाला गास्यन्ति।

९. कुत्र जना गच्छन्ति।

१०. बालेभ्यो लेखिष्यामि।

CHAPTER VII

Exercise 1 : Corrected Vowel Sandhi

१. नास्ति	२. जीवान्त
३. अधीश्वर	४. ऋतूत्सव
५. पितृद्धि	६. परमेश्वर
७. हितोपदेश	८. गण्गोदक
९. तवर्द्धि	१०. महर्षि
११. परैधित	१२. विद्यैव
१३. देवैश्वर्य	१४. अल्पौजस्
१५. गण्गौह	१६. ज्वरौषध
१७. अग्न्यस्त्र	१८. प्रत्युवाच
१९. त्विदानिम्	२०. मात्रानन्द
२१. तेऽपि	२२. सोऽपि
२३. तयाणता: or त आगता:	२४. विष्णविह or विष्ण इह
२५. जेऽति	२६. अग्नये
२७. कस्मायपि or कस्मा अपि	२८. राय: or रा अहे:
२९. ददावन्नम्	३०. नावौ
३१. फले अत्र	३२. गुरवृषि इह
३३. हे ऋषे	३४. अहो बाल

Exercise 2 : Conjugation I, IV, VI plus Sandhi change.

1. The king conquers. नृपो जयति।
2. Trees grow near the village. ग्रामं अभितो वृक्षा रोहन्ति।
3. The horse eats the food. अश्वोन्नं खादति।
4. They run with the boys. बालैर्धावन्ति।
5. They roam with friends. मित्रैरटन्ति।
6. The man and the boys go to the village. नरश्च बालाश्च ग्रामं गच्छन्ति।
7. The son is worthy. पुत्रोऽर्हति।
8. The son wishes. पुत्र इच्छति।

9. The sons conquer. पुत्रा जयन्ति।
10. The husband conquers. पतिर्जयति।
11. The enemy is not worthy. शत्रुर्नार्हति।
12. The fire burned. अग्निर्दहति स्म।
13. The enemy moves. शतुर्चरति।
14. Today the boys see. अद्य बाला: पश्यन्ति।
15. She/he cooks food here. अन्नानं पचति।
16. They left the house. गृहं त्यजन्ति स्म।
17. The mind is here (Here mind). अत्र मनस।
18. Again they cross. पुनरुतरन्ति।
19. He gives food (or The food restrains). अकं यच्छति।
20. I want happiness. सुखं इच्छामि।

Exercise 3 : Sanskrit/English

1. We counsel the servant.
2. The man punishes the boy.
3. The world counts the wealth.
4. The devotee worships Isvara (God).
5. We arrange the beautiful flowers.
6. He proclaims the Truth.
7. The tiger steals the food.
8. Isvara (God) protects the devotees.
9. You (sing.) owe to the man generous rewards.
10. I cover the page with sayings.

Exercise 4 : English/ Sanskrit

१. बालान् अद्य पालयामि।
२. पुष्पानि गणयन्ति स्म।
३. ईश्वरो भक्तान् पूजयति।
४. हे करौ क्षालय।
५. मेघा चन्द्रं छादयन्ति च शठा रत्नानि चोरयन्ति।

६. तथान्नं मक्षस्यिामः।

७. सत्यं चिन्तयामि घोषयामि च।

८. किमर्थं शरीरं छादयसि।

९. शृगालो मांसं चोस्यिति।

१०. किमर्थं चौरं दण्डयथ।

Exercise 5 : English/ Sanskrit

१. मृतं शरिरं अभिधावति।

२. अनिलो ह्रदं अपचरति।

३. रथो वनं अधिगच्छति।

४. मित्रे उद्यानं उपविशतः।

५. ईश्वर आनन्दं लोकाय आनयति।

६. बलं आरोग्यं अनुसरति।

७. पान्था समुद्रं अतिक्राम्यन्ति।

८. चन्द्रं अनुसरामः।

९. नरौ भारौ निक्षिपतः कुपं उपविशतश्च।

१०. दासाः पात्रानि निर्वहन्ति।

Exercise 6 : Sanskrit / English

1. The pupil returns to the village.*
2. The devotee goes beyond grief and obtains immortality.
3. The gardener scatters the seeds in the garden.*
4. The traveller sets out for the mountains.
5. The devotee carries out the holy scriptures.
6. The scriptures summarize the sayings.
7. The crane flies around the village.*
8. The jackal runs toward the deer.
9. Happiness follows union.
10. The boy puts down the book and goes toward the beauty.

CHAPTER VIII

A : Exercise 1 : Sandhi corrections of Sanskrit sentences, with English translation :

१. आरा पुष्पाण्यधुनाच्छादयन्ति।

(Now, the flowers cover the garden.)

२. अश्वाञ्छाम्यामि।

(I calm the horses.)

३. हुताच्चौरौ रत्नानि चोरयतः।

(The two thieves steal the jewels from the family.)

४. दासो बाला लिम्पति।

(The servant annoints the boys.)

५. ज्ञानाच्छीलं रोहति।

(From wisdom, character grows.)

६. परशुस्तरूस्तुदति।

(The axe strikes the trees.)

७. ग्रामाज्जनको गच्छति।

(The father goes from the village.)

B : Exercise 2 : English to Sanskrit, incorporating Sandhi rules through Chapter VIII:

१. वृक्षाद्फलानि पतन्ति।

२. पुत्राञ्जनकः शंसति।

३. माच्छय कुसुमानि।

४. अनिलो वृक्षां लुम्पति।

५. जलं पात्राच्च्योतति।

६. शिशुरतिथींश्चेतति।

७. आसनेन शरीरं शोभति।

Exercise 3 Sanskrit / English

1. The man entered the house.
2. God created truth.
3. The elephant struck the tree.
4. The cranes flew around the lake.
5. The devotees chanted (sang).
6. The person annointed the guru.
7. We threw the food.
8. They experienced the dharma.
9. They two asked.
10. We two wrote.

Exercise 4 English / Sanskrit

१. अश्वा वनमधावन्।

२. अद्य वृक्षावादहन्।

३. मेघाकाशमचलन्।

४. हंसा ह्रदमत्यक्राम्यन्।

५. बालौ आचार्यमन्वगच्छताम्।

६. तथा जनाभक्षयन्।

७. व्याघ्रो वनं प्रत्यगच्छत्।

८. अपठाम।

९. अक्रीडतमधावतश्च।

१०. अपूजयताम्।

११. अद्यान्नमपचत्।

१२. अमुञ्चत्।

१३. सर्वजनागायननृत्यश्च।

Exercise 5 : Correction Sandhi involving the Ablative Case

१. कुपाद्पिबन्ति।

२. आरामाधावन्ति।

३. ज्ञानास्स्मरिष्यति।

४. दुखच्छोचामः।

५. शास्त्रद्यजन्ति।

६. देवाच्चिन्तावः।

७. ज्ञानाद्रोहामः।

८. सत्याज्जयामि।

९. धर्माद्पठामि।

१०. आनन्दाम्माद्यामः or आनन्दाद्माद्यामः।

११. मृत्याद्गूहतः।

१२. हूताद्क्षाम्यन्।

१३. सुखाम्माद्यामः or सुखाद्माद्यामः।

१४. ज्ञानादस्मरन्।

१५. मेघाज्जलम्।

Exercise 6 : Karmadhāraya compounds, Sandhi rules & tense.

१. पर्वताना वृक्षानवादहन्।

of the mountains The trees burned down

(gen., pl.) (Nom. Pl.) (Imperfect, 3rd p. pl.)

The trees of the mountains burned down.

२. अन्धनृपस्य पुत्रोऽपचरति

blind of the king The son leaves.

(gen. sing.) (Nom. sing. + sandhi rule (pres., 3rd. sing.)

The son of the blind king leaves.

३. वृद्धदासस्य इन्धनमधो

old of the servant fuel beneath

(krmdh.) (gen. sing.) (Acc. sing.) (prep.

गृहं निक्षपतिस्म

the house put down (past tense)
(3rd. sing.)

He put the old servant's fuel beneath the house.

४. दिव्याचार्यस्य वचनानि।

divine of the teacher words

(Krmdh.) (gen. sing.) (Nom. pl.)

धर्मम् संक्षिपन्ति।

The Dharma they summarize.

(Acc. sing.) (Pres., 3rd. pl.)

The words of the divine teacher summarize the Dharma.

५. नीलकमलस्य पुष्पानि

blue of the lotus The flowers

(Krmdh.) (gen. sing.) (Nom. pl.)

उद्भवन्ति

come forth

ud + bhavanti : come forth.

The flowers of the blue lotus come forth.

६. शीघ्राश्वयोऽन्नं व्यास्यत्।

swift horses food he scattered.

(krmdh.) (gen., dual) Nom. singl.) 3rd, p. sing., Imperfect).

He scattered the food of the two swift horses.

७. शास्त्रानाम् विश्वपुस्तकानपठन्।

of the sastras all books They studied

(gen. pl.) (Krmdh.) (Acc. pl.) (Imperfect, 3rd p. pl.)

They studied all books of the Śastras.

८. शुक्लकमलस्य पत्रानि क्षोष्यन्ति।
white of the lotus The petals will decay
(Krmdh.) (gen. sing.) (Nom. pl.) 3rd. p. pl., Future)

The petals of the white lotus will decay.

९. वनस्य नवग्रामोऽवादहत्।
of the wood new house burned down
(gen. sing.) (Krmdh.) (Nom. s.) (3rd. p. sing. Imperfect)

The new wooden house burned down.

१०. मनुष्यस्य पुस्तकमपतत्।
of the man The book fell. The man's book fell.
(gen. sing.) (Nom. sing.) (Imperfect, 3rd. p. ing.)

Exercise 7 : English / Sanskrit exercises involving genetive and Karmadhāraya compounds.

१. अचारो मनुष्यस्य।	Man's conduct.
२. हस्तौ दासस्य।	Servant's two hands.
३. नृपस्य दुःखं।	King's misery.
४. फलानि वृक्षस्य।	Tree's fruits.
५. अन्नं अश्वानां।	Horses's food.
६. धनं रामस्य।	Rama's wealth.
७. दुःखं जीवनस्य।	Life's misery.
८. मृगस्य तृणं।	Deer's grass.
९. कृतेऽन्धनरस्य जना। गायन्ति।	For the sake of the blind man the people sing.
१०. पश्चादल्पवृकस्य। शीघ्रजलं द्रवति।	Behind the little tree swift water flows.
११. भक्तानां गुरुः	The devotees have a teacher.

१२. समक्षं नृपस्य स्तिमितजना: In the presence of the king the people are quiet.

१३. अनन्तधनं मम, I have endless wealth.

*(mama is genetive singular for personal pronoun "aham", "I". see Chapter 10.)

Exercise 8 : Sanskrit / English

1. The fire on the mountains burned down the trees.
2. The rays of the sun shine in the sky.
3. Tigers, elephants and monkeys are beasts.
4. Greed does not please the master.
5. Baby! Eat!
6. The poet summarizes from truth.
7. He notices the honest man in the master's house.
8. Death is not the enemy.
9. The sage is (intoxicated with bliss) in the forest.
10. Blades of grass grow on the mountain.
11. She left the relatives because of the quarrel.
12. The sages worship the sun.

Exercise 9 : English / Sanskrit

१. शत्रूनग्रेनृपस्य दण्डयति।

२. किमर्थं वन्यगजा जनानाक्रमन्ति।

३. कदा जिरनि गमिष्यसि।

४. समुद्रात् रामोऽन्नं भक्तेभ्योऽनयति।

५. क्षुद्रेषवो ह्रदेऽपतन्।

६. शास्त्रानि दिव्यनिधिर्भवन्ति।

७. गुरुरभितो गिरिमसीदतगायच्च।

८. कामो दु:खस्य हेतुर्भवति अलं कामेन।

९. वने जना सत्यं सुखं महातनिधीन्धिगच्छन्ति च।

१०. सुन्दरवचनैर्कवेर्बहुभक्ता: पुस्तकानि पठन्ति।

CHAPTER IX

Exercise 1 : Sanskrit / Englsih

1. I shall (set out for) go to the Ganges.
2. The girl performed the vīna for the benevolent king.
3. Because of the King and Queen, the people of the town are happy.
4. The sister grieves with the mother owing to the girl's death.
5. The Queen is not a housewife.
6. Rāma threw the flowers from the shore of the river.
7. The boy's faith (brings together) summarizes knowledge.
8. Twilight brings shade to the town.
9. The poet remembered the Queen with beautiful words.
10. The voice of the lioness is beautiful, but the voice of the jackal is not.

Exercise 2 : English / Sanskrit

१. वाण्या राज्या जना मयन्ति।

२. प्रभुर्ङ्गगा प्रतिगमिष्यति।

३. शत्रव इषून् वीरेषु क्षिपन्ति।

४. अद्य सुन्दरमाला ऋषये दास्यामि।

५. कथम् श्रद्धा सुखमानयति।

६. शर्वर्यां पशवो वने भ्राम्यन्ति।

७. सुन्दरपुष्पानि गिरिं अभितोरोहन्ति।

८. सत्यं निधिर्भक्तैः स्मृतं।

९. साधुः शुभाराग्यं सुखं संयोगं चेश्वरेन सृजति।

१०. लता माला उप वृक्षान् समया तीरम् नद्या रोहति च।

Exercise 3 : Sanskrit / Englsih

1. The mind exists and ignorance departs.
2. I turn my mind to knowledge.
3. Good conduct brings power/energy.
4. In his beak the crow carries meat for himself.
5. I take the rope in my hand.
6. He resorts to yoga of the body.
7. The cow eats the grass of the earth.
8. The two boys restrained the body at night.
9. Because of the guru's advice we two rejoice for ourselves with our bodies.
10. Devotion is satisfaction.

Exercise 4 : English / Sanskrit

१. कृष्णेन क्षणं करोमि।

२. सुन्दरशुक्लमालां पुष्पानां शीर्षं करोमि।

३. शास्त्रेषु मतिं करोमि।

४. चञ्चुर्धन्वा अश्वस्य च न वर्तते।

५. सत्यं दिव्यज्ञानं लभे।

६. गुरुं वने ग्रामं निकषा मन्त्रये।

७. काकः क्षुद्रसर्पं आक्रामति।

८. घटं पूरितं जलेन शीर्षं करोमि।

९. शक्तिं गुरोराद्रिये।

१०. क्रोदादसत्यादज्ञानाच्च निवर्तामहे।

Exercise 5 : English / Sanskrit

१a. अग्निर्वृक्षान् दहति।

१b. अनलो तरुन् दहति।

२a. वृक्षा अग्निना दह्यन्ते।

२b. तरवोऽनलेन दह्यन्ते।

३a. इन्दुराकाशं प्रकाशयति।

३b. चन्द्र आकाशं प्रकाशयति।

४a. आकाशश्चन्द्रेन प्रकाश्यते।

४b. आकाशो विधुना प्रकाश्यते।

५a. नरो नारीं भूषयति।

५b. मनुष्यो नारीं भूषयति।

६a. नारी नरेण भूष्यते।

६b. नारी मनुष्येण भूष्यते।

७a. वृक्षा ग्राममनिलाद्रक्षन्ति।

७b. द्रुमा ग्रामं वायौ रक्षन्ति

८a. ग्रामोऽनिलात् तरुभी रक्ष्यते।

८b. ग्रामो द्रुमैर्वायौ रक्ष्यते।

९a. मेघाः पर्वतानाच्छादयन्ति।

९b. मेघाः शैलानाच्छदयन्ति।।

१०a. शैला मेघैराच्छद्यन्ते।

१०b. गिरयो मेघैराच्छद्यन्ते।

११a. नृपो दासान् निन्दति।

११b. नृपतिर्दासान् निन्दति।

१२a. दासा नृपेण निन्द्यन्ते।

१२b. दासा नृपतिना निन्द्यन्ते।

१३a. नरः सत्यं ईक्षते।

१३b. मनुष्यः सत्यं ईक्षते।

१४a. सत्यं नरेण ईक्ष्यते।

१४b. सत्यं मनुष्येण ईक्ष्यते।

Exercise 6 : Sanskrit / English

1. He thinks.
2. It wanders.

3. The pupil moves.
4. We shall hide for ourselves.
5. They are satisfied for themselves.
6. He suffers.
7. They perish.
8. I show the food to him.
9. She releases for herself.
10. You two summarize.
11. I led.
12. We two eat.
13. She adorns for herself.
14. We consult ourselves.
15. It burned down.

Exercise 7 : English / Sanskrit

१. साविशत्।
२. त्वं गायसि।
३. रामो तत् तस्यै यच्छति।
४. शोकैर्तस्यै सुखं इच्छामि।
५. तदगुणयत्।
६. आवामपचावहे।
७. कन्ये अवगमिष्यतः।
८. आवां पठावः।
९. कन्ययोः पुस्तकानि।
१०. अहं घोषयिष्यामि।
११. आवां निवर्तावहे।
१२. सा रक्ष्यते।
१३. ते (तौ) पुष्येते।
१४. तदनुस्त्रियते।
१५. सर्वपुष्पानि क्षिप्यन्ते।

CHAPTER X

Exercise 1: Sanskrit / English

1. The donor proceeds for himself.
2. The sun shines forth.
3. The conqueror leaves.
4. The daughter and the mother wake up.
5. The father and the brother go.
6. The sister (she) goes to the guru (teacher).
7. The son-in-law learns salvation for himself.
8. The donor supports the people.
9. The sister-in-law bestows happiness on (to) the sister.
10. The leader falls into misfortune because of the treasure.

Exercise 2 : English / Sanskrit Contd.

१. पिता सत्यं शिक्षिष्यति।

२. रामश्च सीता जनान् भरन्ति।

३. किमर्थं भ्राता च ननांदा शत्रवो भवन्ति।

४. जेतारो ग्रामे भक्तानधिक्षिपन्ति।

५. कदा सविता मेघानति निकषा गिरीन् (प्र)काशिष्यते।

६. कार्त्तासनानि करोति।

७. सर्वदहितरो विपद्यन्ते।

८. गोपालश्च सुमातर्जनान् न विस्मरिष्यन्ति।

९. अलं वधेन।

१०. हे गोपाल शिष्या अज्ञनेन जेतुरधिक्षिप्यन्ते।

Exercise 3

१. अन्ध

a. जनैः अन्धैः = जनैरन्धैः

b. नारीषु अन्धेषु = नारीष्वन्धेषु

c. कविना अन्धेन = कविनान्धेन

d. शत्रवे अन्धाय = शत्रवेऽन्धाय

२. शुचिः

a. बालौ शुची

b. जले शुचौ

c. मती शुची

d. दुहितरः शुचयः

३. चरु

a. कुसुमं चरु

b. वारिणा चरुणा

c. बालिकया चरुणा

d. नद्यां चरुणै

४. वक्तृ

a. नृपेण वक्ता

b. मित्राभ्यां वक्तृभ्याम्

c. गृहिणी वक्तां

d. श्वश्रुणां वक्तृणाम्।

Exercise 5 : English / Sanskrit

1. May we rejoice in our asanas.
2. Mother, fondle the baby.
3. Leaders, search for salvation. Do not search for acquirement.
4. May hope be produced.
5. May visionary sight wake up the mind.
6. May the earth endure for itself.
7. Let us not foregt the jest of illusion.
8. May God bestow on us devotion.
9. May we perceive the truth.
10. May you two not suffer.

Exercise 6 : Sanskrit / English

१. दातारो धनं जनेभ्यो ग्रामस्य यच्छन्तु।

२. तद्रोहताम्।

३. जेता जनान् देशस्य मा दण्डयतु।
४. पिता दण्डं क्रोधाम्मा वहतु।
५. भ्रातरश्च स्वसारः शान्तौ जीवन्तु।
६. पापं कारणं दुःखस्य नश्यतु।
७. बाला गृहं मा त्यजत।
८. योगेन सत्यमवगच्छाव।
९. शिक्षामहै।
१०. मोहेन मा पश्यन्तु।

Exercise 7 : Sanskrit / English

1. You, eat ! (Imperative mood)
2. May that protect me. (Imperative mood)
3. May it be pure. (Imperative mood)
4. May the mother-in-law not be angry at the bride. (Potential mood)
5. May the Master advise. (Potential mood)
6. May the student get the poet's books from the housewife. (Potential mood)

Exercise 8 : English / Sanskrit

1. (Potential) चिन्तयेयः।
2. (Potential) गुरुर्तुष्येत्।
3. (Potential) यदि सर्पस्तां दशेत् त्वं म्रियेथः।
4. (Imperative) सत्यं बोधताम्।
5. (Imperative) हे कन्ये शिक्षस्व।
6. (Imperative) ईश्वराय पूजयामहै।
7. (Potential) यदि साधूवचनानि वदेत मुक्तिं लभेत।
8. (Potential) आसनानि कुर्यात।
9. (Imperative) आज्ञानमर्चतां सर्वत्र।
10. (Potential) तम्मां रक्षेत्।

CHAPTER XI

Exercise 1 : Sanskrit / English

1. Rama conquered Ravana.
2. The poet crossed over the mountain.
3. The son left the father.
4. Why didn't the mother cook the food?
5. The devotee knew the scripture.
6. The spoke to the son.
7. The horse carried the man.
8. The tiger crept in the forest.

Exercise 2 : English / Sanskrit

१. भक्तः शिष्यो बभूव।

२. आज्ञानं पिता पुत्राय तस्य ददौ।

३. सीता स्वसृभ्यो तस्योवाद।

४. नारी मृत्युं शिशोः शुशोच।

५. अश्व कासारं पपात।

६. दुहिता मातरं तस्याः शिश्राय।

७. अहं शास्त्रनि सस्मार।

८. पुत्रे मणीञ्जहार।

९. स जहास।

१०. किमर्थं जनो वृक्षान् समया गृहं ददाह।

Exercise 3 : Sanskrit / English

1. The mother, having cooked the food, spoke to the boys.
2. The student, having heard the poet, abandoned evil.
3. The son, having remembered the fathers, spoke.
4. Having eaten honey, the boy drank water.
5. Having considered, the leader served God.
6. The grandson, having consulted the brother, knew.

Exercise 4 : English / Sanskrit

१. जलं समुद्रं प्रति द्रुत्वा जगाम।

२. दुहिता लज्जां स्मृत्वा सह।

३. अन्धनरः शोचित्वा वचनानि गुरोः शुश्राव।

४. बालिका ग्रामं गत्वा साधुभ्यो जनेभ्य प्रवाद।

५. सुरभिवनं गृहं समया स्थित्वावददाह।

६. गजो जलं पीत्वा वनं प्रतिजगाम।

Exercise 5 : English / Sanskrit

1. I wish to conquer anger.
2. She learns (for herself) to meditate.
3. The mother stirs to punish the son.
4. I am pleased to read the scriptures.
5. The girl goes to the guru to breathe.
6. You should (reverently) protect me.
7. The girls are pretty.
8. The fruit is red.
9. The trees are lofty.
10. The town is dirty.
11. Kṛṣṇa is pure.
12. The beloved lotus is white.
13. When the mother leaves, you should come.
14. While I learn (for myself), (you) eat!

Exercise 6 : Sanskrit / English

१. मृगोऽन्नं खादितुमिच्छति।

२. दानान्यस्मभ्यं देष्दुं भ्राता मे गृहं विशति।

३. गीतामिच्छामः श्रोतम्।

४. व्याघ्रो धावितुमारेभे।

५. अर्हसि मां पापाद्रक्षितुम्।

६. नार्यः पृथुनगरं गन्तुमिच्छान्ति।

७. सीतां सुन्दरां बोधामि।

८. यद् वदति तत्सत्यम्।

९. अहं शत्रुनजयमिति सोऽवदत्।

१०. नार्यः प्रबलाः।

११. काशितो गिरिर्दिन्यः

१२. मित्रान्यानन्द्यः।

१३. आसनानि नीरोगानि।

१४. यदा गुरुरवदत् तदावागच्छः।

१५. यावदहमन्नमानयामि प्रतिपालयात्र।

१६. यत्र नरान् मृतान् तत्राक्रन्दाम।

१७. यथानुरागो जीवं भूषयति तथा शान्तिर्लोकं पूरयति।

१८. यतो मित्रानि तामत्यजन् ततः सा न वदति।

१९. यदि नृप आगच्छेत् तर्हि तं नमेः

२०. यद्यपि गुहायां वसामि तथापि ग्रामं स्मरामि।

Exercise 7 : Sanskṛit / Engish

1. She cooks. (present tense, active voice, 3d p.s.)
2. She cooks for herself. (present tense, middle voice, 3 p.s.)
3. Thusly, she cooks.... (present tense, active voice, 3 p.s. with particle marking end of direct speech)
4. When she srings then she will cook. (adverbial clause, present active, 3 p.s.; main clause, future tense, active voice, 3 p.s.)
5. You asked me about my wealth. (concerning wealth/of/me/you, nom. s./question, accurs. s.,/made-p.p.p. accus.s.)
6. Through her tears may the grived mother grow calm. (instrumental pl., nom. s., p.p.p. nom. s., potential mood 3d p.s.)

7. Truth is the light (lamp) of the world. (Nominal construction)
8. In yoga I am made whole. (present tense, active voice, 1 p.s.)
9. She acquires peace. (present tense, active voice, 3 p.s.)
10. It is proper to stand here. (infinitive/nominal clause)
11. Only truth conquers mortality. (middle voice, present tense)
12. Where is your book? (interrogative)

Exercise 8 : English / Sanskṛrt

1. (conjuncive nominal construction) यथा सुराभ पुष्पं तथा शुचिर्मतिः।
2. (imperfect tense, agreement of adj.) शिक्षको बहूनि नवानि वस्तुनि समक्षिपत।
3. (conj. adv. manner) यथा भये ईश्वरस्य कम्पसे तथा भक्तेरीश्वरं पूजयये:।
4. (conj, adv, condition) यदि माता नागच्छेत् शिशवः शोचेयुः।
5. (pres. act.; imperative) सुखमिच्छसि लोभान्निवर्तस्व।
6. (pres. act. 3 p.p) मेघैर्धूल्या च धेनवो तृणं न खादन्ति।
7. (double verb, 1st p.s., active) छायायां वृक्षस्य सीदामि ध्यायामि च।
8. (infinitive cluase) आसनानि शिक्षितुमिच्छामि।
9. (middle voice) नरा फलेभ्यो रोचन्ते।
10. (nominal construction) ग्रामयोरन्नं न जलं च न भवन्ति।
11. (middle voice) ह्रदे ग्रीष्मे प्लोष्ये।
12. (infinitive clause) सत्यं शान्तिमनुरागं च बोधितुं योगं शिक्षे।

VERB PARTS GLOSSARY

Root	Present Tense	Passive	Perfect	Future	Past Passive Participle	Infinitive	English
First Conjugation							
अङ्क्	अङ्क्ते	अङ्क्यते	आनङ्के	अङ्किष्यते	अङ्कित	अङ्कितुम्	to mark
अञ्च्	अञ्चति	अच्यते	आनञ्च	अञ्चिष्यति	अञ्चित	अञ्चितुम्	to worship
अट्	अटति	अट्यते	आट	अटिष्यति	अटित	अटितुम्	to roam
अय्	अयते	अय्यते	आये	अयिता			to go
परा+अय्	पलायते	पलाय्यते	पलाये	पलायिता	पलायित	पलायितुम्	to fly
अर्च्	अर्चति	अर्च्यते	आनर्च	अर्चिष्यति	अर्चित	अर्चितुम्	to worship
अर्ज्	अर्जति	अर्ज्यते	आनर्ज	अर्जिष्यति	अर्जित	अर्जितुम्	to earn
अर्ह्	अर्हति	अर्ह्यते	आनर्ह	अर्हिष्यति	अर्हित	अर्हितुम्	to deserve
अव्	अवति	अव्यते	आव	अविष्यति	अवित	अवितुम्	to protect
ईक्ष्	ईक्षते	ईक्ष्यते	ईक्षाञ्चक्रे	ईक्षिष्यते	ईक्षित	ईक्षितुम्	to see
ईर्ष्य्	ईर्ष्यति		ईर्ष्याञ्चकार	ईर्ष्यिष्यति	ईर्ष्यित	ईर्ष्यितुम्	to envy
ईह्	ईहते	ईह्यते	ईहाञ्चक्रे	ईहिष्यति	ईहित	ईहितुम्	to aim at
उष्	ओषति	उष्यते	उवोष	ओषिष्यति	उषित	ओषितुम्	to burn

Root	*Present Tense*	*Passive*	*Perfect*	*Future*	*Past Passive Participle*	*Infinitive*	*English*
First Conjugation							
ऊह्	ऊहते	ऊह्यते	ऊहाञ्चक्रे	ऊहिष्यते	ऊहित		to infer
एध्	एधते	एध्यते	एधाञ्चक्रे	एधिष्यते	एधित	एधितुम्	to grow
कण्	कणति	कण्यते	चकाण	कणिष्यति	कणित	कणितुम्	to sound
कत्थ्	कत्थते	कत्थ्यते	चकत्थे	कत्थिष्यते	कत्थित		to praise
कम्प्	कम्पते	कम्प्यते	चकम्पे	कम्पिष्यते	कम्पित	कम्पितुम्	to shake
काश्	काशते	काश्यते	चकाशे	काशिष्यते	काशित	काशितुम्	to shine
कास्	कासते	कास्यते	कासाञ्चक्रे	कासिष्यते	कासित	कासितुम्	to cough
कृष्	कर्षति	कृष्यते	चकर्ष	कर्क्ष्यति	कृष्ट	कर्ष्टुम्	to draw
				क्रक्ष्यति		क्रष्टुम्	
क्लृप्	कल्पते		चकल्पे	कल्पिष्यते	क्लृप्त	कल्पितुम्	to be fit
				कल्प्स्यते		क्लृप्तुम्	
क्रन्द्	क्रन्दति	क्रन्द्यते	चक्रन्द	क्रन्दिष्यति	क्रन्दित	क्रन्दितुम्	to cry
क्रम्	क्रमिति	क्रम्यते	चक्राम	क्रमिष्यति	क्रान्त	क्रमितुम्	to go
	क्रमते						

Root	*Present Tense*	*Passive*	*Perfect*	*Future*	*Past Passive Participle*	*Infinitive*	*English*
क्रीड्	क्रीडति	क्रीड्यते	चिक्रीड	क्रीडिष्यति	क्रीडित	क्रीडितुम्	to play
क्लश्	क्रोशति	क्लश्यते	चुक्रोश	क्रोक्ष्यति	क्रुष्ट	क्रोष्टुम्	to cry
क्षम्	क्षमते	क्षम्यते	चक्षमे	क्षमिष्यते	क्षान्त	क्षमितुम्	to bear
				क्षंस्यते		क्षन्तुम्	
क्षर्	क्षरति	क्षर्यते	चक्षार	क्षरिष्यति	क्षरित	क्षरितुम्	to flow
क्षि्	क्षयति	क्षीयते	चिक्षाय	क्षेष्यति	क्षित	क्षेतुम्	to decay
					क्षीण		
क्षीव्	क्षीवति	क्षीव्यते	चिक्षीव				to spit
क्षुम्	क्षोभते		चुक्षुमे	क्षोभिष्यते	क्षुमित		to be agitated
खन्	खनति ते	खायते	चखान	खनिष्यति	खात	खनितुम्	to dig
		खन्यते					
खाद्	खादति	खाद्यते	चखाद	खादिष्यति	खादित	खादितुम्	to eat
गद्	गदति	गद्यते	जगाद	गदिष्यति	गदित	गदितुम्	to say
गम्	गच्छति	गम्यते	जगाम	गमिष्यति	गत	गन्तुम्	to go

Root	Present Tense	Passive	Perfect	Future	Past Passive Participle	Infinitive	English
गर्ज्	गर्जति	गर्ज्यते	जगर्ज	गर्जिष्यति	गर्जित	गर्जितुम्	to roar
गर्ह्	गर्हते	गर्ह्यते	जगर्हे	गर्हिष्यते	गर्हित	गर्हितुम्	to censure
गाह्	गाहते	गाह्यते	जगाहे	गाहिष्यते	गाढ	गाहितुम्	to dive
				घाक्ष्यते		गाढुम्	
गुप्	गोपायति	गुप्यते	जुगोप	गोपिष्यति	गुप्त	गोपितुम्	to protect
						गोप्तुम्	
गुह्	गूहति ते	गुह्यते	जुगूह	गूहिष्यति	ते गूढ	गूहितुम्	to hide
			जुगूहे	घोक्ष्यति	ते	गोढुम्	
गै	गायति	गीयते	जगौ	गास्यति	गीत	गातुम्	to sing
ग्रस्	ग्रसते	ग्रस्यते	जग्रसे	ग्रसिष्यते	ग्रस्त	ग्रसितुम्	to swallow
ग्लै	ग्लायति	ग्लायते	जग्लौ	ग्लास्यति	ग्लान	ग्लातुम्	to be weary
घट्	घटते		जघते	घटिष्यते	घटित	घटितुम्	to happen
घृष्	घर्षति		जघर्ष	घर्षिष्यति	घृष्ट	घर्षितुम्	to rub
घ्रा	घघ्रति	घ्रायते	जघ्रौ	घ्रास्यति	घ्रात	घ्रातुम्	to smell
					घ्राण		

Root	*Present Tense*	*Passive*	*Perfect*	*Future*	*Past Passive Participle*	*Infinitive*	*English*
चर्	चरति	चर्यते	चचार	चरिष्यति	चरित	चरितुम्	to walk
चर्व्	चर्वति	चर्व्यते	चचर्व	चर्विष्यति	चर्वित		to chew
चल्	चलति	चल्यते	चचाल	चलिष्यति	चलित	चलितुम्	to move
चित्	चेतति	चित्यते	चिचेत	चेतिष्यति	चिता	चेतितुम्	to notice
चुम्ब्	चुम्बति	चुम्ब्यते	चुचुम्ब	चुम्बिष्यति	चुम्बित	चुम्बितुम्	to kiss
चेष्ट्	चेष्टते	चिष्ट्यटे	चिचेष्टे	चेष्टिष्यते	चेष्टित	चेष्टितुम्	to stir
च्यु	च्यवते		चुच्युवे	च्योष्यते	च्युत		to fall
च्युत्	च्योतति		चुच्योत	च्योतिष्यति	च्युतित	च्योतितुम्	to drop
जप्	जपति	जप्यते	जजाप	जपिष्यति	जपित	जपितुम्	to mutter
जल्प्	जल्पति	जल्प्यते	जजल्प	जल्पिष्यति	जल्पित	जल्पितुम्	to murmur
जि	जयति	जीयते	जिगाय	जेष्यति	जित	जेतुम्	to conquer
जीव्	जीवति	जीव्यते	जिजीव	जीविष्यति	जीवित	जीवितुम्	to live
डी	डयते	डीयते	डिड्ये	डयिष्यते	डयित डीन	डयितुम्	to fly

Root	*Present Tense*	*Passive*	*Perfect*	*Future*	*Past Passive Participle*	*Infinitive*	*English*
तक्ष्	तक्षति	तक्ष्यते	ततक्ष	तक्षिष्यति	तष्ट	तक्षितुम्	to cut
						तष्टुम्	
तप्	तपति	तप्यते	तताप	तप्स्यति	तप्त	तप्तुम्	to shine
तृ	तरति	तीर्यते	ततार	तरिष्यति	तीर्ण	तरितुम्	to cross
				तरीष्यति		तरीतुम्	
						तर्तुम्	
त्यज्	त्यजति	त्यज्यते	तत्याज	त्यक्ष्यति	त्यक्त	त्यक्तुम्	to leave
त्रप्	त्रपते		त्रेपे	त्रपिष्यते	त्रप्त	त्रपितुम्	to be ashamed
				त्रप्स्यते		त्रप्तुम्	
त्रस्	त्रसति	त्रस्यते	तत्रास	त्रसिष्यति	त्रस्त	त्रसितुम्	to fear
त्रै	त्रायति	त्रायते	तत्रे	त्रास्यते	त्रात	त्रातुम्	to protect
					त्रनण		
त्वर्	त्वरते	त्वर्यते	तत्वरे	त्वरिष्यते	त्वरित	त्वरितुम्	to hurry
					तूर्ण		

Root	Present Tense	Passive	Perfect	Future	Past Passive Participle	Infinitive	English
त्विष्	त्वेषतिते		तित्वेष तित्वेषे	त्वेक्ष्यतिते	त्विष्ट		to shine
दंश्	दशति	इश्यते	ददंश	दंक्ष्यति	दष्ट	दंष्टुम्	to bite
दय्	दयते		दयाञ्चक्रे	दयिष्यते	दयित		to pity
दल्	दलति		ददाल	दलिष्यति	दलित		to burst
दह्	दहति	दह्यते	ददाह	धक्ष्यति	दग्ध	दग्धुम्	to burn
दृश्	पश्यति	दृश्यते	ददर्श	द्रक्ष्यति	दृष्ट	द्रष्टुम्	to see
द्युत्	द्योतते	द्युत्यते	दिद्युते	द्योतिष्यते	द्युतित	द्योतितुम्	to shine
द्रु	द्रवति	द्रूयते	दुद्राव	द्रोष्यति	द्रुत	द्रोतुम्	to melt
धाव्	धावतिते	धाव्यते	दधाव दधावे	धाविष्यति ते	धावित धौत	धावितुम्	to run
धृ	धरतिते	ध्रियते	दधार दध्रे	धरिष्यति ते	धृत	धर्तुम्	to hold
ध्मा	धमति	ध्मायते	दध्मौ	ध्मास्यति	ध्मात		to blow

Root	Present Tense	Passive	Perfect	Future	Past Passive Participle	Infinitive	English
ध्यै	ध्यायति	ध्यायते	दध्यौ	ध्यास्यति	ध्यात	ध्यातुम्	to ponder
ध्वन्	ध्वनति	ध्वन्यते	दध्वान	ध्वनिष्यति	ध्वनित	ध्वनितुम्	to sound
नट्	नटति	नट्यते	ननाट	नटिष्यति	नटित	नटितुम्	to act
नन्द्	नन्दति	नन्द्यते	ननन्द	नन्दिष्यति	नन्दित	नन्दितुम्	to be pleased
नम्	नमति	नम्यते	ननाम	नंस्यति	नत	नन्तुम्	to salute
नर्द्	नर्दति	नर्द्यते	ननर्द	नर्दिष्यति	नर्दित	नर्दितुम्	to roar
निन्द्	निन्दति	निन्द्यते	निनिन्द	निन्दिष्यति	निन्दित	निन्दितुम्	to blame
नी	नयति ते	नीयते	निनाय निन्ये	नेष्यति ते	नीत	नेतुम्	to lead
पच्	पचति ते	पच्यते	पपाच पेचे	पक्ष्यति ते	पक्व	पक्तुम्	to cook
पठ्	पठति	पठ्यते	पपाठ	पठिष्यति	पठित	पठितुम्	to read
पण्	पणते	पण्यते	पेणे	पणिष्यति	पणित	पणितुम्	to bargain
पत्	पतति	पत्यते	पपात	पतिष्यति	पतित	पतितुम्	to fall

Root	*Present Tense*	*Passive*	*Perfect*	*Future*	*Past Passive Participle*	*Infinitive*	*English*
पा	पिबति	पीयते	पपौ	पास्यति	पीत	पातुम्	to drink
पुष्	पोषति	पुष्यते	पुपोष	पोषिष्यति	पुष्ट	पोषितुम्	to nourish
प्याय्	प्यायते		पिप्ये	प्यायिष्यते	प्यान	प्यायितुम्	to swell
					पीन		
प्लु	प्लवते	प्लूयते	पुप्लुवे	प्लोष्यते	प्लुत	प्लोतुम्	to float
फल्	फलति		पफाल	फलिष्यति	फलित	फलितुम्	to result
					फुल्ल		
फुल्ल्	फुल्लति		पुफुल्ल	फुल्लिष्यति	फुल्लित	फुल्लतुम्	to blossom
बाध्	बाधते	बाध्यते	बबाध	बाधिष्यते	बाधित	बाधितुम्	to oppress
बुध्	बोधति ते	बुध्यते	बुबोध	बोधिष्यति ते	बोधित	बोधितुम्	to know
			बुबुधे				
भज्	भजति ते	भज्यते	बभाज	भक्ष्यति ते	भक्त	भक्तुम्	to share
			भेजे				
भण्	भणति	भण्यते	बभ्ण	भणिष्यति	भणित	भणितुम्	to speak

Root	*Present Tense*	*Passive*	*Perfect*	*Future*	*Past Passive Participle*	*Infinitive*	*English*
भाष्	भाषते	भाष्यते	बभाषे	भाविष्यते	भाषित	भाषितुम्	to say
भास्	भासते	भास्यते	बभासे	भासिष्यते	भासित	भासितुम्	to shine
भिक्ष्	भिक्षते	भिक्ष्यते	बिभिक्षे	भिक्षिष्यते	भिक्षित	भिक्षितुम्	to beg
भू	भवति	भूयते	बभूव	भविष्यति	भूत	भवितुम्	to be
भृ	भरति ते	भ्रियते	बभार	भरिष्यति ते	भृत	भर्तुम्	to carry
			बभ्र				
भ्रंश्	भ्रंशते	भ्रश्यते	बभ्रंशे	भ्रंशिष्यति	भ्रष्ट	भ्रंशितुम्	to fall
भ्रम्	भ्रमति	भ्रम्यते	बभ्राम	भ्रमिष्यति	भ्रान्त	भ्रमितुम्	to roam
भ्राज्	भ्राजते	भ्राज्यते	बभ्राजे	भ्राजिष्यते	भ्राजित	भ्राजितुम्	to shine
मील्	मीलति		मिमील	मीलिष्यति	मीलित	मीलितुम्	to close
मुण्ड्	मुण्डति	मुणडय्ते	मुमुण्ड	मुण्डिष्यति	मुण्डित	मुण्डितुम्	to shave
मुद्	मोदते	मुद्यते	मुमुदे	मोदिष्यते	मुदित	मोदितुम्	to rejoice
मृष्	मर्षति	मृष्यते	ममर्ष	मरिष्यति	मृष्ट	मर्षितुम्	to sprinkle
				म्रक्ष्यति			
				मर्क्ष्यति			

Root	*Present Tense*	*Passive*	*Perfect*	*Future*	*Past Passive Participle*	*Infinitive*	*English*
म्ना	मनति	म्नायते	मम्नौ	म्नास्यति	म्नात	म्नातुम्	to think
यज्	यजति ते	इज्यते	इयाज	यक्ष्यति ते	इष्ट	यष्टुम्	to sacrifice
			ईजे				
यत्	यतते	यत्यते	येते	यातिष्यते	यत	यतितुम्	to attempt
यम्	यच्छति		ययाम	यंस्यति	यत	यन्तुम्	to check
याच्	याचति ते	याच्यते	ययाच	याचिष्यति ते	याचित	याचितुम्	to beg
			ययाचे				
रक्ष्	रक्षति	रक्ष्यते	ररक्ष	रक्षिष्यति	रक्षित	रक्षितुम्	to protect
रञ्ज्	रजति ते	रज्यते	ररञ्ज	रंक्ष्यति ते	रक्त	रंक्तुम्	to be coloured
			ररञ्जे				
रम्	रमते	रम्यते	रेमे	रंस्यते	रत	रन्तुम्	to sport
राज्	राजति ते	राज्यते	रराज	राजिष्यति ते	राजित	राजितुम्	to shine
			रराजे				
			रेजे				

Root	Present Tense	Passive	Perfect	Future	Past Passive Participle	Infinitive	English
रुच्	रोचते	रुच्यते	रुरुचे	रोचिष्यते	रुचित	रोचितुम्	to be pleased
रुह्	रोहति	रुह्यते	रुरोह	रोक्ष्यति	रुढ	रोढुम्	to grow
लङ्घ्	लङ्घति ते		ललङ्घ ललङ्घे	लङ्घिष्यति ते	लङ्घित	लङ्घितुम्	to leap
लप्	लपति	लप्यते	ललाप	लपिष्यति	लपित	लपितुम्	to talk
लभ्	लभते	लभ्यते	लेभे	लप्स्यते	लब्ध	लब्धुम्	to get
लष्	लषति ते	लष्यते	ललाष लेषे	लषिष्यति ते	लषित	लषितुम्	to long for
लस्	लसति	लस्यते	ललास	लसिष्यति	लसित	लसितुम्	to shine
लस्ज्	लज्जते	लज्यते	ललज्जे	लज्जिष्यते	लज्जित	लज्जितुम्	to be ashamed
वद्	वदति	उद्यते	उवाद	वदिष्यति	उदित	वदितुम्	to tell
वन्द्	वन्दते	वन्द्यते	ववन्दे	वन्दिष्यते	वन्दित	वन्दितुम्	to salute
वप्	वपति ते	उप्यते	उवाप ऊपे	वप्स्यति ते	उप्त	वप्तुम्	to sow

Root	*Present Tense*	*Passive*	*Perfect*	*Future*	*Past Passive Participle*	*Infinitive*	*English*
वम्	वमति	वम्यते	ववाम	वमिष्यति	वान्त	वमितुम्	to vomit
वस्	वसति	उष्यते	उवास	वत्स्यति	उषित	वस्तुम्	to dwell
वह्	वहति ते	उह्यते	उवाह	वक्ष्यति ते	ऊढ	वोढुम्	to carry
			ऊहे				
वाञ्छ्	वाञ्छति	वाञ्छ्यते	ववाञ्छ	वाञ्छिष्यति	वाञ्छित	वाञ्छितुम्	to wish
वृत्	वर्तते	वृत्यते	ववृते	वर्त्स्यति	वृत्त	वर्तितुम्	to exist
				वर्तिष्यते			
वृध्	वर्धते	वृध्यते	ववृधे	वर्त्स्यति	वृद्ध	वर्धितुम्	to grow
				वर्धिष्यते			
वृष्	वर्षति	वृष्यते	ववर्ष	वर्षिष्यति	वृष्ट	वर्षितुम्	to rain
वे	वयति ते	ऊयते	उवाय	वास्यति ते	ऊत	वातुम्	to weave
			ऊये				
			ऊवे				
वेप्	वेपते	वेप्यते	विवेधे	वेपिष्यते	वेपित	वेपितुम्	to tremble

Root	*Present Tense*	*Passive*	*Perfect*	*Future*	*Past Passive Participle*	*Infinitive*	*English*
वेष्ट्	वेष्टते	वेष्ट्यते	विवेष्टे	वेष्टिष्यते	वेष्टित	वेष्टुिम्	to surround
व्यथ्	व्यथते	व्यथ्यते	विव्यथे	व्यथिष्यते	व्यथित	व्यथितुम्	to suffer
व्रज्	व्रजति	व्रज्यते	वव्राज	व्रजिष्यति	व्रजित	व्रजितुम्	to go
शंस	शंसति	शंस्यते	शशंस	शंसिष्यति	शस्त	शंसितुम्	to praise
शङ्क्	शङ्कते	शङ्केयते	शशङ्के	शङिकष्यते	शङि्क्त	शङि्तुम्	to doubt
शप्	शपति ते	शप्यते	शशाप शेपे	शप्स्यति ते	शप्त	शप्तुम्	to curse
शम्	शमति	शम्यते	शशाम	शमिष्यति	शान्त	शमितुम्	to grow calm
शिक्ष्	शिक्षते	शिक्ष्यते	शिशिक्षे	शिक्षिष्यते	शिक्षित	शिक्षितुम्	to learn
शुच्	शोचति	शुच्यते	शुशोच	शोचिष्यति	शुचित शोचित	शोचितुम्	to grieve
शुभ्	शोभते		शुशुभे	शोभिष्यते	शोभित	शोभितुम्	to shine
श्चुत्	श्चोतति	श्चुत्यते	चुश्चोत	श्चोतिष्यति	श्चुतित श्चोतित	श्चुतितुम्	to ooze

Root	*Present Tense*	*Passive*	*Perfect*	*Future*	*Past Passive Participle*	*Infinitive*	*English*
श्रि	श्रयति ते	श्रीयते	शिश्राय शिश्रिये	श्रयिष्यति ते	श्रित	श्रयितुम्	to reach
ष्ठिव्	ष्ठीवति		तिष्ठेव टिष्ठेव	ष्ठेविष्यति	ष्ठ्यूत	ष्ठेवितुम्	to spit
सञ्ज्	सजति	सज्यते	ससञ्ज	सङ्क्ष्यति	सक्त	सङ्क्तुम्	to cling
सद्	सीदति	सद्यते	ससाद	सत्स्यति	सन्न	सत्तुम्	to sit
सस्ज्	सज्जति ते	सज्यते	ससज्ज ससज्जे	सज्जिष्यति ते	सज्जित	सज्जितुम्	to get ready
सह्	सहते	सह्यते	सेहे	सहिष्यते	सोढ	सहितुम् सोढुम्	to bear
सिध्	सेधति	सिध्यते	सिसेध	सेधिष्यति	सिद्ध	सेधितुम्	to go
सूद	सूदते	सूद्यते	सुषूदे	सूदिष्यते		सूदितुम्	to strike
सृ	सरति	स्त्रियते	ससार	सरिष्यति	सृत	सर्तुम्	to go
सृप्	सर्पति	सृप्यते	समर्प	स्त्रप्स्यति सप्स्यति	सृप्त	सर्प्तुम्	to creep

Root	*Present Tense*	*Passive*	*Perfect*	*Future*	*Past Passive Participle*	*Infinitive*	*English*
सेव्	सेवते	सेव्यते	सिषेवे	सेविष्यते	सेवित	सेवितुम्	to serve
स्खल्	स्खलति	स्खल्यते	चस्खाल	स्खलिष्यति	स्खलित	स्खलितुम्	to stumble
स्था	तिष्ठति	स्थीयते	तस्थौ	स्थाष्यति	स्थित	स्थातुम्	to stand
स्पन्द्	स्पन्दते	स्पन्द्यते	पस्पन्दे	स्पन्दिष्यते	स्पन्दित	स्पन्दितुम्	to throb
स्पर्ध्	स्पर्धते	स्पर्ध्यते	पस्पर्धे	स्पर्धिष्यते	स्पर्धित	स्पर्धितुम्	to challenge
स्फुट्	स्फोटते		पुस्फुटे	स्फोटिष्यते	स्फुटित	स्फुटितुम्	to burst
स्मि्	स्मयते	स्मीयते	सिष्मिये	स्मेष्यते	स्मित	स्मितुम्	to smile
स्मृ	स्मरति	स्मर्यते	सस्मार	स्मरिष्यति	स्मृत	स्मर्तुम्	to remember
स्यन्द्	स्यन्दते		सस्यन्दे	स्यन्दिष्यते	स्यन्न	स्यन्दितुम्	to flow
स्रंस्	स्रंसते	स्रस्यते	सस्रंसे	स्रंसिष्यते	स्रस्त	स्रंसितुम्	to fall
स्रु	स्रवति		सुस्राव	स्रोष्यति	स्रुत		to flow
स्वञ्ज्	स्वजते	स्वज्यते	सस्वजे सस्वञ्जे	स्वङक्ष्यते	स्वक्त	स्वङक्तुम्	to embrace
स्वन्	स्वनति		सस्वान	स्वनिष्यति	स्वनित	स्वनितुम्	to sound

Root	*Present Tense*	*Passive*	*Perfect*	*Future*	*Past Passive Participle*	*Infinitive*	*English*
स्वाद्	स्वादते	स्वाद्यते	सस्वादे	स्वादिष्यते	स्वादित -	स्वादितुम्	to taste
स्विद्	स्वेदते	स्विद्यते	सिष्विदे	स्वेत्स्यते	स्विदित स्विन्न	स्वेदितुम्	to perspire
हस्	हसति	हस्यते	जहास	हसिष्यति	हसित	हसितुम्	to laugh
हृ	हरति ते	ह्रियते	जहार जह्रे	हरिष्यति ते	हसित	हसितुम्	to take
ह्वे	ह्वयति ते	हूयते	जुहाव जुहुवे	ह्वास्यति	हूत	ह्वातुम्	to call
Fourth Conjugation							
अण्	अण्यति	अण्यते	अणे	अणिष्यते	अणित	अणितुम्	to breathe
अस्	अस्यति	अस्यते	आस	असिष्यति	अस्त	असितुम्	to throw
इष्	इष्यति	इष्यते .	इयेष	एषिष्यति	इष्ट	एषितुम्	to go
ऋध्	ऋध्यति	ऋध्यते	आनर्ध	अर्धिष्यति	ऋद्ध	अर्धितुम्	to prosper
कुप्	कुप्यति	कुप्यते	चुकोप	कोपष्यिति	कुपित	कोपितुम्	to angry

Root	Present Tense	Passive	Perfect	Future	Past Passive Participle	Infinitive	English
कृश्	कृश्यति		चकर्श	कर्शिष्यति	कृष्ट	कर्शितुम्	to become
क्रुध्	क्रुध्यति	क्रुध्यते	चुक्रोध	क्रोत्स्यति	क्रुद्ध	क्रोद्धुम्	to be angry
क्लम्	क्लाम्यति	क्लाम्यते	चक्लाम	क्लमिष्यति	क्लान्त	क्लामितुम्	to be tired
क्लिद्	क्लिद्यति	क्लिद्यते	चिक्लेद	क्लेदिष्यति क्लेत्स्यति	क्लिन्न	क्लेदितुम् क्लेत्तुम्	to become wet
क्लिश्	क्लिश्यति	क्लिश्यते	चिक्लिशे	क्लेशिष्यते	क्लिष्ट क्लिशित		to be afflicted
क्षम्	क्षाम्यति	क्षाम्यते	चक्षाम	क्षमिष्यति क्षंस्यति	क्षान्त	क्षमितुम् क्षन्तुम्	to bear
क्षुध्	क्षुध्यति	क्षुध्यते	चुक्षोध	क्षोत्स्यति	क्षुधित क्षुब्ध	क्षोधितुम्	to be hungry
खिद्	खिद्यते		चिखिदे	खेत्स्यते	खिन्न	खेत्तुम्	to suffer pain
जन्	जायते	जन्यते	जज्ञे	जनिष्यते	जात	जनितुम्	to be born
जॄ	जीर्यति	जीर्यते	जजार	जरिष्यति जरीष्यति	जीर्ण	जरितुम्	to grow old

Root	*Present Tense*	*Passive*	*Perfect*	*Future*	*Past Passive Participle*	*Infinitive*	*English*
डी	डीयते		डिड्ये	डयिष्यते	डयित	डयितुम्	to fly
					डीन		
तप्	तप्यते		तेपे	तप्स्यते	तप्त		to heat
तुष्	तुष्यति	तुष्यते	तुतोष	तोक्ष्यति	तुष्ट	तोष्टुम्	to be pleased
तृप्	तृप्यति	तृप्यते	ततर्प	तर्पिष्यति	तृप्त	तर्पितुम्	to be satisfied
				तप्र्स्यति		तर्प्तुम्	
				त्रप्स्यति			
तृष्	तृष्यति		ततर्ष	तर्षिष्यति	तृषित	तर्षितुम्	to be thirsty
त्रस्	त्रस्यति	त्रस्यते	तत्रास	त्रसिष्यति	त्रस्त	त्रसितुम्	to tremble
त्रुट्	त्रुट्यति	त्रुट्यते	तुत्रोट	त्रुटिष्यति	त्रुटित	त्रोटितुम्	to break
दम्	दाम्यति	दम्यते	ददाम	दमिष्यति	दान्त	दमितुम्	to be tamed
दिव्	दीव्यति	दीव्यते	दिदेव	देविष्यति	द्युत	देवितुम्	to play
दीप्	दीप्यते		दिदीपे	दीपिष्यते	दीप्त	दीपितुम्	to shine
दुष्	दुष्यति	दुष्यते	ददोष	दोक्ष्यति	दुष्ट	दोष्तुम्	to be wrong

Root	Present Tense	Passive	Perfect	Future	Past Passive Participle	Infinitive	English
दू	दूयते		दुदुवे	दविष्यते	दूत		to suffer
दृप्	दृप्यति	दृप्यते	ददर्प	दर्पिष्यति	दृप्त	दर्पितुम्	to be glad
द्रुह्	द्रुह्यति	द्रुह्यते	दद्रोह	द्रोहिष्यति	द्रुग्ध	द्रोहितुम	to hate
				ध्रौक्ष्यति	द्रुढ	द्रोग्घुम्	
						द्रोढूम्	
नश्	नश्यति	नश्यते	ननाश	नशिष्यति	नष्ट	नशितुम्	to perish
				नक्ष्यति		नंष्टुम्	
नह्	नह्यति ते	नह्यते	ननाह	नत्स्यति ते	नद्ध	नद्धुम्	to bind
			नेहे				
नृत्	नृत्यति	नृत्यते	ननर्त	नर्तिष्यति	नृत्त	नर्तितुम्	to dance
				नर्त्स्यति			
पद्	पद्यते		पेदे	पत्स्यते	पन्न	पत्तुम्	to go
पुष्	पुष्यति	पुष्यते	पुपोष	पोषिष्यति	पुषित	पोषितुम्	to nourish
				पोक्ष्यति	पुष्ट		

Root	Present Tense	Passive	Perfect	Future	Past Passive Participle	Infinitive	English
प्री	प्रीयते		पिप्रिये	प्रेष्यते	प्रीत	प्रेतुम्	to feel affection
बुध्	बुध्यते		बुबुधे	भोत्स्यते	बुद्ध	बोद्धुम्	to know
भ्रंश्	भ्रश्यति	भ्रश्यते	बभ्रंश	भ्रंशिष्यति	भ्रष्ट	भ्रंशितुम्	to fall
भ्रम्	भ्राम्यति	भ्रम्यते	बभ्राम	भ्रमिष्यति	भ्रान्त	भ्रमितुम्	to roam
मद्	माद्यति	मद्यते	ममाद	मदिष्यति	मत्त	मदितुम्	to be glad
मन्	मन्यते		मेने	मंस्यते	मन	मन्तुम्	to think
मुह्	मुह्यति	मुह्यते	मुमोह	मोहिष्यति	मुग्ध	मोहितुम्	to faint
				मोक्ष्यति	मूढ	मोग्धुम्	
						मोढुम्	
युज्	युज्यते		युयुजे	योक्ष्यते			to concentrate
युध्	युध्यते		युयुधे	योत्स्यते	युद्ध	योद्धुम्	to fight
राध्	राध्यति	राध्यते	रराध	रात्स्यति	राद्ध	राद्धुम्	to grow
रुष्	रुष्यति	रुष्यते	रुरोष	रोषिष्यति	रुष्ट	रोषितुम्	to be angry
				रोक्ष्यति			
लष्	लष्यति ते	लष्यते	ललाष	लषिष्यति	लषित	लषितुम्	to wish
			लेषे				

Root	*Present Tense*	*Passive*	*Perfect*	*Future*	*Past Passive Participle*	*Infinitive*	*English*
ली	लीयते		लिल्ये	लेष्यते लास्यते	लीन	लेतुम् लातुम्	to stick
लुट्	लुट्यति	लुट्यते	लुलोट	लोटिष्यति	लुटित	लोटितुम्	to roll
लुभ्	लुभ्यति	लुभ्यते	लुलोभ	लोभिष्यति लोप्स्यति	लुब्ध	लोब्धुम्	to covet
विद्	विद्यते		विविदे	वेत्स्यते	वित्त	वेत्तुम्	to be
व्यध्	विध्यति	विध्यते	विव्याध	व्यत्स्यति	विद्ध	व्यद्धुम्	to pierce
शप्	शप्यति ते	शप्यते	शशाप शेपे	शप्स्यति ते	शप्त	शप्तुम्	to curse
शम्	शाम्यति	शम्यते	शशाम	शमिष्यति	शान्त	शमितुम्	to grow calm
शुध्	शुध्यति	शुध्यते	शुशोध	शोत्स्यति	शुद्ध		to be pure
शुष्	शुष्यति	शुष्यते	शुशोष	शोक्ष्यति	शुष्क	शोष्टुम्	to be dried
शो	श्यति	शायते	शशौ	शास्यति	शात शित		to sharpen

Root	*Present Tense*	*Passive*	*Perfect*	*Future*	*Past Passive Participle*	*Infinitive*	*English*
श्रम्	श्राम्यति	श्रम्यते	शश्राम	श्रमिष्यति	श्रान्त	श्रमितुम्	to be tired
सिध्	सिध्यति	सिध्यते	सिसेध	सेत्स्यति	सिद्ध	सेधितुम्	to reach
सिव्	सीव्यति	सीव्यते	सिषेव	सेविष्यति	स्यत	सेवितुम्	to sew
सो	स्यति	सीयते	ससौ	सास्यति	सित	सातुम्	to destroy
स्निह्	स्निह्यति	स्निह्यते	सिष्णेह	स्नेहिष्यति	स्निग्ध	स्नेग्धुम्	to feel affection
				स्नेक्ष्यति			
स्विद्	स्विद्यति	स्विद्येते	सिष्वेद	स्वेत्स्यति	स्विदित		to sweat
					स्विन्न		
Tenth Conjugation							
इष्	इच्छति	इष्यते	इयेष	एषिष्यति	इष्ट	एषितुम्	to wish
उञ्छ्	उञ्छति		उञ्छाञ्चकार	उञ्छिष्यति	उञ्छित		to glean
कृत्	कृन्तति	कृत्यते	चकर्त	कर्तिष्यति	कृत्त	कर्तितुम्	to cut
कृष्	कृषति ते	कृष्यते	चकर्ष	कर्क्ष्यति ते	कृष्ट	क्रष्टुम्	to plough
				क्रक्ष्यति ते		कर्ष्टुम्	

Root	*Present Tense*	*Passive*	*Perfect*	*Future*	*Past Passive Participle*	*Infinitive*	*English*
कृ	किरति	कीर्यते	चकार	करिष्यति	क्रीर्ण	करितुम्	
				करीष्यति		करीतुम्	
क्षिप्	क्षिपति ते	क्षिप्यते	चिक्षेप	क्षेप्स्यति ते	क्षिप्त	क्षेप्तुम्	to throw
			चिक्षिपे				
गृ	गिरति	गीर्यते	जगार	गरिष्यति	गीर्ण	गरितुम्	to devour,
				गरीष्यति			swallow
जुष्	जुषते	जुष्यते	जुजुषे	जीविष्यते	जुष्ट		to like
तुद्	तुदति ते	तुद्यते	तुतोद	तोत्स्यति ते	तुन्न	तोदितुम्	to strike
			तुतुदे				
तृह्	तृहति	तृह्यते	ततर्ह	तर्हिष्यति	तृढ	तर्हितुम्	to kill
				तर्क्ष्यति			
त्रुट्	त्रुटति	त्रुट्यते	तुत्रोट	त्रुटिष्यति	त्रुटित	त्रोटितुम्	to tear
दिश्	दिशति ते	दिश्यते	दिदेश	देक्ष्यति ते	दिष्ट	देष्टुम्	to show
			दिदिशे				

Root	*Present Tense*	*Passive*	*Perfect*	*Future*	*Past Passive Participle*	*Infinitive*	*English*
आदृ	आदृियते		आदद्रे	आदरिष्यते	आदृत	आदर्तुम्	to honour
नुद्	नुदति ते	नुद्यते	नुनोद	नोत्स्यति ते	नुत्त		to impel
			नुनुदे		नुन्न	नोदितुम्	
वि आ पृ	व्याप्रियते		व्यापप्रे	व्यापरिष्यते	व्यापृत		to be engaged
प्रच्छ्	पृच्छति	पृच्छ्यते	पप्रच्छ	प्रक्ष्यति	पृष्ट	प्रष्टुम्	to ask
भ्रस्ज्	भृज्जतिते	भृज्जयते	बभर्ज	भर्क्ष्यति ते	भ्रष्ट	भर्ष्टुम्	to fry
			बभ्रज्ज	भ्रक्ष्यति ते		भ्रष्टुम्	
			बभर्जे				
			बभ्रज्जे				
मस्ज्	मज्जति	मज्ज्यते	ममज्ज	मङ्क्ष्यति	मग्न	मङ्क्तुम्	to sink
मिल्	मिलति ते	मिल्यते	मिमेल	मेलिष्यति	मिलित	मेलितुम्	to join
			मिमिले				
मुच्	मुञ्चति ते	मुच्यते	मुमोच	मोक्ष्यति ते	मुक्त	मोक्तुम्	to release
			मुमुचे				

Root	*Present Tense*	*Passive*	*Perfect*	*Future*	*Past Passive Participle*	*Infinitive*	*English*
मृ	म्रियते		ममार	मरिष्यति	मृत	मर्तुम्	to die
मृश्	मृशति	मृश्यते	ममर्श	मर्क्ष्यति	मृष्ट	मर्ष्टुम्	to consider
				म्रक्ष्यति		म्रष्टुम्	
लिख्	लिखति	लिख्यते	लिलेख	लेखिष्यति	लिखित	लेखितुम्	to write
लिप्	लिम्पति ते	लिप्यते	लिलेप	लेप्स्यति ते	लिप्त	लेप्तुम्	to anoint
			लिलिपे				
लुप्	लुम्पति ते	लुप्यते	लुलोप	लोप्स्यति ते	लुप्त	लोप्तुम्	to break
			लुलुपे				
विद्	विन्दति ते	विद्यते	विवेद	वेदिष्यति ते	वित्त	वेदितुम्	to gain, get
			विविदे		विदित	वेत्तुम्	
विश्	विशति	विश्यते	विवेश	वेक्ष्यति	विष्ट	वेष्टुम्	to enter
सिच्	सिञ्चति ते	सिच्यते	सिषेच	सेक्ष्यति ते	सिक्त	सेक्तुम्	to sprinkle
			सिषिचे				
सृज्	सृजति	सृज्यते	ससर्ज	स्रक्ष्यति	सृष्ट	स्रष्टुम्	to create

Root	Present Tense	Passive	Perfect	Future	Past Passive Participle	Infinitive	English
स्पृश्	स्पृशति	स्पृश्यते	पस्पर्श	स्प्रक्ष्यति	स्पृष्ट	स्प्रष्टुम्	to touch
				स्पर्क्ष्यति		स्पर्ष्टुम्	
स्फुर्	स्फुरति		पुस्फोर	स्फुरिष्यति	स्फुरित		to throb
Tenth Conjugation							
अर्थ्	अर्थयते	अर्थ्यते	अर्थयाञ्चक्रे	अर्थयिष्यते	अर्थित	अर्थयितुम्	to request
अंश्	अंशयति		अंशयामास	अंशयिष्यति			to divide
ईर्	ईरयति ते	ईर्यते	ईरयाञ्चकारचक्रे		ईरयिष्यति ते	ईरित	to move
कथ्	कथयति	कथ्यते	कथयामास	कथयिष्यति	कथित	कथयितुम्	to tell
कर्ण्	कर्णयति	कर्ण्यते	कर्णयामास	कर्णयिष्यति	कर्णित	कर्णयितुम्	to pierce
क्षप्	क्षपयति	क्षप्यते	क्षपयामास	क्षपयिष्यति	क्षपित	क्षपयितुम्	to send
क्षल्	क्षालयति	क्षाल्यते	क्षालयामास	क्षालयिष्यति	क्षालित	क्षालयितुम्	to wash
गण्	गणयति	गुण्यते	गणयामास	गणयिष्यति	गणित	गणयितुम्	to count
गुण्	गुणयति	गण्यते	गुणयामास	गुणयिष्यति	गुणित	गुणयितुम्	to multiply

Root	*Present Tense*	*Passive*	*Perfect*	*Future*	*Past Passive Participle*	*Infinitive*	*English*
घुष्	घोषयति	घोष्यते	घोषयामास	घोषयिष्यति	घुषित		to proclaim
चिन्त्	चिन्तयति ते	चिन्त्यते	चिन्तयामास	चिन्तयिष्यति ते	चिन्तित	चिन्तयितुम्	to think
चुद्	चोदयति ते	चोद्यते	चोदयामास	चोदयिष्यति ते	चोदित		to direct
चुर्	चोरयति ते	चोर्यते	चोरयामास	चोरयिष्यति ते	चोरित	चोरयितुम्	to steal
चूर्ण्	चूर्णयति	चूर्ण्यते	चूर्णयामास	चूर्णयिष्यति ते	चूर्णित		to crush
छद्	छादयति ते	छायते	छादयामास	छादयिष्यति ते	छादित	छादयितुम्	to cover
तड्	ताडयति	ताड्यते	ताडयामास	ताडयिष्यति	ताडित	ताडयितुम्	to beat
तर्क्	तर्कयति	तर्क्यते	तर्कयामास	तर्कयिष्यति	तर्कित	तर्कयितुम्	to guess
तर्ज्	तर्जयते	तर्ज्यते	तर्जयाञ्चक्रे	तर्जयिष्यते	तर्जित	तर्जयितुम्	to threaten
तुल्	तोलयति	तोल्यते	तोलयामास	तोलयिष्यति	तोलित	तोलयितुम्	to weigh
दण्ड्	दण्डयति	दण्ड्यते	दण्डयामास	दण्डयिष्यति	दण्डित	दण्डयितुम्	to punish
पाल्	पालयति	पाल्यते	पालयामास	पालयिष्यति	पालित	पालयितुम्	to protect
पीड्	पीडयति	पीड्यते	पीडयामास	पीडयिष्यति	पीडित	पीडयितुम्	to hurt
पूज्	पूजयति	पूज्यते	पूजयामास	पूजयिष्यति	पूजित	पूजयितुम्	to adore

Root	Present Tense	Passive	Perfect	Future	Past Passive Participle	Infinitive	English
पूर्	पूरयति	पूर्यते	पूरयामास	पूरयिष्यति	पूरित	पूरयितुम्	to fill
भक्ष्	भक्षयति	भक्ष्यते	भक्षयामास	भक्षयिष्यति	भक्षित	भक्षयितुम्	to eat
भर्त्स्	भर्त्सयते	भर्त्स्यते	भर्त्सयाञ्चक्रे	भर्त्सयिष्यति	भर्त्सत	भर्त्सियितुम्	to threaten
भूष्	भूषयति ते	भूष्यते	भूषयामास	भूषयिष्यति ते	भूषित	भूषयितुम्	to adorn
मण्ड्	मण्डयति	मण्ड्यते	मण्डयामास	मण्डयिष्यति	मण्डित	मण्डयितुम्	to adorn
मन्त्र्	मन्त्रयते	मन्त्र्यते	मन्त्रयाञ्चक्रे	मन्त्रयिष्यते	मन्त्रित	मन्त्रयितुम्	to consult
मान्	मानयति ते	मान्यते	मानयामास	मानयिष्यति ते	मानित	मानयितुम्	to respect
मार्ग्	मार्गयति	मार्ग्यते	मार्गयामास	मार्गयिष्यति	मार्गित	मार्गयितुम्	to seek
मार्ज्	मार्जयति	मार्ज्यते	मार्जयामास	मार्जयिष्यति	मार्जित	मार्जयितुम्	to wipe
मिश्र्	मिश्रयति	मिश्र्यते	मिश्रयामास	मिश्रयिष्यति	मिश्रित	मिश्रयितुम्	to mix
मृग्	मृगयते	मृग्यते	मृगयाञ्चक्रे	मृगयिष्यते			to hunt
रच्	रचयति	रच्यते	रचयामास	रचयिष्यति	रचित	रचयितुम्	to arrange
रूप्	रूपयति ते	रूप्यते	रूपयामास	रूपयिष्यति ते	रूपित	रूपयितुम्	to consider
लक्ष्	लक्षयति ते	लक्ष्यते	लक्षयामास	लक्षयिष्यति ते	लक्षित	लक्षयितुम्	to define

Root	*Present Tense*	*Passive*	*Perfect*	*Future*	*Past Passive Participle*	*Infinitive*	*English*
लोक्	लोकयति ते	लोक्यते	लोकयामास	लोकयिष्यति ते	लोकित	लोकयितुम्	to see
लोच्	लोचयति ते	लोच्यते	लोचयामास	लोचयिष्यति ते	लोचित	लोचयितुम्	to see
वञ्च्	वञ्चयते	वञ्चयते	वञ्चयामास	वञ्चयिष्यति ते	वञ्चित	वञ्चयितुम्	to cheat
सान्त्व्	सान्त्वयति	सान्त्वयते	सान्त्वयामास	सान्त्वयिष्यति	सान्त्वित	सान्त्वयितुम्	to soothe
सूच्	सूचयति	सूच्यते	सूचयामास	सूचयिष्यति	सूचित	सूचयितुम्	to pierce
स्पृह्	स्पृह्यति	स्पृह्यते	स्पृह्ययामास	स्पृह्यिष्यति	स्पृहित	स्पृह्यितुम्	to desire

BIBLIOGRAPHY

Monier—Williams, The Sanskrit Language,1962, Chowkhamba Series XXI, Varanasi, India.

——A Sanskrit—English Dictionary, Oxford University Press

R. G. Bhandarkar, The First and Second Book of Sanskrit 36th ed. 1971, Karnatak Publishing House, Bombay.

W. D. Whitney, A Sanskrit Grammar, 1961 edition, Motilal Banarsidas, Delhi—6.

A. A. Macdonell, A Sanskrit Grammar for Students 3rd. edition, Oxford University Press.

——A Vedic Reader for Students, Oxford Univ. Press. Madras.

J. Gonda, A Concise Elementery Grammar for the Sanskrit Language 1966, University of Alabama Press, U.S.A.

E. D. Perry A Sanskrit Primer, 9th edition 1965, Columbia Unvi. Press, N. Y.

V. K. L. Sastri & L. A Sastri, Dhatarupa—Manjari, 1970 edition R. S. Vadhyar & Sons, Kalpathi, South India.

R. Antoine, Volume I & II, A Sanskrit Manual, 6th edition Xavier Publications, Calcutta.

M. R. Kale A Higher Sanskrit Grammar, 1969 Motilal Banarsidass, Delhi—6.

H. H. Wilson Sanskrit Language and Introduction to Grammar Chowkhamba Sanskrit Series XI, Varanasi—1.

J. M. Tyberg, First Lesson in Sanskrit Grammar and Reading Ist. edition 1964, Aurobino Ashram, Pondicherry, India.

M. Coulson Introduction to the Classical Language of Sanskrit 1976, University Press, Oxford, England.

G. Mukhopadhyaya & G. Bhattacarya, A Trilingual Dictionary 1976, Sanskrit College, Calcutta.

C. R. Lanman, A Sanskrit Reader for Students, 1952 Harvard University Press, Cambridge, Mass. U.S.A.

J. Beames, A Comparative Grammar of Modern Aryan Languages of India, 1970 Munshiram Manoharlal, New Delhi.

R. N. Safaya The Teaching of Sanskrit, 1962 Punjab Kotab Ghar, Mai Hiran Gate, Jullundur.

S. K. Belvakkar Systems of Sanskrit Grammar, 1976 Bharatiya Vidya Prakashan, Delhi—7, India.

S. Varma Vakyapadiyam of Sri Bhartrihari, 1970, Munshiran Manoharlal, New Delhi, India.

Paul Brunton, Indic Philosophy and Modern Culture 1939, E.P. Dutton & Co., New York.

Satischandra Chatterjee, The Fundamentals of Hinduism 1950, Das Gupta & Co. Ltd., Calcutta.

Frederick Max Mueller, The Six Systems of Indic Philosophy 1928, Longmans, Green & Co., New York.

Sarvepalli Radhakrishnan, et. al., History of East & West Philosophy 1953, 2 volumes, George Allen & Unwin Ltd. London.

——The Priciple Upanishads, revised edition 1935 George Allen & Unwin Ltd. London

——The Bhagavad Gita, 1967, G. Allen & Unwin Ltd., London

——The Principle Upaniṣads, G. Allen & Wnwin Ltd., London 1935.

——Eastern Religion & Western Thought, Clarendon Press, Oxford.

Prabhu Dutt Shastri, The Essentials of Eastern Philosophy, 1928 Macmillan Co., New York.

Henrich Zimmer & Joseph Cambell, Philosophies of India Bollingen Series XXVI, 1951, Pantheon Books, New York.

T,M,P,Mahadevan, Selections from 108 Upaniṣdas with English Translations, G.A. Natesan & Co. Madras

Annie Besant, A Introduction to Yoga 1920, Theosophical Publishing House, Madras.

Alain Danielou, The Method of Re—Integration of Yoga 1949, Christopher Johnson, London.

Ernest Wood, Great Systems of Yoga 1954, Philosophical Library Publications, New York.

Dr. Shakuntala Rao Sastri, The Bhagavad Gita, 1971, Bharatiya Vidya Bhavan, Bombay.

Alain Danielou, Hindu Polytheism, 1964, Bollingen Foundation LXXIII, New York.

I. K. Taimini, The Science of Yoga (Patanjali Sutras) 1961, Theosophical Publishing House, Adyar, India.

R. S. Kelkar The Life of A Yogi, 1973, 112 Rabindra Nagar, New Delhi—3.

A. A. Macdonell India's Past, 1927, Clarendon Press, Oxford

Swami Sivananda, The Bhagavad Gita, 1957, Rishikesh-Calcutta 1.

——All About Hinduism, 1956, Rishikesh—Calcutta 1.

A. A. Macdonell, A History of Sanskrit Literature 1961, Munshi Ram Manohar Lal, Delhi-6.

Ernest Wood, Yoga Wisdom, 1970, Philosophical Library, Yew York.

——Mind and Memory Training, 1961, Philosophical Library, New York.

Y.Keshava Menon & Richard F. Allen, The Pure Principle (of Shankar) 1960, Michigan State University Press, U.S.A.

Sri Aurobindo, Eight Upaniṣads, 1953, Aurobindo Ashram, Pondichery, So. India.

——A Vedic Glossary, 1962, Aurobindo Ashram, Pondicherry, So. India.

Anilbaran Roy, Essays on The Gita, 1954, Aurobindo Ashram, Pondicherry, So. India.

A. Chatterjee & D. Datta, Introduction to The Indic Philosophical Systems, 1960, University of Calcutta.

T.M.P.Mahadevan, Outlines Hinduism, 1960, Washington Square Press, New York.

Monier-Williams, Nalopakhyanam, 1965, Chokhamba Sanskrit Series LIII, Varanasi-1.

J.F.Staal, A Reader on the Sanskrit Grammarians, 1972, M.I.T. Press, Cambridge, Mass.,U.S.A.

Sri Bhartṛihari, Vākyapadīyam (Brahmakānda) 1970 Munshiram Manoharlal, Delhi-6

B. K. S. Iyengar, Light on Yoga, 1974, Allen-Unwin Paperback, London.

Swāmi Hariharānanda Aranya,Yoga Philosophy of Patanjali, 1965, University of Calcutta.

M.R.Kale, Pancatantra of Visnusarman for student, 1969 Motilal Banarasidass, Delhi-6.

Romain Rolland, Prophets of the New India, 1930 Albert and Charles Boni, New York.

M. Anantanārāyanan, Thirty Verses of Sri Ramana Maharshi, 1955, Sri Ramanasramam, Tiruvannamalai, So. India.

"K" Sat-Darshana Bhashya and talks with Maharshi, 1968, Sri Ramanasramam, Tiruvannamalai, So. India.

●●●